FRITZ AND TOMMY

FRITZ AND TOMMY

ACROSS THE BARBED WIRE

PETER DOYLE AND ROBIN SCHÄFER

FOREWORD BY AL MURRAY

The
History
Press

Für unsere Eltern

Cover illustrations: *Front*: A German soldier lights a cigarette for
a British soldier, 1918. (Universal History Archive/UIG via
Getty Images); rear: German prisoners acting as stretcher-bearers.

First published 2015

The History Press
The Mill, Brimscombe Port
Stroud, Gloucestershire, GL5 2QG
www.thehistorypress.co.uk

British Library Cataloguing in Publication Data.
A catalogue record for this book is available from the British Library.

ISBN 978 0 7509 5684 0

Typeset in 10.5/14pt Bembo by The History Press
Printed and bound in Malta by Melita Press

The Great War has always been a story about two opposing sides. Here in the pages of *Fritz and Tommy* we at last have that story, told in stark relief and in a meaningful and often very moving way. In nearly forty years of reading about the Great War this is arguably one of the most important books I have come across. It is simply essential reading for anyone with an interest in World War One.

PAUL REED, HISTORIAN

Fritz and Tommy ingeniously unpicks the traditional straitjacket of 'national memory' in World War One by using diaries and letters home to show both the similarities and the differences between British and German soldiers. Engaging, poignant and hugely informative, it is an inspired concept, brilliantly executed.

ROGER MOORHOUSE, HISTORIAN AND AUTHOR OF *THE DEVILS' ALLIANCE: HITLER'S PACT WITH STALIN, 1939-1941*

In this excellent book Peter Doyle and Robin Schäfer weave together personal testimony, memoirs and contemporary writing to illustrate the contrasts, similarities and shared experience of British and German soldiers on the Western Front. The result is a fascinating, thought-provoking and frequently touching story of men at war.

SPENCER JONES, MILITARY HISTORIAN AND AUTHOR OF *COURAGE WITHOUT GLORY: THE BRITISH ARMY ON THE WESTERN FRONT 1915*

This is a wonderful account of the day-to-day lives of the British and German soldiers who fought the Great War. It cuts through the gloss of a hundred years of distortion and propaganda to reveal the faces of the real men who lived and died in the mud and blood of the trenches.

GILES MACDONOGH, HISTORIAN AND AUTHOR OF *AFTER THE REICH*

Fritz and Tommy is a triumph. A time machine. Open it, step inside, and you are back in that hot distant summer of 1914. Travel with the combatants as they scribble their letters from those opening days of the war, to the shattered rubble of fallen empires and devastated landscapes of 1918. The young men are long gone. In this remarkable book they live again. Sit with them. Hear their tales.

MAJOR NIGEL PRICE, EX-7TH GURKHA RIFLES, AS 'ANTHONY CONWAY',
AUTHOR OF THE CASPASIAN NOVELS AND *THE MOON TREE*

This remarkable book is a fitting memorial to the men and women of both nations who served in the Great War.

LORD FAULKNER OF WORCESTER, CHAIRMAN OF THE ALL-PARTY
PARLIAMENTARY WAR HERITAGE GROUP

When it is peace, then we may view again
With new-won eyes each other's truer form
And wonder. Grown more loving-kind and warm
We'll grasp firm hands and laugh at the old pain,
When it is peace. But until peace, the storm
The darkness and the thunder and the rain.

CAPT. CHARLES HAMILTON SORLEY
KILLED IN ACTION, LOOS, 13 OCTOBER 1915

Contents

Foreword/*Vorwort*

The First World War, as anyone sensible will tell you, is the event that birthed the modern world, that set the twentieth century's tumultuous events in motion, that unleashed the forces that devastated the world as empires collapsed and new ones rose. While this all might be true, you might also say it's somewhat impersonal. The First World War wasn't about tectonic plates grinding against one another so much as ordinary men facing each other across no-man's-land in countless battlefields all over the world, in a war that both sides saw as a war for survival.

Peter and Rob – Tommy and Fritz, respectively – have done what many have been unable to do in the wake of the First World War's centenary, and put aside the whoever and, dare I say, the whatever about how the war began, and looked at those ordinary men and their attitudes. Diaries, letters home, written without the benefit of hindsight, without the outcome or the terrible butcher's bill at the end of the war in mind.

'Fritz and Tommy' came from countries you might be tempted to describe as 'the same but different'. Their armies had their own powerful traditions, and had spent the decades running up to the outbreak of war admiring each other and comparing themselves. When war came, both institutions were sorely tested by the deadlock that followed – the personal accounts in *Fritz and Tommy* take us into these challenges – and German and British soldiers continued to admire and compare as much as they were told to hate each other.

As the First World War becomes more distant in time, and the ancient animosities fade, a book like *Fritz and Tommy* helps to peel another layer from the historical onion. There's lots to learn from this book, and maybe some of the glib answers about the First World War will be replaced by sterner questions. Why do men fight? And why, even when things are as bad as they were, do they continue to fight?

Al Murray

Introduction/ *Einführung*

You have to know that in some places our trench is only 15 metres away from the enemy. You won't believe it, but last night a Tommy called us in German! *Haben Sie Zigarren?* One of my men threw some over the parapet and they seemed to have reached their destination as a few minutes later something landed in our trench. First we thought it was a grenade, but it turned out to be a small metal tin full of chocolates! After that there was silence. The English are a lot different to the French. I will send you the tin as it is quite decorative! Has Werner been promoted yet? I hope to meet him in Cologne soon …

LEUTNANT WALTER BLUMSCHEIN, 3 FEBRUARY 1916

There has been no firing here today as far as I know as Fritz seems to be quite as sentimental as we are over Christmas. It is nice to feel that this awful war is so contrary to the spirit of Christ that they try and stop it on His Birthday. Why they don't attempt to do so every day beats me.

RFN WILLIAM C. TAFFS, 1/16TH QUEEN'S WESTMINSTER RIFLES,
26 DECEMBER 1915

Fritz and Tommy. Two protagonists in a war that claimed over 10 million military lives and that was fought on five continents. Who were they? What drove them to fight? And what was it like for them both, separated by lines of trenches and fields of cruelly-barbed wire?

The First World War/ *der 1. Weltkrieg*, defined Europe. While it is true that the wars of European liberation and confederation that erupted each decade of the late nineteenth century created new nation states, the Great War was a conflict that shaped the continent we know today. Old empires fell, monarchies were toppled, new nations created. From the ruins of a Europe wracked by two world wars arose the vibrant confederation we know today. But with the causes, effects and grand strategies of the war discussed now – a hundred years on – with renewed vigour, there is also a human story.

The British saw almost 900,000 military deaths during the First World War, and the Germans more than twice this, at over 2 million (and with some 750,000 civilians dead through malnutrition): 2 per cent of the British population, 4 per cent of the German one. Add to this the millions who returned home with memories, wounded, maimed and mentally scarred – the war left an indelible mark on both countries. As we personally reflect upon these figures we can think of our forebears: *Wehrmann* Peter Gilgenbach, wounded on the Marne in September 1914; Pte William Black, killed at Bellewaarde in Flanders in 1915; Pte Thomas Roberts, killed in action at Passchendaele in August 1917, Pte Albert Howard, who died of wounds at Arras in October 1918, aged just 18; or brothers Joseph and August Reinhardt who were both killed near Luxemont-et-Villotte within just two days of each other. Framing experiences in this way we can consider the lives of these men as they faced their enemies across the barbed wire, and those of their extended families – the shared experience of humanity.

More than 100 years have passed since the war broke onto the world stage in June 1914. Over this century, and clouded by the impact of another, even more terrible conflict, the origins of the Great War and the nature of its battles and leaders have been much discussed. Almost before the war's end, books and articles sought to address the balance of war guilt, and consider accusations of incompetence by leaders. Yet above this climate of accusation and counter-accusation, there remains a simple truth – that soldiers on both sides believed in the cause they were fighting for. They fought to protect their homes, their families, and their way of life. They fought for King and Country/*für König und Vaterland*, and they believed that God was on their side/*Gott mit uns*.

In 1916, the famous novelist Sir Arthur Conan Doyle wrote of the soldiers of 1914. In Britain, he recalled, 'A just war seemed to touch the land with some magic wand, which healed all dissensions and merged into one national whole …', while the German soldiers 'were filled with patriotic ardour and a real conviction that they were protecting their beloved Fatherland. One could not but admire their self-sacrificing devotion.' Although as the war dragged on, the appetite for war lessened – particularly in Germany, with many soldiers calling for a compromise peace – those men who marched home in 1918, and who had seen such sacrifices, did so with pride. With no old soldiers of the conflict left to express this view, our task is to interpret what they left behind, their letters, writings and interviews. And drilling down deeply into these, we find the experience of the front-line soldiers, those men who endured life 'in the trenches'.

For most people, trench warfare *is* the First World War. Though the war extended across four continents, from the wet Flanders Plain to the steppes of Russia, from the deserts of the Middle East to the Alps, life 'in the trenches', as depicted in France and Belgium, continues to fascinate. Assisted by numerous sharply focused photographic images, the perception of life in the Great War is one of men and animals struggling to survive, making the best of a life of utter squalor before being sent 'over the top' in large set-piece battles. These views endure, informed not only by the rich photography, but also by the legacy of war art, literature and poetry that came pouring out in the ten-year period after the war's end. Tellingly, for the most part these stories have been from the Allied side, the victors, and the life of the average Imperial German soldier overshadowed by events forged when the Treaty of Versailles was signed in June 1919.

The war between Fritz and Tommy commenced once the British Expeditionary Force, landing in France in early August, took up its pre-determined position in the line in support of the French. Arriving on the continent, the British soldiers were taken in by the sights, sounds and smells, the waving crowds and the strange accents. Regulars – many of the British troops had experienced the rigours of international duties, and had acted as guardians of Empire in far-flung outposts, across India, in Africa, the Caribbean and even the Mediterranean – they were used to foreign postings; after all, over half the British army of 1914 was spread overseas. And they were well trained. In the aftermath of the disastrous opening campaigns of the Anglo-Boer War of 1899–1902, when the Boer citizen-soldiers had painfully exposed the inadequacies of the British regular army, things had been tightened up considerably. New manuals were developed, insistence on adequate musketry training increased, and all arms were trained to a high degree to meet their responsibilities as international policemen of Empire. And yet, that next foe would be one of the most highly organised, efficient and powerful of European nations – one that had been described in the British press just seventeen years previously as 'a perfect machine', a machine only too capable of defeating Britain on the field of battle:

The German Army is the most perfectly adapted, perfectly running machine. Never can there have been a more signal triumph of organisation over complexity. The armies of other nations are not so completely organised. The German Army is the finest thing of its kind in the world; it is the finest thing in Germany of any kind. Briefly, the difference between the German and, for instance, the English armies is a simple one. The German

Army is organised with a view to war, with the cold, hard, practical, business-like purpose of winning victories. And what should we ever do if 100,000 of this kind of army got loose in England?

G.W. STEEVENS, DAILY MAIL, 1897

The first British soldiers to be captured in 1914 saw for themselves the power of their enemies:

Once we passed a train with heavy artillery on specially constructed wagons, and we saw several trains of ordinary field artillery. These trains of troops, munitions, motor-cars, coal, and a hundred other weapons of war that were hidden from view, the whole methodical procession of supplies to the Front, were most suggestive of power, of concentration, and organisation of effort. Most impressive was this glimpse of Germany at war. It is difficult to convey the impression to those who have not seen Germany in a state of war. Men who have been at the Front see little of the power which is behind the machine against which they are fighting.

LT MALCOLM VIVIAN HAY, 1ST GORDON HIGHLANDERS, 1914

In summer 1914, the German army in the west stood at about 1.6 million strong. This machine, programmed to win, swept through the borders of Belgium as it took its part in unleashing the Schlieffen Plan, the German war plan that had been developed in 1904. With a wary eye on revenge-hungry French to the west – allied to the Russians in the east – the plan envisaged a great arcing movement that would involve seven armies wheeling around, constrained only by the Channel coast. The plan demanded that the German armies pass with speed through the low countries. No delays could be tolerated, and no resistance from civilians allowed. In August 1914, any who stood in their way were dealt with, summarily, and the Germans marched on, their sights set on the encirclement of Paris:

I had just declared in the Reichstag that only dire necessity, only the struggle for existence, compelled Germany to march through Belgium, but that Germany was ready to make compensation for the wrong committed. What was the British attitude on the same question? The day before my conversation with the British Ambassador, Sir Edward Grey had delivered his well-known speech in Parliament, wherein, while he did not state expressly that England would take part in the war, he left the matter in little doubt. One needs only to read this speech through carefully to learn the reason of England's intervention in the war. Amid all his beautiful phrases about England's honour and England's obligations we find it over and over again expressed that England's interests – its own interests – called for participation in war, for it was not in England's interests that a victorious, and therefore stronger, Germany should emerge from the war.

Reichskanzler Theobald von Bethmann-Hollweg, 4 August 1914

When the Germans crossed the Belgian border, the British guarantee to support the independence of the 100-year-old state was tested. And though the *Entente Cordiale* between France and Britain was no formal military alliance, there was equally no chance that Britain would stay out of the war. The growing challenge to Britain's maritime hegemony – and the possibility of the fall of the Channel ports – were significant and tangible. Britain was to support the French, and come to the aid of 'gallant little' Belgium. From August 1914, the miniscule British army faced its toughest enemy in the Germans, who outnumbered them ten times, and who were an unfamiliar foe.

Almost as the first six British divisions crossed the English Channel, the propaganda battle began. Attributed to the German Kaiser was an infamous, contemptuous view of the British, a matter widely reported in the British press in August 1914:

THE KAISER'S SPITE

At a conference, held last Wednesday week, at the Imperial headquarters at Aix-la-Chapelle, of his general officers commanding divisions and brigades of the German Northern Army, it is said that the Kaiser issued this grim order:–

It is my Royal and Imperial command that you concentrate your energies, for the immediate present, upon one single purpose, and that is, that you address all your skill and all the valour of my soldiers to exterminate, first, the treacherous English; walk over General French's contemptible little army.

That explains why the flower of the German Army was flung against the British troops.

Yorkshire Evening Post, 29 August 1914

Uir aben zwar nicht geschlagen die Feind ; aber
eine neue Weltrekord — im Laufen .

Goot gracious me ! Here
kom der British.

Above: 'We have not beaten
the enemy, but we have set
a new world record – in
running.' British soldier
pictured in German
propaganda – always thin,
awkward and oddly dressed.

Left: Conversely, the
Germans were usually
portrayed as overweight
buffoons in British
propaganda.

Contemptible? The term was quickly adopted as a badge of honour by the British soldiery, fuelled on by the press reports. The idea that the British would be swept aside was fiercely opposed by the men themselves:

> He [the Kaiser] is trying … to break through Britain's contemptible little army but he shall get a prod and a very good one at that.
> Cpl J. Bremner, Royal Garrison Artillery, 27 January 1915

But an absence of documents and supporting statements undermine the existence of this order. The Army Historical Branch could track nothing down, and neither could Major General Sir Frederick Maurice; the MP Arthur Ponsonby dismissed it as a clever British propaganda ploy. In fact, the German High Command had greater respect for the British army than has so far been considered. The Germans never underestimated their enemies:

> The BEF is a first-class opponent. The officer corps is recruited from the best classes. It is united and morale is excellent.
> German Army Memorandum, 1914

> [English officers] studied on the battlefields of Manchuria and they can be found on the manoeuvre grounds of all major military powers, always ready to observe, compare and to learn. What they have learned they take home to England where it is evaluated by the General Staff which in its current form has only recently been set up by Haldane, before making the information accessible to the army. Large scale manoeuvres are today just as common in England as they are on the continent … countless battlefields all over the world and a glorious history stand proof to the fact that he [the English soldier] was always ready to fight and to die bravely for the honor of his arms. The English Army, set into a natural, warlike state by an outstanding reformer and trained by its appointed leaders commands the respect even of continental armies.
> German General Staff, 1909

Despite this, the propagandists – reacting to the actions of the German army in Belgium and France in 1914 – ensured that the enmity of the two nations would deepen from very early on. Pre-war, intellectuals had a respect for German learning, but even this would be tested and challenged in the wake of the enhanced tale-telling of atrocity stories, in newspapers, on posters, in everyday life:

'The helpful English (when spotting the *Pickelhauben*) – running away in fright.'

Surrender was a constant theme in British propaganda representations of the Germans.

'ONCE A GERMAN, ALWAYS A GERMAN'
REMEMBER!
This Man, who has shelled Churches, Hospitals, and Open Boats; this
Robber, Ravisher and Murderer, And This Man, who after the War, will want
to sell you his German Goods, ARE ONE AND THE SAME PERSON!
Men and Women of Britain! Have nothing to do with Germans Until the
Crimes Committed by Them against Humanity have been expiated!

POSTER BY DAVID WILSON, 1918

For the Germans, the perception of British perfidy in siding with the French,
meant that the 'Hymn of Hate' targeted its greatest enemy:

Hymn of Hate

French and Russian, they matter not,
A blow for a blow and a shot for a shot!
We love them not, we hate them not,
We hold the Weichsel and Vosges gate.
We have but one and only hate,
We love as one, we hate as one,
We have one foe and one alone.
He is known to you all, he is known to you all,
He crouches behind the dark grey flood,
Full of envy, of rage, of craft, of gall,
Cut off by waves that are thicker than blood.
Come, let us stand at the Judgment Place,
An oath to swear to, face to face,
An oath of bronze no wind can shake,
An oath for our sons and their sons to take.
Come, hear the word, repeat the word,
Throughout the Fatherland make it heard.
We will never forego our hate,
We have all but a single hate,
We love as one, we hate as one,
We have one foe and one alone –
ENGLAND!

ERNST LISSAUER, 1914

Retouched image from the *Illustrated War News* (1915) depicting the incredible events of Christmas 1914.

But what was the actual relationship between the Germans and the British troops? Though shaped by the virulent propaganda at home, this relationship was also born from the actions of the soldiers at the front.

It is the Christmas Truce of 1914 that has captured the imagination of many, for it was across the frozen fields of France and Flanders that the soldiers of both nations met each other on equal terms without enmity – albeit briefly. The motives for the truce have been much discussed, and whether it was through curiosity, cynical opportunity to examine the trenches of the enemy, or simply the chance to give the war a rest, Briton and German met in no-man's-land without weapons. There are many accounts. At Frelinghien and Houplines, British soldiers of the 6th Division met their German counterparts face-to-face:

On Christmas morning some of us went out in front of the German trenches and shook hands with them, and they gave us cigars, cigarettes, and money as souvenirs. We helped them bury their dead, who had been lying in the fields for two months. It was a comical sight to see English and German soldiers, as well as officers, shaking hands and chatting together. When we had buried their dead one of the Germans danced and another played a mouth organ. We asked them to play us at football in the afternoon, but they had no time. They seemed a decent crowd to speak to, and I got into conversation with one who had worked at Selfridge's in London, and he said he was sorry to have to fight against us. Well I don't expect we shall shake hands with the enemy again for a long time to come.

RFN ERNEST W. MUNDAY, 3RD RIFLE BRIGADE, 26 DECEMBER 1914

At Aubers, a German infantryman recorded his experiences of this spontaneous event:

25 December 1914. Today the troops on both sides seem to be in tacit consent not to shoot at each other, not a single shot is fired. In front of another company Germans and Englishmen met between the trenches and agreed upon a ceasefire. If we were to open fire again we were asked to fire five shots into the air; a warning signal which the English would then answer in the same manner. At another place Schnaps and cigarettes were exchanged. Later our Oberleutnant ordered the company to assemble and gave us a severe reprimand. Each and every one of us would get court martialled and every Englishman that came over to our trenches was to be taken prisoner. Later we received an incredible amount of presents and merrily celebrated Christmas. Bolsinger is dead and tomorrow we may well be too so let us be merry as long as it is possible. Merry Christmas and a happy new year!

26/27 December 1914. We and the English soldiers have agreed upon a ceasefire. We met between the trenches and exchanged cigarettes for tea. Spoke to three English soldiers, one of them a corporal. I gave him an open letter for Elisabeth in England and dictated him her address, he promised to deliver it. Actually they were not Englishmen but Scots. Scottish Guards; strong men all of them, even though they appeared to be even more dirty than we were. Their uniform is cut similar to my hiking suit and has about the same colour. They also wear puttees and laced boots.

LTN. HEINRICH EBERHARD, INFANTERIE-REGIMENT NR. 158

The Truce would soon be left behind as the war deepened, and there would be many fierce encounters to come. The relationships between the armies cannot simply be defined by its incredible events – but it does underline the interest with which both sides viewed each other.

This book represents the first time that two authors – one British, one German – have attempted to examine the lives of their forebears in a single volume, comparing them. There are distinct differences. The standard of German education meant that many low-rank letter writers were articulate, while the cards and notes written by British other ranks were often stilted and formulaic. And with German letters and cards written in their billions, the system of local and base censorship soon went into abeyance, with German soldiers describing in some detail the nature of their surroundings, the state of the trenches, the progress of battle. British letters, strongly controlled and actively censored, were that much more cautious. Despite these constraints, what emerges is the depth of meaning that is carried by the details of their writing and the words used by the combatants. Was the relationship between enemies just what was represented by the propagandists of both sides? Through their writing we hope to find out. In this book, we examine the time of mobilisation, life at the front, the sustaining of morale, the act of battle and of death, and the end of the war.

To us, the very act of writing this book is a simple act of remembrance of those men, of Fritz and Tommy, who fought and returned, to the *Heimat* and Blighty, and to the millions who were left behind in the fields of *Westfront/* the Western Front. We dedicate it to their memory.

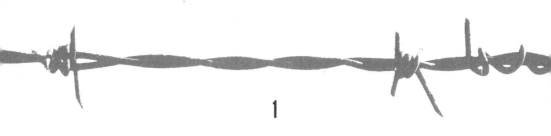

1

The Armies/ *Die Armeen*

Why did I volunteer? Certainly not because of any kind of enthusiasm for war or because I think it is a major thing to shoot people or to get a war decoration of some kind. The opposite is the case, war is a wicked thing and I also think that by using more skilful diplomacy it should have been possible to avoid it.

But now that there is a war, it is quite natural that I unite my own personal destiny with that of the German people. And even though I am sure that I would have been able to achieve better things for *Volk* and *Vaterland* in peacetime than in war it feels wrong to undertake such calculating observations. It is like comparing one's own value with that of a drowning man to find out if he is worth saving ….

KRIEGSFREIWILLIGER FRANZ BLUMENFELD, RESERVE-FELDARTILLERIE-
REGIMENT NR. 29, 24 SEPTEMBER 1914

Then the first war broke out and the early news of the invaders terrorising the women made me feel that must not happen here so I decided to enlist.

PTE HUMPHREY MASON, 6TH OXFORDSHIRE AND BUCKINGHAMSHIRE
LIGHT INFANTRY

The armies of Britain and Germany were distinctly different. In organisation, national characteristics, recruitment and logistics, the two armies moulded and shaped their soldiers. It is necessary to examine their differences in some depth.

The Germany of 1914–18 was forged from the wars of unification, the *Reichseinigungskriege*, fought between 1864 and 1871, which led to the creation of the *Deutsches Reich*. In particular, the Franco-Prussian War of 1870–71 saw the total defeat of the French army, and the reputation of the armies of the newly unified German state, the *Deutsches Heer*, was second to none. The German military system was superbly efficient and was locked into everyday life. It committed almost all males to a period of service that would carry them through from young man to older reservist. And every man was efficiently trained according to a system that prepared the German army for its ultimate challenge when world war erupted in August 1914.

For Britain, a maritime nation with a significant array of overseas possessions, the events on the continent were seemingly remote, and there was a reliance on the navy to represent its greatest force of arms. While the German forces were engaged in Europe, the purpose of the British army was very different; it was there simply to provide an Imperial police force, used to maintain borders and put down insurrections or unrest. It was used in fighting 'brush-fire' wars against native rebellions.

Following the *entente cordiale* of 1904, the possibility that Britain might have to field an army in Europe meant the creation of an expeditionary force of six divisions of all arms and a single cavalry division. Each division, based across Britain until needed, had a war establishment of some 18,000 men, 12,000 of which were infantry, and the remainder artillery – together with, in 1914, twenty-four machine guns and seventy-six artillery pieces. Each infantry division was composed of three brigades (*c.* 4,000 men), each brigade of four battalions (*c.* 1,000 men each). Battalions were derived from each regiment, and it was highly unusual for battalions from the same regiment to be brigaded together. The regular infantry divisions that were embodied in 1914 and destined to serve overseas were supplemented by others that were assembled to carry forward the British responsibilities that deepened from 1914. First, there was the assembly of regular battalions recalled or returned from overseas service as new regular divisions. Second, the 'first line' Territorial battalions were formed into divisions of men who had volunteered to serve overseas; second line battalions, formed to serve at home, would wait their turn. Finally, there were 'New Army' divisions, composed of the volunteers for Kitchener's Army from 1914. They would amass some seventy-four infantry divisions by the war's end. Added to this were three regular cavalry divisions and four mounted yeomanry. Each was supported by regular, Territorial and 'New Army' artillery, engineer and support troops.

On mobilisation in 1914, and conforming to French practice, it was decided to group British divisions into corps each comprising two divisions, such that the British Expeditionary Force, when it landed in France, consisted of three army corps. In all these units, additional manpower was available in attached army, corps, division and brigade troops, and headquarters staff. As the war progressed, so the drain of manpower increased; by late 1917 the number of brigades per division was reduced by one. In 1914, the cavalry division was organised differently, with four brigades of three regiments each (together with attached troops), having a strength of 9,000 men, 10,000 horses, twenty-four machine guns and twenty field guns. It was with this structure that the British army went to war, and it was this structure that provided the expeditionary force that landed in France in August 1914.

In comparison with the British unified system, the *Deutsches Heer* was a federal force that comprised armies of the four kingdoms of Prussia, Bavaria, Saxony and Württemberg, together with representatives across the twenty-one minor states of the *Deutsches Reich*. Of these nations, only Bavaria employed a separate numbering system, the other states following that of the Prussians. Taken together, however, in July 1914 these contingents meant that *Heer* could muster a strength of 840,000 men: the second largest army on the continent, second only to the Russians. And within a week of war being declared, with the reserves called up, that figure was pushed up to nearly 4 million men, and reached a peak of around 7 million in 1917.

It was the Kaiser who held overall command of the *Heer* – including the Bavarian contingent – and exercised control through the Ministry of War and the *Großer Generalstab* (Great General Staff). The basic peacetime organisational structure of the *Heer* was a hierarchal system, with *Armee-Inspektionen* (army inspectorate), *Armee-Korps*, *Divisionen*, and *Regimenter*. The Bavarian Army served on the Western Front as an integral component of the German army, while the armies of Saxony and Württemberg formed self-contained army corps. The minor German states, kingdoms and duchies also provided separate units of mostly regimental size that served as part of the Prussian contingent.

Armee-Korps were virtually independent formations receiving orders directly from the Kaiser. Composed of two infantry divisions, each division was formed from two brigades with two infantry regiments each and two cavalry brigades with two cavalry regiments each together with a *Fußartillerie* ('foot artillery' – mobile field artillery) regiment. In addition, each *Korps* had single *Jäger* (elite light infantry), pioneer, and train battalions, and other support troops. The *Infanterie-Division* was the basic tactical unit. In summer 1914, in addition to the units of the *Garde-Korps*, there were forty-two regular divisions in the Prussian Army (including four Saxon and two Württemberg divisions), and six divisions in the Bavarian contingent. As the war progressed, reserve divisions were formed as the need for more men increased.

The basic combat unit was the regiment. Early war German infantry regiments typically had a strength of 3,300 officers, NCOs and men, and one machine-gun company with six heavy MG08 machine guns. By summer

German recruits muster in 1915.

1918, the serious shortage of personnel forced a reduction to about 700 men while many battalions with fewer than 650 men were reduced to three rifle-companies. By 1916 so-called *Sturmbataillone* (assault battalions) were formed on army level. These units were not only elite shock troops at the front, but also acted as schools for regular infantry units.

German regiments were raised and maintained at a local level. Large cities and towns could muster an entire regiment, while smaller rural areas would be responsible for raising a company or battalion for the local regiment, which meant that the whole system became ingrained deeply into the social structure of the country. During peacetime, military service was very much like a social club. One could serve the entire twenty-two years required by the army alongside one's family, friends and neighbours; this forged very strong bonds of loyalty and friendship to a regiment, a factor that was useful for morale in battle:

My address is 11/55 – 11th company, Regiment Nr. 55 in Detmold. Tomorrow
we will hopefully receive our uniforms and in the meantime we are sitting
around in the barracks. Here and among the reservists I have met many old
friends and acquaintances, so all is well. A 1000 kisses, your son Paul

MUSK. PAUL VIETMEYER, INFANTERIE-REGIMENT NR. 55

The downside, always the case with local regiments and equivalent to the
experience of the British, was that during the war small towns might find
many of their young men killed, wounded or missing in a single day.

The 22 October 1914, a day that no member of the regiment will ever
forget. A foggy, chilly and damp morning; a rosy-fingered dawn on the
horizon. A day that had brought nameless grief and sorrow to the relatives
and families at home. Countless people were talking to each other on the
streets of Hannover and Hildesheim, asking for news of their 215th regiment. For hours mothers and fathers were waiting on the station platforms
where the trains carrying the wounded were coming in, until the news
arrived: 'Fallen on the field of honour' or 'missing'. 'Missing' – what a terrible word, which turned the feeling of trembling suspense into a horrible
suffering. Countless requests at the central registration office remained
without answer. The regiment had hundreds of soldiers missing. Some
clarity was gained, but the ultimate fate of 50 comrades will forever stay a
mystery. They rest as unknown soldiers in the cool, foreign soil.

HISTORY OF RESERVE-INFANTERIE-REGIMENT NR. 215

If, in 1914, the British army could trace its origins back 300 years, this could
be matched equally by the Germans. The oldest regular German regiments had histories that stretched back to the early seventeenth century. In
at least three major conflicts – the Seven Years War, the American War of
Independence and, most notably, the Napoleonic Wars – German states and
their armies stood as allies alongside the British, earning battle honours that
would be recognisable by regiments on both sides of the North Sea. But not
all regiments in the *Deutsches Heer* could claim this longevity; there were
the thirty-three so-called 'Young Regiments' – raised in 1896 – that had no
antecedents, and consequently possessed no battle honours. They would have
their chance to earn them in the coming conflict – as could the Reserve
Regiments formed on and shortly after mobilisation in 1914.

Following the reforms of the British army in 1908, in 1914 there were sixty-
one British regular infantry regiments, ranked in an order of precedence set

by tradition which placed the five regiments of Foot Guards above the county regiments of Infantry of the Line, the rifles sitting towards the end of this list. Each infantry regiment was named, usually after the county of association, having left their numbers behind following reform. Each one had two regular battalions allied with a county or region, and each was given a home depot. The third or Special Reserve Battalion was designed to gather recruits for the regular battalions, while the fourth, fifth and often sixth battalions belonged to the Territorial Force – though Irish regiments were never to have Territorial battalions. There were also five all-Territorial regiments.

The naming and numbering of German regiments was complex. In 1860, Prussia started numbering its regiments in a system that did not follow any particular chronology, and after the Austro-Prussian War of 1866 the Prussian-annexed states integrated their armies into this system. Württemberg and Saxon units were numbered according to the Prussian system, while Bavaria maintained its own (thus, the *2. Württembergisches Infanterie-Regiment* was *Infanterie-Regiment Nr. 120* under the Prussian system). But initial numbers were just part of the story. In addition to them, all regular regiments possessed a name, a state or provincial number, and usually an honour title too.

In common with the British army, many regiments carried the title 'Grenadier' or 'Fusilier' – throwbacks to an earlier age – and many proudly displayed regimental traditions on their helmet plates, or on their uniform. One such title is the award of the battle honour 'Gibraltar' to both British and German regiments, a function of the siege that took place in 1779–83, during the American War of Independence. With German-born King George III of Great Britain and Ireland also the Duke of Hanover, three Hanoverian infantry regiments were sent with five British units to defend Gibraltar in 1775. For their endurance and loyalty, during three years of siege they were granted the battle honour 'Gibraltar'. The descendents of all these regiments – the British Suffolk, Dorsetshire, Essex and Northamptonshire regiments, and the Highland Light Infantry, and the German *Füsilier Regiment General Feldmarschall Prinz Albrecht von Preußen (Hannoversches) Nr. 73, Infanterie-Regiment von Voigts-Rhetz (3. Hannoversches) Nr. 79*, and *Hannoversches Jäger-Bataillon Nr. 10* – shared the Gibraltar title. It must have been an unusual sight for British soldiers mindful of regimental history to meet Germans proudly wearing their cuff title. It was certainly an honour that celebrated stormtrooper Ernst Jünger was proud to wear:

> Whenever we appeared on some sector of the front, we heard the shouts of '*Les Gibraltars, les lions de Perthes*'.
>
> LTN. ERNST JÜNGER, FÜSILIER-REGIMENT NR. 73

Mobilisation

At 7:30am all reservists in our street and from the neighbourhood assembled and together we marched out to report at the barracks. On the way more men and young volunteers attached themselves to our column. Countless people lined the roads, they cheered and sang 'Die Wacht am Rhein' and 'Deutschland über alles'. Young boys carried their fathers' luggage. What a great and moving experience it was ....

SCHÜTZE W. HIMMES, RESERVE-INFANTERIE-REGIMENT NR. 91, 2 AUGUST 1914

For the Germans, the First World War was fought mainly by armies of conscripted citizen-soldiers, as had been done since the early nineteenth century. Under the Imperial Constitution of 16 April 1871, every able-bodied German male between the ages of 17 and 45 was liable for compulsory military service. Exemptions from service were allowed on the grounds of family distress, as well as the continuation of education.

German military service was divided into four phases. After active service, the conscript passed in turn to the reserve, the *Landwehr*, and the *Ersatz-Reserve* (supplementary reserve), amounting to twenty-two years of service. Active service in the *Heer* meant two years in the infantry or a non-mounted artillery unit. Three years were demanded by cavalry and mounted artillery.

Personnel discharged from active service passed into the *Reserve*, and all soldiers were expected to have served a combined total of seven years. Reservists had to take part in regular training courses and army manoeuvres spanning up to eight weeks a year. A transfer to the *Landwehr* followed. Service in the *Landwehr* typically lasted for another five years (for infantry, for example), but was reduced to three years where the original active service had also demanded three years. *Landwehrmänner* were required to participate in two manoeuvres each year amounting to four weeks in a year. Personnel surplus to requirements (*Restanten*) were transferred into the *Ersatz-Reserve*, which acted as a ready manpower pool for active units. Finally there was the *Landsturm*, comprising men aged between 17 and 45 who did not qualify for one of these service groups.

Inspection at 3:45pm. It has been too long since I have been a soldier. I do not think that I will be able to survive the first enemy attack and I can only hope to get used to all this again.

DIARY OF AN UNKNOWN LANDSTURM SOLDIER

All young men in a calendar year were grouped together and referred to as a *Jahrgang* (year group), a group that would serve together in the future. Though the conscript system was highly organised, there was still a chance for a young *Landsturm* soldier to choose to volunteer before his year group was due to be called for active service. If he was physically and mentally able, the volunteer might qualify for a fashionable regiment or could follow a family tradition of serving in a noted unit.

The final decision on which arm of service a conscript would be serving in was made by the *Ober-Ersatzkommissionen*, based on his physical and mental abilities. While this system worked well in peacetime, the sheer volume of volunteers in the early weeks of August 1914 rendered it virtually inoperative. To cope with the massive numbers of *Kriegsfreiwillige*, individual units often distributed them randomly, but during the course of the war and after the first rush of euphoria had died down, the system was largely back in place again. Another class of volunteer was the *Einjährig Freiwilliger* – young men of 'suitable social class' and education who could enlist as a 'one-year volunteer' in order to shorten their active service period:

> Highly honoured Professors!
>
> As our beloved Fatherland is in grave danger I have decided to give my strength and blood to Kaiser and Reich and to take part in the fighting that needs to be done. Now, since 16 August, I am a soldier and I take the liberty to send my Professors the most heartfelt wishes! I have joined *Infanterie-Regiment 23* as a One Year Volunteer and I am now part of *3. Ersatz-Kompanie.*
>
> Your always grateful student
> Kriegsfreiwilliger Otto Schlechter, Reserve-Infanterie-Regiment Nr. 23, 31 August 1914

To be allowed to join in this way, a recruit had to pass a special one-year certificate in his *Gymnasium* (grammar school). This would earn him the right to choose the unit he wished to serve with – though he was still expected to equip, feed and house himself from his own pocket. In an infantry unit this amounted to between 1,750 and 2,200 marks – a substantial sum of money. Joining as a volunteer was a considerable decision for a young man to take:

> My parents!
> I decided to write to you, not because I am afraid of a debate but because I want to give you time to muse about your decision. This letter is not the

result of a spontaneous idea, I have given everything a long thought, weighed the pros and cons and came to the same result, over and over again. One thing I have to emphasise: whatever your decision is, I will accept it without complaint as my experiences taught me that parents are always right.

But now let me tell you the reason I am writing this letter. I want to move into the field! All of my colleagues, from school and from work dropped everything to follow the call of the Kaiser. Do you want your son to be the exception? Their parents and siblings cry, but they are proud of their sons and brothers. Men between the age of 25 and 40 years have already taken up arms, even though they had to leave their women and children and even though there is the uncertainty that their loved ones might now succumb to hunger and need. And I, having no such obligations, am supposed to continue standing behind a shop counter to sell rolls of yarn to our customers and to answer countless questions about why I have not joined up yet?

I have the strength to defend my family and fatherland, but I prefer to work in this shop as this is a lot safer! Dear parents, would you want me to say that? Certainly not, because you would be ashamed of me.

A Leutnant who regularly visits our shop, but so far has not been granted the honour of serving at the front told me that at the moment there are so many volunteers that uniform stocks have been temporarily exhausted. Now they are offering that every volunteer will be trained to become an *Unteroffizier*. This training will last for three months. Conditions: 1) A One-Year Certificate; 2) 300 Marks to pay for expenses; 3) I have to buy my own uniform, underwear, socks etc. The training will begin on 11 August and minors need the written and signed consent of their parents to join!

If I supply all this I will be an NCO in three months. If not, I might get called up in a few weeks anyway and then I will only be an enlisted man – what do you prefer? Please remind yourselves that uncle Karl sent both his sons to serve under the colours! I will visit you at 10 o'clock to receive your answer.

KRIEGSFREIWILLIGER HANS BUCKY, INFANTERIE-REGIMENT NR. 153

At seven in the morning the artillery barracks here in Oldenburg started recruiting volunteers. There must have been around 1,500 young men on the square, but they only accepted 440 who were then divided into four depots with 110 men each. I am now in the 3rd depot and already met some old friends here.

GEFREITER OTTO BORGRÄFE, FELDART.-REGIMENT NR. 62, 15 AUGUST 1914

In August 1914, the *Reserves* were called up and the *Deutsches Heer* required only twelve days to expand from about 840,000 to a total of 3.5 million soldiers. Upon mobilisation, the *Reserve* and *Landwehr* regiments were activated:

> This morning we were sworn in. At 8:10 am we assembled and marched to the church. Pastor Wilksen delivered a sermon in which he highlighted the righteousness of the German cause. At 10:20 we assembled on the barrack's square at the Zeughausstrasse to take our oaths. On the square there were six artillery pieces on which we had to place our left hands, the right hand raised to deliver the oath. The recruits were grouped by nationality and confession and everyone delivered the oath as it fitted his religion and on his local ruler. I was sworn in on His Royal Highness the Grand Duke Friedrich August of Oldenburg. The whole ceremony lasted for about an hour.
>
> GEFR. OTTO BORGRÄFE, ERSATZABTEILUNG FELDARTILLERIE-REGIMENT
> NR. 62, 23 AUGUST 1914

Personnel from *Reserve* regiments were used to bring the regular active regiments to *Kriegsstärke* (war strength), while *Landwehr* soldiers were moved up to bring *Reserve* units up to strength. The *Landwehr* regiments were the last to depart the garrisons, and were often not fully manned:

> After I left, Gustav accompanied me to the station and at 10:27am, I and the other Reservists, among them Stuck, Schwarze and Weingarten, took the train to Detmold. All stations are bustling with activity and trains packed with soldiers roll by, most of them go towards Cologne. Everyone is singing and there is a cheerful atmosphere. We arrived at Detmold at 12:00 and reported at the barracks. After the paperwork had been done we marched into the 'Preussischer Hof' where we were accoutered in the dining hall. I had difficulty to find a fitting tunic and trousers and as I did not find a pair of riding breeches I had to content myself with a pair of cloth trousers. I did not even find a cap and the helmet I got is too large. I and about 20 other NCOs are now attached to the reserve baggage train.
>
> UNTEROFFIZIER DER RESERVE HERIBERT BORNEMANN, TRAIN-BATAILLON 7,
> 4 AUGUST 1914

As units departed, they were replaced by corresponding cadre units, the so-called *Ersatzbataillone* (replacement battalions), three of which were put in

Recruits of *Feld-Artillerie Nr. 56* in 1914.

place for each of the unit's active, *Reserve* and *Landwehr* components. Through these units, the *Feldtruppenteil* (field unit) would receive its flow of trained replacements:

> I was recovering from my wound and by the beginning of January I had recovered so far that I was to do garrison duty again. There is lots of work in the *Ersatzbataillon*. On 20 January a company of 100 recruits arrived. They are supposed to receive a further 6–8 weeks of training, so they are not going to be sent into the field soon. They are a keen lot and full of ardour, but a good number of them will fall down on the job as the physical strain seems to be too much for them. I suppose 10–15 per cent are unfit for service.
>
> UFF3. WALTHER PAUER, KÖNIGLICH BAYERISCHES 11.
> INFANTERIE-REGIMENT, 25 FEBRUARY 1915

While the German system worked well in times of peace, the horrendous casualties suffered in combat during the war greatly reduced its effectiveness. The first result of that was a continual lowering of the induction age as the fighting at the front wore down the available manpower reserve. By 1918, the members of *Jahrgang* 1920 were being called to service, fully two years ahead of time. These were the young soldiers so often pictured as prisoners of war by the Allies, eager to portray the defeat of Germany.

While Germany espoused its system of military compulsion, Britain stuck rigidly to the principle of a volunteer army. Haldane's reforms ensured that, for infantry regiments, there would be at least two regular battalions for the county regiments, recruited locally. There was also a special reserve battalion which remained at the county depot and supplied drafts of reservists, and at least a further two Territorial battalions. It was this system that ensured there was an efficient means of expanding the army, using the local Territorial Associations that existed to serve to support their Territorial battalions, now affiliated to the regulars. The idea was to provide an expanding reserve:

> It was Mr Haldane's intention to make the County associations the medium for indefinite expansion of the forces in case of need ... the County Associations justified Mr Haldane's faith in them, and their zeal and ability were of the utmost value to the War Office and the country.
>
> BRIG.-GEN. J. EDMONDS

In the early stages of the declaration of war, the British system snapped into place. Regular troops on leave were recalled, while those men who had recently left the army, and who were liable for a normal five-year service (Category B men) in the reserves were called back to the colours, and formed a significant component of the regular army battalions. Reservists in Category A could be called back for any perceived need; Category B men required a general mobilisation. The words of reservists have largely been overlooked in the mass of volunteers and conscripts:

> Being a Reservist, I was naturally called to the colours on the outbreak of war between England and Germany on August 4th, 1914, so I downed tools; and, although a married man with two children, I was only too pleased to be able to leave a more or less monotonous existence for something more exciting and adventurous.
>
> PTE FREDERICK BOLWELL, LOYAL NORTH LANCASHIRE REGIMENT, 1914

British soldiers in camp; Grenadier guardsmen relax in their hut.

Reservists reporting to the regimental depot had to start again from scratch, including seeking out their uniforms from the store:

> On August 5th 1914, I reported to my regimental depot being an Army reservist. What a meeting of old friends! All were eager to take part in the great scrap which every pre-war soldier had expected. In the mobilisation stores, every reservist's arms and clothing were ticketed, and these were soon issued with webbing equipment.
>
> PTE R.G. HILL, 1ST BATTALION ROYAL WARWICKSHIRE REGIMENT,
> 6 AUGUST 1914

The Territorials, known sneeringly as 'Saturday night soldiers', had signed on for a typical commitment of four years, and were required to attend regular parades at the local drill hall and an annual summer field camp. 'Time expired' men could sign on again for another four years. It was expected that the Territorial Force would form the 'Second Line' – Britain's home defence with no overseas obligation, but they could be expanded in times of need. But it was obvious that even with the actions of the County Associations, it would be difficult to get sufficient men to supply a major commitment overseas:

> The Battalion has volunteered for foreign service, and will go as a battalion. Eighty per cent volunteered, and of the remaining 20 per cent some have applied for commissions. We have started recruiting again to fill up from 800 to 1,000, so as to go at full strength.
>
> PTE D.H. BELL, LONDON RIFLE BRIGADE, 28 AUGUST 1914

Things changed dramatically when Field Marshal Lord Kitchener was brought in to lead the War Office. Despite his lack of political acumen, with his breadth of experience in the Victorian 'small wars', he was an obvious choice as a war leader for the government. And he soon shocked the cabinet with his assessment of the probable length of the war. Kitchener was summoned to the War Office to take on the direction of the war and to take a seat in the cabinet. Impatient with the current recruiting system, and in the knowledge that maintaining an adequate flow of soldiers to the front would be of great importance, the Secretary of State for War made a direct appeal to the public for more men. The first appeal was for 100,000 men, an appeal that would be driven by his own image pasted up on bill-boards and recruiting offices:

> The task the Government set itself was a formidable, nay, a staggering one. It was in the first place to take 500,000 raw men from the streets, from the clubs, from the fields, from the villages, towns and cities of Great Britain, and not only to train them in the art of war in the shortest space of time that it is possible to train soldiers, but also to prepare the equipment, the arms, and the munitions and stores of war.
>
> EDGAR WALLACE, 1916

To assist Kitchener in his work, the Parliamentary Recruiting Committee was formed in August 1914, a cross-party body administered by officers of the major political parties. Senior representatives of the Liberal and Unionist parties worked hard at developing means of persuading their fellow men to join the colours. With public meetings and a flurry of posters, the PRC became an active body that would ensure that Britain was united in sending its men as quickly to the front as possible.

The 'First Hundred Thousand' (K1), were recruited within days of Kitchener's appeal, and the war minister was to issue four further appeals through the late summer and early autumn of 1914. Recruiting offices sprang up across the country, with local municipal buildings and mobile recruiting offices pressed into service, usually bedecked with banners and posters:

> The enthusiastic response to Lord Kitchener's appeal for men is the pride
> of our country and the dread of our enemies. In his great speech at the
> Guildhall, Mr Asquith mentioned that from 250,000 to 300,000 men had
> offered themselves and been accepted. Since then the 500,000 have been
> secured and we have advanced into the second half million.
>
> THE WAR ILLUSTRATED, 19 SEPTEMBER 1914

Would-be soldiers were given the briefest of medicals before being formally 'attested' as soldiers of the king. Queues formed outside well-founded or hastily contrived recruiting offices up and down the country, with a crush of men waiting to 'sign on' and receive their first symbolic wages, the king's shilling binding them to military service.

Initial recruitment to Kitchener's army was steady, but was significantly boosted following the British retreat from Mons in August. The men of K1, K2 and so on took their places in the ranks of the existing army system, but very soon energetic and influential individuals were forming whole battalions, men who joined to train together and serve together. The concept was born following a request from the City of London to raise a whole battalion of 'stockbrokers' in August 1914. But the proliferation of the concept was in large part due to the action of Lord Derby, who introduced the notion that men of the 'commercial classes' might wish to serve their country in a battalion of their comrades, their 'pals'. The 'Liverpool Pals' was the result. The implication was that middle-class men would not be forced to serve alongside men they would neither know nor understand – men of 'lower social class'. It was a resounding success, though it would lead ultimately to the devastating losses felt by some local communities.

Following Liverpool's example, there was a rush to form 'City' and 'Pals' battalions from men with similar backgrounds and circumstances. Each battalion was raised by local dignitaries, who fed, clothed and equipped them until the unit was taken over by the War Office to become service battalions (numbered in sequence after the Territorials) – of the county regiments. Recruitment avalanched, reaching 1,186,357 by the end of 1914.

The flow of men to the colours continued almost unabated throughout 1914 and into 1915. Yet with the initial rush of men to join in the early stages of the war, it was inevitable that there would others less keen. Voluntary recruitment took a sharp dip in 1915, and declined month-on-month from its peak in August 1914. Emergency action was required to address this decline, and Lord Derby was appointed 'Director of Recruitment' in October 1915. The first steps to compulsion had already been taken with the National Registration Act of July 1915. The Act required every citizen between the ages of 15 and 65 to register their name, place of residence, nature of work and other details, and receive a National Registration Card. By October 1915 there were 21,627,596 names on the register, of which 5,158,211 were men of military age. Of this figure, 1,519,432 men were identified as being in reserved occupations, vital to the war effort. But by the autumn of 1915, the numbers actually joining was falling at an alarming rate. Lord Derby drew up a scheme that would force the issue. The 'Derby Scheme' proposed the voluntary attestation of all men between 18 and 40, to be called to the colours in batches:

> I have just received 4 recruits in my platoon all married men whose ages average 27 and I suppose they belonged to one of the Derby Groups. I wonder how they like it? I really feel sorry for them as they must have all given up their homes and they have only been training 3 months.
>
> 2Lt Arthur H. Lamb, 1st Lancashire Fusiliers, 3 October 1916

Lord Derby invited all eligible men to attest by 15 December 1915, but over 2 million of the 3.5 million men available for military service failed to attest. With the failure of Derby's scheme, compulsion to join came with the Military Service Act of January 1916. Now, all fit single men between the ages of 18 and 41 would be compelled to join the colours, married men joining them in the second Military Service Act of May 1916:

> What is your opinion of the Army Bill? I think it is a good one don't you? It is really only compulsion for those absolute slackers who have no earthly excuse. After all 3 million at least of us have not been compelled to join.
>
> Rfn William C. Taffs, 1/16th Queen's Westminster Rifles,
> 12 January 1916

Three further Acts, in April 1917, January 1918 and April 1918, would find ways of 'combing-out' more men for military service (the last reducing the recruitment age to 17, while, at the same time, increasing it to 55). Not everyone would have to serve; volunteering to work in a munitions factory was one way out:

> I am sorry to hear Will has got some more papers. I only hope he can keep clear of the Army, nobody knows what it's like only those that are in it. You have to be on parade and all cleaned up first thing in the morning. When he goes up, if they ask him to go in a labour battalion do try to put him in one. Tell him to say he would be more use in a munition factory, because if he gets in the Army they will keep him on odd jobs and it's hard to get your ticket.
>
> GNR ALBERT ROBBINS, ROYAL FIELD ARTILLERY, 1917

And for some men of conscience, the donning of a military uniform, and the act of supporting a war, was something they could not countenance. Conscientious Objectors – COs or 'conchies' – were not universally admired by some soldiers:

> Really, Gertie, one cannot help feeling mad, sorry, and amused at some of the 'objectors'. How some of them can get up and tell the world at large what weird consciences they have beats me.
>
> RFN WILLIAM C. TAFFS, 1/16TH QUEEN'S WESTMINSTER RIFLES,
> 8 MARCH 1916

Other men were unfit to serve; military medical examinations would test them – and do so repeatedly through the war – to ensure no fit man would escape service:

> I there and then fell in with a batch of men going up for medical inspection. We were then examined by two doctors very thoroughly. The next place to visit was the Quarter Master's Stores, there to be fitted up with uniform, equipment, etc. After that, as it was quite dark, we retired for the night, but not before we had all taken advantage of a little refreshment.
>
> PTE FREDERICK BOLWELL, LOYAL NORTH LANCASHIRE REGIMENT, 1914

Some men counted themselves lucky not to be called to serve:

> Dear Win. Just to let you know, I was examined yesterday after waiting 6 hours. Hot stuff aren't they? Well they have rejected me. I have *not* been passed for any branch of Service. Love F.S.
>
> POSTCARD TO WIN DELLOW, NORTH LONDON, 1916

Uniforms and Equipment

Of all the nations, arguably it was the soldiers of Germany and Britain that were best equipped for the war; both had developed field uniforms in practical colours that sought to blend their soldiers into the background of the average battlefield – and while *Feldgrau* (field grey) and Drab (otherwise known as khaki) soldiers met each other in 1914, other nations were still encumbered by more gaudy blue, and in some cases red, uniforms that made them stand out in the field of battle.

The contrasts between the German soldier and his British counterpart were well known in the propaganda of the day. In Britain, the essence of the German soldier was portrayed in his high boots and his spiked helmet (replaced by the equally distinctive *Stahlhelm*) – as well as the peakless cap of other ranks. British propaganda mocked these items as ill-fitting and clumsy, and end-of-war photographs for public consumption sought to ridicule their enemies with photographs of slight, bespectacled, boys in ill-fitting uniforms and over-large helmets. Such images are at odds with the depictions of young men with good military bearing in family photographs of their *Soldaten*, wearing their uniforms with pride:

> We have now been equipped with the fieldgrey gown, belts, buckles, bayonets and helmets. I can imagine now how the heroes of 1870 must have felt. I have never been so proud.
>
> KRIEGSFREIWILLIGER WERNER ALPHEUS, RESERVE-INFANTERIE-REGIMENT NR. 215

From the perspective of the German public, the British soldier, in ragged puttees or dressed in kilts sporting dish-like helmets, was equally bizarre:

> Soon the fighting moved further towards the town. Here the enemy occupied every house and from every window a machine gun fired. Here we needed to move fast, and as you well know, I am capable of this. Then I took off my backpack and dashed to a house which had not been occupied; we numbered around 20 men and we were fired upon from all directions. Here we took the first prisoners: Highlanders with short skirts. I am however convinced that they wear trousers underneath those.
>
> UNTEROFFIZIER ALWIN GOTTSCHLICH, INFANTERIE-REGIMENT NR. 76,
> MONS, 23 AUGUST 1914

In 1914, most British soldiers went to war in a peaked cap designed to accompany the wool serge uniform, but not designed to protect the head from anything other than the elements. The peaked cap would be the most significant identifying feature of most British soldiers – though Scots had their own 'bonnets'. Scot or Englishman, his profile could not have been more different than that of the German, who sported the *Lederhelm* (known as the *Pickelhaube* outside German army circles) in early war. Not all of these helmets were spiked – ball-top versions were worn by the artillery – and there was some variation in the helmet during its period of existence. Highly prized as an Allied trophy, there were numerous variants depending on, for example, state of origin, or rank of its owner:

> The Germans are about 100 yards away. They look pretty formidable in their Pickelhaubes and bearskin packs. I have got to leave my equipment and Millar his pack as to retrieve either means that we are either going to be shot or taken prisoners. In any case, we should have been shot thirty seconds ago if the 'Jerries' could shoot.
>
> PTE EDWARD ROE, 1ST EAST LANCASHIRE REGIMENT, 1 SEPTEMBER 1914

And from its early war grandeur of boiled leather and brass, the complex and no doubt expensive *Lederhelm* was simplified. Leather passed to steel and pressed felt, brass fittings to dull zinc before its universal replacement by the steel helmet, or *Stahlhelm*, in 1916. The *Lederhelm* was not the only headgear, of course. There were peakless field caps or *Feldmützen* – more often than not ridiculed in numerous British propaganda postcards, which pictured the cap perched on the shaven heads of obese soldiers – and its peaked variety, the *Dienstmütze*, usually worn by officers and NCOs. Both caps bore cockade discs showing their state and service. But that wasn't all. *Jägers* wore distinctive shakos, and there was the oilcloth high hat worn by the *Landsturm*. Like the British regimental cap badge, there was a bewildering array of caps, cockades and state insignia.

In northern Europe, the field uniforms of both nations were woollen, designed to be serviceable in cold weather, and when Fritz met Tommy on the battlefields of France and Flanders in 1914, they did so in woollen uniforms:

> The English are all slim, strong chaps … They did not have a single cigarette stub, instead they had pipes. In order to save tobacco, they smoked them unlit. Nearly all of them had their hands in their pockets; almost all were

bareheaded. The khaki material of the English uniforms is much sturdier than our *Feldgrau* …

Hauptmann Paul Oskar Höcker, Landwehr-Infanterie-Regiment
Nr. 20, 1914

The British uniform jacket for the most part looked very different from that of his German counterpart, though like it, the British uniform was loose-fitting – in order that layered undergarments could be worn. Fitting it to new recruits was often a challenge:

Off went our tailor-mades and on went our ready-mades, which fitted us only where they touched. The tunics were very slack and were particularly ill fitting at the neck. What a job it was putting on puttees and trying to get them to look smart … We must have looked strange. Surely only our mothers would have recognised us on our first appearance in uniform.

Rfn Gerald Dennis, King's Royal Rifle Corps

This morning we got clothed. At 6:40 we assembled and marched to the regimental quartermasters store. There we received blue tunics, trousers, caps and neck stocks all of which are of fourth grade quality. My tunic looked a bit scruffy, but after giving it some work with a brush it is not as bad as I thought it to be. Trousers and cap are very good.

Gefr. Otto Borgräfe, Ersatzabteilung Feldartillerie-Regiment Nr. 62,
16 August 1914

Fitting difficulties are where the similarities ended. The German field service uniform was issued in 1910 in *Feldgrau*, or field grey. Like its British counterpart was introduced to replace a more brightly coloured uniform – *Dunkelblau* or dark blue:

When we return to the barracks a number of carts loaded with brand new fieldgrey uniforms have arrived. Finally we get rid of our old blue rags. Soon I am fully clothed and start packing and never have I enjoyed packing more. At 6, I say farewell to the comrades that have to stay behind. I receive my iron rations, a pack of field dressings and a brand new grey uniform coat of good quality. An hour later the battalion commander inspects us and offers us a brash good-bye. At night no one is able to sleep, it is our last night as recruits and probably the last night we will be able

44

to sleep in a bed. At 4am after the waking call we get issued with seven cartridge frames and half a pound of sausage each. It's a cold morning. We finally march to war.

KRIEGSFREIWILLIGER R. SCHOLDER, FELDARTILLERIE REGIMENT NR. 37,
10 MAY 1915

The early German *Waffenrock* was plain in appearance from the front, with two side pockets closed by buttons, and eight visible tombak zinc metal buttons bearing the Imperial crown – or lion for soldiers from Bavaria. These buttons were never intended to be polished; this contrasted directly with the British jackets, with their five large brass buttons that had to be cleaned once out of the line. German rifle regiments, the *Jäger*, wore a 'grey-green' *graugrün* version of the *Waffenrock*, and were further distinguished by green piping to their jackets – in contrast with the red of the infantry. There were obvious links between German and British rifle regiments, and even as late as 1916, the regimental nicknames of the King's Royal Rifle Corps were described as:

'The Greenjackets,' from the colour of the uniform; 'The Jaegers'; … and quite recently has been dubbed 'The Kaiser's Own' from the fact that the regimental badge, a Maltese Cross, closely resembles the Iron Cross.

ANON, 1916

British Service Dress differed from the cleaner lines of the German *Waffenrock* in having a pair of box-pleated patch pockets with button-down flaps at the upper chest, and a pair of deep pockets let into the tunic skirt. The *Waffenrock* had only two buttoned pockets – but was distinguished by its piping, its distinctive divided skirt to the rear, with buttons, and variable cuffs, described as either *Brandenburg* (with a vertical buttoned flap) or Swedish (with buttoned turn-back). German cavalry uniforms were rather more variable, however; those worn by *Kürassiere, Dragoner* and *Jäger zu Pferde* had stand-up collars; *Ulanen* and *Chevaulegers* – Bavarian lancers – wore a special double-breasted tunic known as the *Ulanka*, while hussars wore the elaborate braided *Attila*.

The British uniform jacket lacked a belt, though in many cases, the standard webbing belt was worn on parade. For the Germans, the leather *Feldkoppel* worn by all ranks with clasp-like buckle was distinctive, the plate bearing the crowns of the respective states (other than the simple unadorned Hanoverian horse of Hesse) and mottoes to match as if to proclaim the right of the soldiers

45

who wore them, men of destiny with God on their side: *Gott mit Uns* ('God with us' – Prussia, Baden); *In Treue fest* ('Firm in loyalty'– Bavaria); *Providentiae memor* ('Mindful of Destiny' – Saxony); and *Furchtlos und Treu* ('Fearless and Loyal' – Württemberg).

Shoulder straps on both German and British other ranks' uniforms were significant in that they bore regimental insignia. For German other ranks, it was the number or monogram of the regiment worked in red for the most part, with its fastening button also bearing the regimental number. For the British, regiments were distinguished by brass shoulder titles, but a range of other insignia were also used. For both armies, in an attempt to deny the enemy of valuable information if captured, regimental insignia like these was either removed or covered up. Shoulder straps were also significant for officers' ranks in the German army; flat silver-edged straps denoted *Leutnant*, *Oberleutnant* and *Hauptmann*; larger twisted silver cord straps for *Major*, *Oberstleutnant* and *Obers;* and larger twisted silver and gold cord for general officers. British officers, by way of contrast, mostly bore their rank stars and crowns on their sleeves – though some units, the Guards for example, bore them on the shoulder straps. This became more common later in the war, to reduce recognition by the enemy.

Perhaps the most surprising component of the British army, if only from the perspective of the Germans, was the kilted highlanders. Many Scottish regiments wore the kilt, which was warm to wear with its many folds of woollen tartan, the downside of these folds being their propensity to harbour lice, as well as their ability to soak up vast amounts of water. The bright colours of some regimental tartans was also a problem, such that the kilt was usually worn covered by a wrap-around simple apron of khaki cloth in the field. The Scot was identified by his kilt in many German accounts:

> The English here are mostly Scots and even though they are strong men they wear short skirts (no trousers), which only just cover their knees. There is nothing a German soldier is afraid of.
>
> Unidentified German soldier, 11 October 1914

Kilted soldiers were also admired by some civilians in the battlezone, an unusual sight for many:

> We were the first British troops in Armentieres. As we marched through, the civilians went frantic with delight. The Germans had been there for a week, and had committed the usual excesses of troops flushed with

The German *Waffenrock* uniform.   The British Service Dress uniform.

victory. The highlanders in our brigade caused much amusement, the female part of the population shrieking with laughter at the dress of the 'Mademoiselle Soldats'.

PTE R.G. HILL, 1ST ROYAL WARWICKSHIRE REGIMENT, AUGUST 1914

With sniping a constant menace in the trenches, some protection of the head was essential – especially as trench parapets were constantly being blown down, putting the occupants of the trench at risk. Steel helmets were an innovation intended to reduce the head injuries that were all-too prevalent amongst men living and working in these ditches close to head height. Soldiers were vulnerable to snipers, but they were also subject to the random tragedies of spent bullets, and from air burst shrapnel and shell fragments. For most nations, 1915 was the pivotal year, as trench warfare became the norm. Clearly there was a need for increased head protection, and this was to be introduced late in the year, with innovation by the French, Germans and British – all of whom produced markedly different steel helmets to achieve the same effects.

Due to the high number of head wounds, the German High Command authorised the development of a steel helmet and in December 1915, military physician Friedrich Schwerd and Professor August Bier of the technical institute in Hanover developed a prototype for field trials. Their helmet was fabricated with high quality chromium–nickel steel and featured a visor and sloping skirt which protected the wearer's neck and ears. The helmet was a great success and by November 1918 some 7.5 million had been produced:

> When I come home I will bring my steel helmet with me; it is causing quite a stir here. One rifle bullet pierced the left side, went straight through and exited on the right side. It only grazed my head!
>
> CHRISTIAN TRAMSEN, GERMAN SOLDIER, 9 MAY 1917

Scots soldier of the Seaforth Highlanders with kilt and sporran.

The British steel helmet was designed in 1915 by John Leopold Brodie, an engineer. Brodie proposed a simple, easy to manufacture, dish-like helmet that could be punched from a single sheet of steel, with a liner that would resist impact. The shape of the helmet, with the bowl and extended rim, was designed to resist spent bullets, as well as shrapnel falling from above. After some trials, the helmet was adopted on 24 September 1915. It was battle tested in the Ypres Salient and was a success; over 1 million were supplied to the army by July 1916 – in time for the Battle of the Somme:

> You asked me to sketch one of the shrapnel helmets. Well there's absolutely nothing in them really, as they are more like an inverted pie dish that anything with a rubber buffered bandeau (I hope this is the right way to spell it). Still this is the best I can do.
> RFN WILLIAM C. TAFFS, 1/16TH QUEEN'S WESTMINSTER RIFLES, 20 APRIL 1916

The principal load-bearing equipment set used by the British was designated 'The Pattern 1908 Web Infantry Equipment'. The official guide that accompanied it praised its versatility, its balance, its flexibility, and its lack of constricting chest straps. All of these made the equipment easy to wear and fit for purpose. With supply difficulties, the webbing was replaced by a leather version (the 1914 pattern). Later in the war, the typical infantryman would also carry the respirator (in its appropriate haversack) and steel helmet. His burden would grow steadily:

> Yesterday we marched back … in grilling heat. What with their box respirators with extensions, steel helmets, rifles, ammunition, packs, etc, there is little doubt that the infantry soldier is getting over-loaded for marching. His equipment grows as the inventions for killing grow. Already he must carry between 70 lbs and 80 lbs.
> LT-COL ROWLAND FEILDING, 6TH CONNAUGHT RANGERS, 14 JUNE 1917

In the main, British equipment was admired by the Germans:

> All positions from which the English had fled have revealed weapons and equipment. I have to admit that the English, in the light of their experiences, had provided their soldiers with very good equipment. The leather of the backpacks is excellent. We felt almost envious of the two outside breast pockets, which were sewn onto their tunics. In each of their backpacks there was a mess tin and a shaving kit. Their rifles are perfect. However in the trouser

NCO of IR 119 (Württemberg) in full kit.

British soldier of the Essex Regiment equipped with 1908 pattern webbing equipment, and the SMLE rifle and bayonet.

pockets of each Englishman there is a weapon which is extremely effective in close combat. It is a folding dagger, with which they cut joints of meat and in addition – possibly after an attack – the throats of the enemy after an ambush. Among the prisoners were of all branches of the English Army: cavalry, artillery, infantry. Also Scottish Highlanders whose bare knees show beneath a diced tartan kilt. These are elite troops, but prisoners never the less.

HAUPTMANN PAUL OSKAR HÖCKER, LANDWEHR-INFANTERIE-REGIMENT
NR. 20, 1914

While the 1908 webbing equipment was an integrated 'waistcoat', the German system required cartridge pouches, bayonet, entrenching tool and 'bread bag' to hang off the leather belt, putting strain on the waist. Support for the belt was provided by shoulder straps that were integral to the calfskin pack known as the *Tornister*. In common with the British, supply was a problem, and by the end of the war a variety of replacement or ersatz materials were used in its manufacture. The German system, simple as it was, was tiring to wear.

The German backpack or *Affe* (monkey) usually weighed between 11 and 13kg. It usually contained: Messkit straps (*Kochgeschirr-Riemen*), *Mantelrolle/ Zelt* straps (*Mantelriemen*), tent accessories (*Zeltzubehörbeutel*), rolled-up over-coat (*Mantel*) and tent quarter (*Zeltbahn*), messkit (*Kochgerschirr*), a spoon/ fork utensil (*Essbesteck*), a tin of vegetables (*Gemüsekonserve*), two bags of rusk (*Zwiebacksäckchen*), two cans of coffee (*Kaffedosen*), a bag of salt (*Salzsäckchen*), a tin of meat (*Fleischbüchse*) and a tin of lard (*Fettbüchse*), a pair of ankle boots (*Schnürschuhe*), a shirt (*Hemd*), a pair of socks (*Strümpfe*) or foot cloths (*Fußlappen*), a handkerchief (*Taschentuch*), a pair of underpants (*Unterhosen*), a scarf (*Halstuch*), a field cap (*Feldmütze*), toiletry items (*Waschzeug*), rifle clean-ing kit (*Gewehrreinigungsbeutel*), tin of leather grease (*Lederfett*), cleaning kit (*Putzzeug*), brass-cleaning kit (*Messingputz*), paybook (*Soldbuch*), song book (*Feldgesangbuch*) and spare cartridges (usually three clips of five, fifteen rounds in total). The 'monkey' soon passed into legend:

The Monkey

And every infantryman knows this instrument of torture, his bugbear;
His tormenter, is this thing, that he calls a monkey.
Constantly, to make him wail
Dragging him up hill and dale,
He bears him like the bagpipes,
Piggyback, bathed in sweat he gripes.
The monkey feels no remorse,
And always stuffs his guts.

But in the evening when he gets home
That monkey comes into his own.
They open up his gibus tum,
And out rolls food and cheer and rum.
For tucker and what a lot I got
Is hidden in his distended pot.
And when it calls for a welcome nap
Then it shuts its monstrous trap.
The monkey rolls up in a ball
And makes a bed that's not bad at all.

GERMAN POSTCARD, c. 1915

The principal weapon of the British soldier from 1904 was the Short Magazine Lee–Enfield rifle, the SMLE to most soldiers. The charger system used by the SMLE allowed for five rounds to be loaded at a time, the magazine holding ten all together. Well-trained soldiers could fire around fifteen aimed bullets a minute with the SMLE – while the record, set in 1914, was thirty-eight bullets fired in a minute, a prodigious rate of fire.

The standard long arm of the German army was the *Gewehr 98*, a manually operated, magazine-fed, controlled-feed bolt-action rifle that fired a powerful 7.92mm cartridge and had seen its first combat use during the Boxer Rebellion in 1901. It was a reliable and accurate weapon, but its length of 1.25m made it difficult to handle in the confined spaces of a trench:

> At very close range, a very hot fire-fight developed. I stood taking aim alongside a pile of wood. My adversary was twenty yards ahead of me, well covered, behind the steps of a house. Only part of his head was showing. We both aimed and fired almost at the same time and missed. His shot just missed my ear. I had to load fast, aim calmly and quickly, and hold my aim. That was not easy at twenty metres with the sights set for 400 metres, especially since we had not practised this type of close-in fighting in peacetime. My rifle cracked; the enemy's head fell forward on the step.
>
> OBERLEUTNANT ERWIN ROMMEL, INFANTERIE-REGIMENT NR. 124

To improve the rifles' value in trench combat conditions, special kits were made to modify existing rifles in service. These included a twenty-five-round 'trench' magazine or *Grabenmagazin* and a stamped sheet steel breech cover which was intended to protect the action from dirt, mud and dust. While this was a great idea in theory, the cover had a tendency to rattle, creating noises that could give a soldier's position away to the enemy and thus it was seldom used. Nevertheless, the SMLE was much admired by the Germans:

> Compared to our hand held primary weapon the English rifle is undoubtedly more modern. Its foresight, for example, is framed by two curved blades which allows for easier aiming. Its rear sight is calibrated to a maximum range of up to 2000 metres. Its bolt is designed similar to that found on our rifles, but it's more crudely made. It can chamber up to 11 rounds, which are bit less powerful than ours, whereas our rifle can only chamber five. Its stock holds a small compartment with a bottle of oil, something that would be quite desirable for us as well.
>
> GEFR. HANS PAULS, INFANTERIE-REGIMENT NR. 58, 24 NOVEMBER 1914

Training

With mass recruitment came issues of space; the increasingly rapid flood of men that were joining the ranks of the British army in 1914–15 meant that new accommodation would be needed. The response was to build hutted encampments; while the new camps were being built, tented accommodation was provided – adequate for a two-week Territorial field camp, but hardly the perfect setting to train an amateur army to the peak of military effectiveness. With the weather worsening into the autumn of 1914, this was not an ideal situation, and muddy conditions made things unpleasant for many recruits:

> We are up to the knees in mud and water it is not fit for pigs never mind men here. I expect to be home for Christmas.
> PTE W. ASTBURY, 5TH CHESHIRE REGIMENT, PARK HALL CAMP, OSWESTRY

> Don't know if you would like to hear what we do each day. Anyway it is this:
> Rise 5.30, wash and shave till 6.15. Physical drill till 7 and then knock off for breakfast. After this one cleans one's boots etc and very carefully cleans one's carbine for Parade at 9. Drill or marching till 12.30 and then Dinner till 2.30 when we parade till 4.30. Then we are finished for the day – this is the ordinary day's work.
> RFN WILLIAM C. TAFFS, 1/16TH QUEEN'S WESTMINSTER RIFLES, 1915

With the men settled in their camps, the main job of the army instructors was to create a fit, efficient fighting force attuned to discipline and steady under fire, who took training seriously. As stated in the British manual *Infantry Training 1914*: 'The object to be aimed at in the training of the infantry soldier is to make him, mentally and physically, a better man than his adversary on the field of battle.' With large numbers of civilians coming into the army, training involved a simple diet of physical training, utilising the application of the Swedish drill system of 'physical jerks', as well as long runs and route marches in full equipment. It was *Infantry Training 1914* that set out the training course syllabus: 1, the development of a soldierly spirit; 2, instruction in barrack and camp duties; 3, physical training; 4, infantry training; 5, marching and running; 6, musketry instruction; 7, movements at night; 8, guards and outposts; 9, duties of soldier in the field; 10, use of entrenching equipment; and 11, bayonet fighting. The

British soldiers at rest after a route march.

average recruit might expect to receive training in all of these on his six-month journey to becoming a soldier:

> Well I spent about fifteen weeks there [at Kinmel Park Camp], that was at the 64th TRB [Training Reserve Battalion]. I had a pretty stiff training. I had not realised what the army was like until then. I could not get used to the food for a week or more. Now after we had been there just over three months I got moved to another camp a little lower down the park, still my pal was with me. Whilst I was there I finished my firing course, which I had partly what [sic] done in the other camp. I will tell you about Kinmell Park. It is a nice place, about nine miles from Rhyl. Holds a good thousands rather muddy whenever it rains. Well I left there after a few weeks and still my pal was with me. Well this time I left for Litherland Camp just by Liverpool, to join a service Battalion. I did not like leaving Kinwell Park [sic] with after getting used to everyone there, but I learnt after a few weeks that it was quite a comfortable camp and in a suitable place for pleasure, for you all know you want something to put your thoughts into, to hide the army.
>
> PTE PHILIP WHITEHEAD, 3RD ROYAL WELSH FUSILIERS, 1917

The training was hard for some men:

> Rather a trying day. Exceedingly hot. Busy at judging distances, fire control, and company drill, Swedish drill and semaphore. We dug 'trenches', supposedly under fire, lying face downwards and scratching out a shelter with our little entrenching tools – a frightful Sweat.
>
> PTE D.H. BELL, LONDON RIFLE BRIGADE, 29 AUGUST 1914

> Well I have settled down to my new life alright because it's no use breaking your heart here, just as that song says pack up your troubles in your old kit bag and smile. You should have seen us today on bayonet fighting we were half mad the man who can pull the ugliest face and do the most shouting is the best.
>
> PTE PERCY EDWARDS, 3RD SOUTH WALES BORDERERS, 1918

German infantry training was based on the Infantry Drill Regulations or the *Exerzier-Reglement für die Infanterie* (*Ex.R.f.d.I.*) of 1906, and the German field service regulations, the *Felddienstordnung* of 1908, which continued to stress that victory in battle could best be gained by a bayonet charge and, as a pre-condition to this, by obtaining fire superiority. German infantry would enter a battlefield in close formation and approach the enemy while being supported by fire of the divisional artillery. In case the artillery preparation had not been sufficient to keep the enemies' heads down, the closed columns would break up to form smaller formations, which would advance in bounds, rushing from cover to cover until reaching a covered position less than 500m from the enemy, where the individual units were to form into a single line and then to commence firing. Once the enemy was pinned down and was unable to return fire effectively the infantry would use that advantage to initiate a bayonet charge. To be able to train and lead their subordinates in that way officers were advised to cultivate the initiative and self-reliance of their soldiers:

> Each unit commander, from company level upwards, is directly responsible for the correct training of his subordinates and he must not be restricted in the choice of his means. Their superiors are obliged to intervene only when faults and lags are observed.
>
> GERMAN INFANTRY DRILL REGULATIONS, 1906

The backbone of the concept was the German NCO. The *Unteroffiziere* in the German army had either been made up from the ranks or appointed after graduating from one of the nine *Unteroffiziersschulen* (NCO academies), in which the sons of former soldiers received a free education. Due to these academies and the German educational system in general the German NCO and indeed most of the enlisted men were literate. Being an NCO came with a high social status and major inducements. Social status and security attracted high quality and ambitious candidates. While early in the war the German army was reluctant to allow its NCOs to formally command even the smallest of units this quickly changed as the war dragged on. From early 1915 onwards it was a common sight to see an NCO in command of a company:

> The comradeship we experience here is heart warming. Our *Unteroffizier* is an amicable and cheerful Rhinelander and like most of the other *Unteroffziere* he is about 38 or 40 years old. Last week he helped me to get out of my boots as my feet were so swollen that I could not get out of them on my own. He also helped me to pack my backpack and to roll my coat and the tent-square. A really nice man who cares for his subordinates like a father.
> Reservist Richard Sinawitz, Reserve-Infanterie-Regiment Nr. 35,
> 20 October 1914

Each year in October German infantry regiments would receive their new recruits. Common to all armies, developing a routine was a significant matter:

> Now let me tell you about the daily routine. In the morning, usually about 6:30am we assemble. We then march out into the heath for field exercises: fanning out in dispersed skirmish lines against a designated 'enemy', movement within a skirmish line, going prone into cover and moving into position. To do that the group has to crawl on the belly, the rifle sling between the teeth towards their group leader. As I am usually the group leader I have to do little crawling. I only crawl until I am in a position to open fire on the designated enemy. That is all very interesting and I love doing it. Then suddenly there is a shout of: 'Attack! Get up! Marsch! Marsch!' and we jump up and rush forward. Then to the command of 'Get down!' we go prone again. In the evenings there is usually some bayonet fencing or aiming practice. Tomorrow there will be a live-firing exercise again.
> Musk. Kurt Meyer, 1. Ersatz-Bataillon Infanterie-Regiment. Nr.56,
> 18 January 1915

Usually a recruit's day would start at about 5.30 a.m. after which the recruits would wash, clean and put on their uniforms and equipment, make their beds, clean their rooms and then receive breakfast in the garrison's mess hall. The rest of the day was divided into periods of theoretical and practical training which were absolved under the eyes of an especially appointed training officer. Theoretical training was conducted in the classroom. In most cases, the first three months were spent with individual training:

> Wake up call at 4:45am, fatigue duty (sweeping the parade square etc) until 5:00am, washing and preparing for service up until 6:30am when there is a lecture followed by an interaction-hour, that means questions and answers. At 7:45 assembly in full gear. After a 15 minute breakfast break the forenoon is now filled with drill on foot, gymnastics and especially gun-drill and aiming practice. One is constantly on the move and sheds a lot of sweat. Lunchbreak is at 11:15 and the time until 2:15pm is filled with doing the laundry, studying for the theoretical lessons and drinking coffee. The evening up until about 6:30pm is filled with a number of varying activities. Telephone training, guard duty exercises, lectures at the guns and the aiming circle, aiming at static and moving targets. Even at 10pm we're still practicing with the guns, now with lanterns. The whole gun laying procedure is very interesting. The One-Year-Volunteers have two extra lectures with an officer two times a week and riding lessons have now started as well. I will do my best, but I am sure my knee will go on strike. At 6:30 we usually receive mail and dinner afterwards. Each day there is an inspection of some kind. Next week training with the battery starts. That means we will drive out to exercise in the open terrain. Soon, I think in a about a month, we will be sent to the front.
>
> KANONIER HELLMUTH GOLDEN, ERSATZ-ABTEILUNG FELD-ARTILLERIE-REGIMENT NR. 11, 14 SEPTEMBER 1916

The focus of practical training was put on the effective use of arms, including bayonet drill, the use of terrain in combat conditions, and marching and exercise in accordance with the drill manuals. A special focus was laid on use of the rifle or the *Braut des Soldaten* (the soldier's bride). This included range estimation, target designation and marksmanship. Rifles were not locked away when not being used and usually stored on racks in the hallways near the recruit's quarters. That enabled the men to practise drill even in their off-duty times. To keep track of his abilities as a marksman, each German soldier was required to keep a *Schiessbuch* (shooting book), into which he could enter the results of a prescribed firing table which he had to complete with at least minimum standards and which he had to repeat until he managed to do so. The combined results of all company members were then entered into the *Kompanie-Schiessbuch.*

> There are a lot of things to learn here, but I like the shooting most. Today we have been shooting again, amidst a scurry of snow. I could hardly see the targets, but I made a good job of it. At the moment half of our company has an extra hour of marksmanship training at noon. Last week there was a shooting competition where I scored 41 rings. Today I scored 39 and we only need to hit 30. Tonight there will be a night march with full kit.
> PETER SCHMELZER, I. ERSATZ-BATL., INFANTERIE-REGIMENT NR. 493,
> 14 JANUARY 1916

> Service here is more or less the identical to that in the barracks but it seems that it is to start all over again! When our Hauptmann welcomed us he said that we had learned nothing so far! Yesterday we had to do manual labour for 3 ½ hours and started building a shooting range on which we will train in the coming weeks. We will probably stay here for 6–8 weeks.
> KARL LINDNER, REKRUTENDEPOT 7, I. BAYERISCHES ARMEEKORPS,
> 22 JANUARY 1915

Another important part of rifle drill, which was regulated in a special shooting regulation (*Schiessvorschrift für die Infanterie*) was platoon fire drill, the goal of which was to direct the massed fire of the platoon onto an enemy target. Every recruit was trained to deliver rapid fire or *Schnellfeuer* of eight–ten aimed rounds a minute, but due to ammunition expenditure *Schnellfeuer* was only to be used when repelling enemy assaults or cavalry attacks. Even officers were required to train competitively with the rifle:

> Beloved parents, finally I have the time to write. Day and night we march. You can probably imagine that after a 40km march, with full monkey, tent square and coat, cartridge pouches, spade, breadbag and rifle, I rather use my free time to catch some sleep. We already conducted three live firing exercises and will have another one on Tuesday. Our company has already dug a trench. On Sunday there was a 'skirmish' between Birnbau and Schwering, that means one battalion vs. another battalion.
> RES. EMIL GREMLER, 2. ERSATZ-BATL. RES.-INF.-RGT. NR. 46, 2 MAY 1915

The responsibility of training the men properly lay solely in the hands of the regimental commanders, who usually left the details on how it was done to their officers who in turn relied heavily on their NCOs. As a result of this, the quality of training in the early months of the war could differ. Those units who were lucky enough to have been trained in peacetime or during the war by younger and more modern officers and NCOs – who understood the demands of modern warfare and the devastating killing power of the modern breech loading rifle – went into battle in loose skirmish lines with enough room and freedom to make use of all available cover. Soon after the outbreak of the war most officers and NCOs of this calibre had been transferred to the front, so many units raised in the early months of 1914 – and especially those soldiers of the quickly raised *Reserve-Infanterie* regiments who were hastily trained and thrown into battle in October and November – were trained by older and old-fashioned superiors using the out-dated 1888 regulations, which ignored the lessons learned during the Boer War. It was these men who marched into the British rifle fire in dense columns in 1914. Due to the lessons learned from these early mistakes, a certain amount of front-line personnel was regularly rotated to the regimental *Ersatz* units to train and educate recruits according to the latest developments of the front, while depots were set up in occupied territory behind the front lines where soldiers from Germany could enjoy a further period of training based on the latest standards and experienced front-line personnel.

The length and intensity of the training varied a lot. Where soldiers trained in peacetime had enjoyed up to three years of training followed by regular exercises, many of the volunteers and recruits in the early stages of the war had to make do with a training period of six to eight weeks followed, if they were lucky, by a couple of weeks of extra training when they arrived at the *Ersatz-Depots* behind the front. In the later stages of the war, the situation improved and training phases of six months, followed often by further training behind the front were the norm:

We look quite inhuman having been dressed in six grade fatigue uniforms and people have been warned to inspect us as they might burst their midriff from trying to restrain their laughter. So far we have learned: *Links um!* (Left face!), *Rechts um!* (Right face!), *Kehrt!* (About turn), and *Augen geradeaus!* (Eyes Front!). What a rifle is no one has told us yet.

We feel quite useless and the mood has suffered considerably from the boredom. This morning there was a sigh of joyful relief as there was a bit of drill exercise, but that was already over at noon. Maybe it will be better tomorrow.

KRIEGSFREIWILLIGER RUDOLF EMMERICH, ERSATZ-INFANTERIE-REGIMENT
NR. 32, 11 AUGUST 1914

There would also be specialist training:

I am currently in a machine gun training class. This only lasts for six days, so I have to exert myself to learn as much as I can. There will be an inspection by the regimental commander on the sixth day. Nevertheless I really enjoy it so far, there is hardly anything as interesting as the German machine gun. So well made, so immaculately designed, but also simple and effective to use. Tomorrow we will begin to shoot it, but it is obvious that a six day training period can only be superficial.

L. FELDWEBEL ADOLF TREBER, KÖNIGLICH BAYERISCHES 23. INFANTERIE-
REGIMENT, 4 JANUARY 1917

Adequately equipped and trained, the soldiers of both nations prepared 'for the front':

Now on Nov 8th an order came through that we had to stand to and not leave Barracks, pack up and get ready to move, we filled the ration carts in the afternoon. When it came about seven o'clock they let us out. On the Sunday we had to stop in again until night, all the people were up at the camp. Now on the 5th/17 Monday we got ready, kit and everything packed up and at about half past ten marched on the square. We marched off and down to Seaforth Station headed by the band. Down at the station the people were crowded around us. We did not know right where we were going.

PTE PHILIP WHITEHEAD, 3RD ROYAL WELSH FUSILIERS, 8 NOVEMBER 1917

We had no send off, whatsoever; no shaking hands or wet handkerchiefs – any one not knowing a war had been declared would have had no suspicion that these men were starting out on active service.

PTE FREDERICK BOLWELL, LOYAL NORTH LANCASHIRE REGIMENT, 1914

If they were lucky, men would be inspected by a general or the king himself – and then the journey to the trenches:

The King came to review us today and I can tell you it was a sight. We then all marched past him and then we formed a guard of honour to the station. It was a sight I shall never forget. I expect we go on Saturday, the King told our Colonel. Your Loving Brother, Walter

PTE W. ASTBURY, 5TH BATTALION CHESHIRE REGIMENT, 1915

There was similar devotion to the Kaiser in the Fatherland:

War demands an iron discipline and a concentration of force. Combat demands thinking leaders and self-reliant riflemen who, out of devotion to their warlord and to the Fatherland, display a strong will to win even when their leaders have fallen.

GERMAN INFANTRY DRILL REGULATIONS, 1906

The king and Lord Kitchener review troops who are on their way 'to the front'.

Crown Prince Wilhelm inspects the troops near Bapaume, October 1916.

Then came the command 'shun! Face right!' His Majesty, our Kaiser, came striding down the front of the assembled men. My heart was beating with excitement; soon I would be able to look into His Majesty's eyes. He came closer and soon he stood in front of me. Pointing at my Iron Cross 1st Class he asked: 'Well? How have you earned that?' – 'On patrol duty in Eastern Prussia and during the recent battles here in the West your Majesty' – 'Where from?' was another question he asked. 'From Thuringia, I am from Saxe-Meiningen' was my answer. 'I see, carry on like this!' his Majesty said, shook my hand and left. I had been bestowed with the highest honour a warrior could hope to receive.

UFFZ. KARL SCHUSTER, RESERVE-INFANTERIE-REGIMENT NR. 232

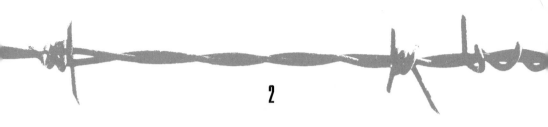

2

In the Field / *Im Feld*

Crossed the border into enemy territory. Three hearty shouts of Hurrah from the men for our Fatherland.

Schütze Franz Koeppe, Infanterie-Regiment Nr. 160,
19 October 1914

We were among the first English troops of the Expeditionary Force to put foot on French soil, and the excitement was great. Over the whole of the distance we travelled we were hemmed in by crowds shouting *Vive l'Angleterre*.

Pte Frederick Bolwell, Loyal North Lancashire Regiment, 1914

For the British, the journey to France was an adventure. It is probable that few men had ever travelled to the continent before the war and the ideas of what it might be like ran riot with their minds. It didn't help that Field Marshal Lord Kitchener had instructed them to steer clear of temptation in advance of their journey, on a slip of paper issued to every man:

You are ordered abroad as a soldier of the King to help our French comrades against the invasion of a common enemy … Remember that the honour of the British Army depends on your individual conduct. It will be your duty not only to set an example of discipline and perfect steadiness under fire but also to maintain the most friendly relations with those whom you are helping in this struggle … In this new experience you may find temptations both in wine and women. You must entirely resist both …

Field Marshal Lord Kitchener, August 1914

The British soldiers' first impression of France was not always a complimentary one:

British troops in France, waiting for transport to move 'up the line'.

We embarked for France and landed at Boulogne on the morning of August 23rd. What a contrast between us and the slip-shod undersized French territorials who were guarding the docks! In their baggy red trousers and long blue coats, they looked like comic-opera soldiers. We looked smart in our new khaki, and training had made us broad chested and clean-looking.

Pte R.G. Hill, 1st Battalion Royal Warwickshire Regiment, 6 August 1914

At Le Havre we were met by two men of the French Army, who to our unaccustomed eyes appeared very strange in their red trousers and blue coats. We promptly dubbed them 'The Pantomime Army.'

Pte Frederick Bolwell, Loyal North Lancashire Regiment, 1914

Though for others the thought of being somewhere 'foreign' was enticing:

> Just a few lines to let you know that I received your welcome letter
> Sunday morning quite safe … Dear Mother France is a grand place and
> we have a lovely church close to the camp and mass is at half past nine on
> Sunday morning.
> PTE WILLIAM COTTER, 2ND ROYAL DUBLIN FUSILIERS, 16 SEPTEMBER 1918

The regular troops that landed in 1914 were very quickly transferred to the
front in order to tackle the German advance; just over two weeks after arriving they were to face the Germans in what would become the first contact
between German and British troops on opposing sides. And from late 1914
through to 1918, the war would be dominated by siege tactics, 'in the trenches'.

Journey to the Trenches

> Sailed for France Aug 15th and arrived at L'Havre Tue, Aug 18th then on to
> Rouen and landed the same afternoon. We stayed here about 3 days, had a
> good look round the place and then left for Amiens arriving on Fri. 20th,
> left here on Sunday for Bohain. This was very close to the fighting and had
> to leave very hurriedly as the Germans were advancing at a terrible rate.
> PTE HENRY W. TALBOT, ARMY SERVICE CORPS (MOTOR TRANSPORT),
> AUGUST 1914

> Regiment in a splendid state and on the way to the western border.
> Everywhere we get a magnificent welcome. These are glorious days!
> LTN. B. ANDRAE, LEIB-DRAGONER REGIMENT NR. 24, LEIPZIG,
> 10 AUGUST 1914

Supplying the siege war meant a journey to the front line and a train that
went back as far as the home country. For the Germans, this meant a reliance
on the European rail structure, which, soon after the start of the war, was
taxed beyond its limits. With the Germans fighting along the whole 700km
front from the Swiss Frontier to the North Sea coast, moving supplies and
men to where they were needed was a serious undertaking. Especially early
in the war, German railheads could be as far as 160km behind the front, so
great distances had to be covered in horse-drawn vehicles and on improvised
narrow-gauge railroads:

Our journey to Belgium was very interesting. We traversed the Lahn valley towards Marburg and Coblenz. From there to Trier and on into Luxembourg. The closer we got to the border the louder the cheers of the population. The train has just crossed the border into Belgium. A minute ago we have passed an old battlefield, mass graves, discarded rifles, abandoned guns and a Belgian village, which has been completely destroyed.

GEFREITER FRITZ APPEL, INFANTERIE-REGIMENT NR. 68

Yesterday evening at the station we had to wait for 7 hours before it was our turn. First train carried about 600 men from the *Ersatz-Bataillons* of Reserve 39 and 57, followed by transport with replacement mounts for the cavalry and artillery. To this was added a wagon carrying a number of elderly *Landsturm* pioneers. During this time at least a dozen other trains, carrying soldiers and supplies for the front came through without stopping.

GEORG WEGENER, RESERVE-HUSAREN-REGIMENT NR. 5

The conditions were basic:

We occupy a railway wagon of the 2nd Class. It has a bathroom and is very comfortable. Johann is in the wagon next to ours and supplies us with everything we need. There is food and drink aplenty, too much some would say. Even at night elegant ladies of the upper classes were waiting on the platforms to supply us with all kinds of good things and during the journey all kinds of people assaulted the train to hitch a ride. As transport commander it is my job to decide who to take with us. As there are already 200 officers and men, their horses and 28 vehicles on the train this was no easy task. 13 nurses, who asked me to get to them to the battlefields as soon as possible were billeted in the servant's wagon as well as a wife of a wounded Hauptmann. I have also taken three young lads who have left school and wanted to join as volunteers. Our march through Leipzig was true triumphal procession with a stirring crowd and lots of flowers.

HAUPTMANN HANNS VON EINSIEDEL, JÄGER-BATAILLON NR. 12

Sunday, 9 August: On the train. Red Cross supplies us with coffee, lemonade, apple juice. I now have diarrhoea from drinking too much. At 12:00 there is coffee and sausages.

Monday, 10 August – Fell asleep and so I missed a nice, hot bowl of meat stew. I share the wagon with 28 other men. Everyone is joking and it's nearly impossible to stop laughing. All railway wagons have been decorated

German troops on their way to the front, 1917.

with funny slogans i.e. 'my sabre tip is itching', 'The Tsar invited us to tea,
in case of bad weather the war will commence indoors'.

ANONYMOUS GERMAN DIARY FRAGMENT, 1914

For the British, the supply line crossed the English Channel with all its attendant problems – men crossing in the numerous ships and steamers would
scan the sea for U-boats and other craft intent on sinking them with their
human cargoes on board. The British component of the line was relatively
small, at first from the medieval town of Ypres in the north, to the industrial
landscape of the Lens coalfield in the south. With the French holding most of
the line, much of the burden fell on them to face the Germans, but gradually
the British front extended as the British war machine developed.

British soldiers arriving in France invariably progressed from the Channel ports through the base camps and on the long journey to the front:

30 January 1916 Arrived 5.00 am Southampton Docks. Went on board the Mona Queen at 5.00pm for France.
31 January 1916 Arrived at Le Harve at 8.15 am. Marched through the town to Mess Camp, arriving about 4.00 pm. Dry but very cold.
    SGT FREDERICK J. COMPTON, 16TH CHESHIRE REGIMENT, JANUARY 1916

The destination of the cross-Channel troop ships was Boulogne, Calais, Rouen or Le Havre:

After leaving we had a good run to Folkestone and went straight on to the boat and it began to snow. We left at once and waited outside harbour for 2 hours and then had a quick run over to Boulogne snowing all the time. At B we went up the quay in a blinding snowstorm and were … divided into groups of Divisions and Army Corps, etc and the rest marched up to Rest Camp moving all the whole officers kits went up by lorry.
    PTE VIVIAN V. STEVENS, ARMY SERVICE CORPS (MOTOR TRANSPORT),
                                                    14 MARCH 1916

I have been in the rest camp at Calais all the time there is plenty of work here making trenches and plenty of food and the best Calais is a fine place.
    PTE WILLIAM COTTER, 2ND ROYAL DUBLIN FUSILIERS, 5 OCTOBER 1918

For most, arrival at their destination would involve a further period of training – battle-hardening and acclimatisation to local conditions that saw, in France at least, the use of vast base camps (known as 'infantry base depots') and harsh training in so-called 'bull rings', such as those at Étaples and Le Havre:

Evening found us at the great base camp at Etaples in a vast wilderness of tents and buildings. For mile on mile the camp stretched along the dunes. I was awed at the vast array which spoke of the growing might of the British Expeditionary Force.
    LT CHARLES DOUIE, 1ST DORSETSHIRE REGIMENT

Thirty thousand men learnt the advanced lessons of war on the 'Pimple.' They bayoneted, manoeuvred and trained from seven in the morning until four in the afternoon … They listened to the most bloodthirsty lectures ever conceived, from the lips of hard-bitten instructors who had seen everything since Mons.

Pte Arthur E. Lambert, 2nd Honourable Artillery Company, 1916

8th July 1916 Le Havre. Day drill at Bull Ring. Work good.
9th July 1916 Church parade at Bull Ring in afternoon. Work good and was praised
11th July 1916 Bull ring all day. Soft day.

Cpl Albert Howard, 9th King's (Liverpool) Regiment, 1916

Learning new tactics and weapons meant that sometimes even the base detail was dangerous:

We were throwing live bombs this morning and a piece of one dropped at my feet although I was standing a least a hundred feet away. Of course if it had hit me it would not have hurt me much but the Sub taking us was rather surprised at its travelling so far. I collared the piece and I shall try and keep it as a memento.

Rfn William C. Taffs, 1/16th Queen's Westminster Rifles, 25 April 1916

When we learned that there was to be a hand grenade throwing competition all the company Feldwebels started practising as well. Derksen of 10/236, Krebs of 11/236, Leonhard of 12/236 and myself. My dog 'Piefke' which excelled at rat hunting and thus was the only dog that Major Ebel allowed in III Battallion, was with us as well. We were practising with live grenades when all of a sudden Piefke dashed after a thrown grenade and picked it up by the handle and turned around to bring it back to us. Terrified we four started running like we had never run before. The fuse delay time was long over when we stopped and Piefke proudly delivered the dud grenade.

Feldwebel Bielert, Reserve-Infanterie-Regiment Nr. 236

Life at the camps was intense:

Just a line to let you know I am, so far, safe in France. I am at the Base where there are 100,000 troops in one huge camp. We had a lovely crossing escorted by three destroyers and one aeroplane and all wore lifebelts while crossing the Channel. We are about 40 miles from the firing Line and we can just faintly hear the guns. I suspect we may be here a few days and it will be quite alright if you will write me to above address. I wish I was back in Whitchurch, but still it is no use worrying I am here and have got to stick it.

2Lt Arthur H. Lamb, 1st Lancashire Fusiliers, 16 July 1916

At Camp put ten into a tent and had a rush for food. At 5.30 paraded and were divided into four groups two to go off 9.30 in morning, rest later in the day. Received one holey blanket a piece with their compliment of live stock complete and after a scrum at Canteen in Cigs scare, returned to rest about 8 o'c snowing all the while and bitterly cold.

Pte Vivian V. Stevens, Army Service Corps (Motor Transport),
14 March 1916

Though accommodation was often in huts, with the increasing number of troops arriving in France there was invariably a crush that would only be handled through the use of tents. These were fine if the weather was good and the ground underfoot had not descended into a morass:

We are having rain here just like at Richmond and as we are again under canvas we are not feeling at all as if we are in a foreign country – Still I shall feel happy when I bow my head and step into a bell tent for the last time. I have seen very little of the town and am afraid I shall see very little more as the place is out of bounds.

Rfn William C. Taffs, 1/16th Queen's Westminster Rifles,
7 December 1915

We are warm in our tents and well we might there is 18 in our tent. I am liking hear [sic] but I don't know how long we shall be hear [sic]. It will be up the line for us soon I expect. I will send you a field P. card when we go up and then you will know I am somewhere nearer the fighting.

Pte Arthur Thorp, 13 April 1916

The journey 'up the line' from the base camps was fraught with fear and expectation. With censorship in place whilst 'Somewhere in France' the British soldier invariably went to 'the front' or 'in the trenches'. In any case, it was not possible to keep one's family informed of the journey:

Travelling in France these days is slow, and not always sure; that is, one is not sure of anything. We set out yesterday afternoon, armed with three and a half days' rations, to reach a destination known as 'The Front'.

CAPT. G.M. BROWN, 9TH SUFFOLK REGIMENT, 1916

For the Germans the journey to the front was equally trying, though there was the anticipation of joining their comrades. Many kilometres of marching, marching, marching:

In column the battalion marches along the mud clogged roads, indifferent, nearly asleep. Instinctively everyone follows the man in front of him, closely behind so not to lose him in the dark. Only sometimes there is a silent course when somebody stumbles, if the weight of a machine gun on a shoulder gets too heavy or when the straps of the backpack cut into the flesh. Otherwise there is only the steady, scuffing, heavy rhythm of the march. Give us a rest – give us a rest – rest – rest – rest …

LTN. FRIEDRICH KLEINE, INFANTERIE-REGIMENT NR. 459

Day after day we have to march and there is not a lot of time to rest. In the last couple of days we have marched nearly 80 kilometres! We have heard that a comrade in 6th company has shot himself because he could not bear it anymore. You can't imagine what we have to go through.

WILHELM HEIGL, KÖNIGLICH BAYERISCHES 14. INFANTERIE-REGIMENT

Just a few lines to let you know I am well. Life here is generally good, but the food could be better. Army bread is all we are getting. We have to march 20–25 kilometres a day with fully packed 'monkeys'. This is quite a lot, especially as we have only just started to carry backpacks at all. We usually spend the nights in barns where we sleep in the hay. We rarely wash, but I have already washed myself once. There are a lot of turnips here which are quite tasty. We eat a lot of them as an addition to our meals. Sometimes we sleep inside rooms and houses. The people speak Flemish which is terribly hard to understand, but I am able to use my knowledge of French to good effect. They are generally very friendly and sometimes frightened. We requisition their hay and use their stoves to make coffee. When they are unwilling to comply the revolver usually sets them straight. On the 14th we had to arrest the mayor and two citizens of a nearby village as they had fired on one of our pickets.

KRIEGSFREIWILLIGER WILHELM HERWIG, RESERVE-INFANTERIE-REGIMENT NR. 233,

10 OCTOBER 1914

In some parts of the line, men would move through the abandoned towns and broken cities, marvelling at the nature of the warfare that wrought this destruction:

> The town here is extraordinary, with masses of masonry lying about in the streets. Great houses with not a pane of glass in the windows and their doors standing open. Great skeletons of houses with just the four walls standing and the window places gaping empty and then a little ray of light from some door or window where some shopman more daring than the rest has crept back to sell his wares. The soldiers flock in and out and in the small Inns they discuss the war and all the latest stories.
>
> 2Lt Arthur R. Stanley-Clarke, 1st Dorsetshire Regiment,
> 12 March 1915

The British soldiers' journey from the base camps to the front line was all too often in notoriously slow-moving trains, housed in trucks marked '*Hommes 8, Chevaux 40*':

> At Le Havre Railway Station we were packed into horse-boxes, 36 men and NCOs in each box, the total often reaching nearly 50 men.
>
> Pte Frederick Bolwell, Loyal North Lancashire Regiment, 1914

Travelling at speeds that approached walking pace, the journey was long, drawn out and frustrating. At the very least, it was a relief to know that finally, they were to go 'up the line':

> On 3rd April left Folkestone about 9 o'clock landed France Boulogne about dinner, had dinner and then left for Etaples, landed just after tea got put in tents for the night, the morning after we removed a little farther up the camp, there we were in tents. We stayed at Etaples from the 3rd/18 to the 7th same date. Then on the 7th, Sunday we left about half past six and got in cattle trucks, had a ride all night and landed at a place which they called Casae [Cassel] a few miles from the line. We marched up into a small camp where we had something to eat, then we had another march which I shall never forget. This was a depot for the R.W.F. We stayed there a night and on the following day April 9th/18 had another small march down towards the line, there we pitched our tents.
>
> Pte Philip Whitehead, 3rd Royal Welsh Fusiliers, April 1918

British soldiers asking the French engine driver for water – the journey to the front was incredibly slow, and tea made in this way relieved the boredom. The soldiers wear goatskins issued in 1914 to combat the cold – they were nicknamed 'stinkers'.

With frequent halts along the way, soldiers would walk up to the engine in order to beg water for tea – that brew so universally admired by the British soldier:

Do you know how to make tea, I wonder? Take enough of the tea mixture (supplied by the Army, consisting roughly of five parts of moist sugar to two of inferior tea) to cover the bottom of a mess tin, then walk to the front of the train; this is generally about 700 yards away, since one is sure to be in the last carriage … then in your best French ask the driver for some hot water.

If successful in your request, a blast of steam suddenly issues from an unexpected quarter in the side of the engine, shortly followed by a fountain of hot, if slightly brackish water. Suspend the tin by a handkerchief under this, and after leaving it for a few minutes to draw, one's tea is ready. The more fortunate ones soak an old condensed milk tin in the stew to obtain cream.

CAPT. G.M. BROWN, 9TH SUFFOLK REGIMENT, 1916

Reaching the railheads in France and Belgium, the onward journey was invariably on foot. Carrying the full equipment meant that this was a tiring experience for the average man, whatever their nationality:

The post has again been delayed owing to our moving again. We had a 17 mile trek yesterday and we are now in quite a pretty little village in a valley. It's a gorgeous day today and everything is looking its best. It was rather a strain yesterday but only 4 of our chaps fell out and they went until they dropped. We were again congratulated by the Colonel on our marching. It may interest you what I carried to give you some idea of the weight. I will make a list and put it on a separate piece of paper. Will you keep it for me?

Full equipment (water bottle, sword, entrenching tool)
120 Rounds ball cartridge
1 Overcoat
1 Macintosh
Holdall (hussif, knife, fork, spoon, shaving tackle, toothbrush and powder)

1 Mess tin and Cover	1 Cup
1 Balaclava	1 Tin bully beef
1 Muffler	1 tin grocery [ration]
2 pairs socks	6 big biscuits
1 shirt	Rifle cleaning outfit
Stationery	1 Rifle
1 Towel and soap	6 Candles
2 Respirators and goggles	1 bottle eau de cologne
1 Tin chocolate	1 tin cocoa
Cigarettes, Tobacco, and 2 pipes	1 day's Rations
1 Plate	

RFN WILLIAM C. TAFFS, 1/16TH QUEEN'S WESTMINSTER RIFLES,
13 MARCH 1916

Tomorrow we will have to march 30 kilometres, but that is not difficult for me. I hiked longer distances with father. Our *Affen* will be transported on the baggage cart so we will not have to carry those. Like every infantryman I am equipped with infantry trousers, short boots, tunic and I wear a light felt helmet, which is a bit too large so underneath it I wear a cloth cap to make it fit better. Over my shoulder there is my rifle, which is new, well maintained and a real beauty. We call it the infantryman's bride. Around my hips is the *Koppel* with a number of attachments including: a bayonet, a *Beilpicke*, two cartridge pouches with 60 cartridges, a Mauser pistol, a breadbag with 30 rounds for the Mauser, rations, gloves, a canteen with coffee, a pocket knife, etc. Coat and tent square have been rolled and are attached to the *Affe*. We have all equipped ourselves with sturdy long walking sticks which help us to march through the thick mud. This we have copied from the Russians who call these sticks 'Nokosch'.

Anton Kratz, Infanterie-Regiment Nr. 57, 10 October 1914

Interactions with the locals often relied on body language, gestures and speaking loudly; those soldiers with knowledge of French – or the confidence to try to use it, even with Flemish-speaking Belgian locals – would be in demand amongst their comrades, especially when there was the opportunity of buying or bartering food and drink from them:

Do you know, I acted as interpreter to four other Subs and made some French soldiers understand what I wanted – so you see I am a bit of a linguist! I left my sword at a small cottage opposite No 3 camp at Le Havre, it belongs to a lawyer and I gave the sword in charge of the housekeeper as no-one but I was carrying one. They say it gives one away too much and that the Germans always bring down anyone carrying one so I thought discretion was the best part of valour.

2Lt Arthur R. Stanley-Clarke, 1st Dorsetshire Regiment,
26 October 1914

I was a scream yesterday in the shops. My French is the absolute limit. I go in the shop with a carefully prepared sentence, they never understand but only laugh at. I beat about the bush an awful lot until the place is a mass of broad grins. I always manage to get what I want eventually, if it is in the shop. The other chaps with me laugh too, but I notice they get me to get the things for them.

Rfn William C. Taffs, 1/16th Queen's Westminster Rifles, 18 May 1916

Arriving in the battlezone was often a challenge for the senses:

> We were travelling nearly all day and of course it rained hard all the time
> and so we all got thoroughly wet and very muddy, as every road is a river of
> muddy slime and the whole country is again just a damp desolate wilder-
> ness of mud. I have never known anything so awfully depressing and utterly
> cheerless! It's just terrible and people at home have no idea what it is like
> out here, a perfect H on Earth!!
>
>   2Lt Arthur H. Lamb, 1st Lancashire Fusiliers, 21 February 1917

> What impressed one more than anything was the sight of the country
> round us. Running right across our lines away into the German lines was a
> road – once a main road with trees each side and full of traffic, and now –
> I can hardly describe it as one looks along it as dawn was breaking – every
> tree as far as one could see shot to pieces! Splintered trunks standing out
> against the sky line. Shell holes – broken stone work – torn barbed wire –
> equipment old and broken – dead Germans – rifles – absolute despairing
> ruin everywhere so intense that one could almost touch it and tore one's
> felling to shreds. I am afraid this sounds like Rosa N. Carey at her worst
> but it made a tremendous impression on me and I shall never forget it.
> I wish some great artist or author could see it and feel it as I did and make
> it permanent as a picture or an article.
>
>   Sgt Oswald S. Blencowe, 18th Royal Fusiliers, 26 January 1916

Arrival in the battlezone was usually the soldiers' first experience of artillery fire. The new men soon picked up the slang of the old hands. Shells
would no longer be known by their calibre – instead they would be 'Jack
Johnsons' and '*Schwarze Sau*', 'Whizz-bangs' and '*Ratsch-bumm*', 'Coal-boxes'
and '*Kohlenkasten*':

> There is a small village in front of us which Fritz used to occupy and all
> the morning he has been dropping great whacking shells onto it and we
> are just hoping now he does [not?] turn his attentions to this old muddy
> trench! I talk about a village but it is merely a rubble heap literally nothing
> else but small piles of bricks that were once homes and which our artillery
> has turned into the aforesaid piles of rubbish!!!
>
> The country here is all desolate and destroyed by the tide of War and
> covered with relics, rifles, bombs, equipment, letters, photos and every
> conceivable thing and also other more horrible sights I dare not speak to

you of, it is all too horrible and I am quite sick and tired of it, mummy dear, and oh! How much I do pray to God to bring me soon back to you. I simply trust in Him and for the meanwhile I must try and endure like a man, for the sake of the men. I believe they think I like it !!!! But I don't and no words can express the unspeakable horror of this war. It is far far worse than I ever realised it to be and I say this that people at home cannot do too much for the boys out here, the brave Tommies whom we look after; they are fine, mummy dear, and I have seen and do see each day the sufferings they endure and they are very real! Forgive me writing like this and I know you think about us out here but there are people at home by the thousand, sitting before the fire and in every luxury who are content to read the official reports of 'British progress' etc and if they could only realise what it means. I know every inch of ground gained is at a fearful cost!

2Lt Arthur H. Lamb, 1st Lancashire Fusiliers, 22 October 1916

We have had rather an excited week here. After 20 hours in the train we arrived here (that is at five o'clock the next morning, last Sunday). We were taken out to do a little firing. We were formed up and marched off in a field. We had not been on the move mins when Wizz Bang, our first shell made a hole where we had just stood. So that was a bit of a scare. They shelled us all that day and night intermittently and the next day fairly fiercely so when we were told B coy were to go up to the 1st firing line that night we had our baptism of fire, and it was not strange when we got there.

Rfn William C. Taffs, 1/16 Queen's Westminster Rifles,
25 December 1915

The destination of all the soldiers was 'the trenches' – with some apprehension.

In the Trenches

The Western Front, the western theatre of operations of the German army who was also fighting in the east on a two-front war, became an entity once the opposing forces had entrenched across northern Europe, in late 1914. And it was on the Western Front that trenches became the dominant feature of warfare. The importance of massed artillery and the firepower that could be brought to bear by the infantryman or by machine guns was testimony to that. Men naturally went to ground, and in so doing pitted the artilleryman against the engineer. In truth, the only way that this situation could change was through reliance on the only arm capable of effecting it – the infantry, who ultimately would have to rise from the trenches in a frontal assault.

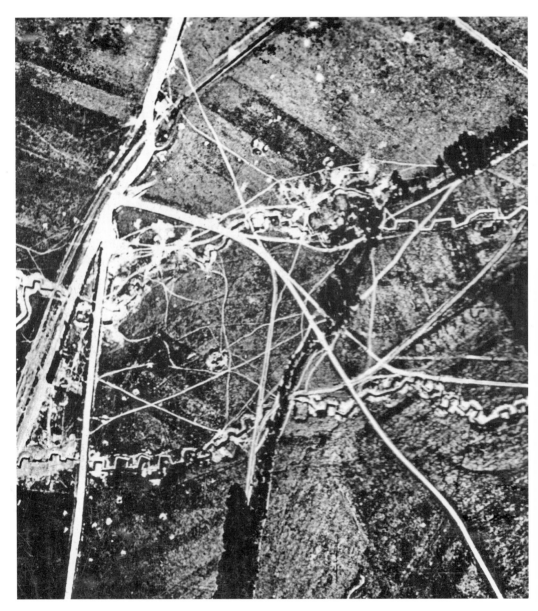

Aerial view of 'the trenches'; this is a British reconnaissance photograph of the German trench system known as the *Siegfriedstellung* – the Hindenburg Line to the British.

As men went to ground, so there evolved a system that both sides understood only too well. Each trench was meant to be deep enough to give adequate protection to the men within; each one was equipped with traverses and bays that were designed to prevent enfilade fire along its length, limiting the effect of bursting shells, or of machine guns aimed along a captured trench. From humble beginnings there evolved a complex trench architecture as men strove to improve the ground underfoot, or to prevent the trench slopes from collapsing. Each nation had its preferred system of trench construction, but needless to say, the workings of a captured trench was clear to soldiers of either side.

Maps were produced that made the complexity of the trench systems intelligible to officers as they came up to the line; these were surveyed with great accuracy and depicted the trenches of enemies and friends alike – though the ever-cautious British only marked their own trenches on to their own maps for fear of them being captured, despite the fact that enemy aviators were all too capable of observing their own trenches in full glory, producing the aerial photographs that would be used to make more maps:

> In modern war impressive things are done. A while ago I had the chance to have a closer look at one of our maps on which the enemy trench system could be seen in every detail. It even showed camouflaged artillery positions! Of course I cannot tell just how up to date this map was, but it seemed to be a comprehensive and detailed view. The enemy trench system was subdivided into numbered sections and even sported the enemy's terrain designations!
>
> UFFZ. FRANZ SEEGERS, RESERVE-INFANTERIE-REG. NR. 73, 30 MARCH 1915

Most trench activity went on at night. Reliefs and replacements arrived, picking their way through complex trench systems that were mapped out in intricate detail – but which may well have come about by accident, at points where the opposing sides halted on their onward advances. During the day, trenches saw limited activity; at night, there were working parties in no-man's-land, checking defences, reconnoitring and probing enemy positions, gathering intelligence. Barbed wire parties worked to strengthen their obstacles while machine gunners nervously fingered their grips; star shells and very lights were sent up to illuminate the night sky and trap the enemy in silhouette against it.

At all times there was a randomness to death, from stray spent bullets, aimed sniper fire or artillery. All through this, men on both sides of the barbed wire tried to scrape an existence, 'standing to' on the fire step at dawn and at dusk to ward off the possibility of attack. With fear subsided, men would go about their lives as best they could.

Going into the trenches for the first time was viewed with apprehension by men of both sides; trench life commenced from late 1914 and would define the war for most of its life:

We have moved during last night some three miles nearer the trenches. Another battalion has gone into the trenches before us and we are their reserve for ten days when we go in. We are in a large town, billeted in a damp, dark, dirty cellar; most horrible place; but we have to go into cellars as the Hun is rather fond of shelling the place.

This town is a sight; imagine a place like Sale simply razed to the ground! Not a house or a church or a wall standing, the work of the German gunners. It is a scene of utter desolation and I never conceived such a thing could be and it shows what a terrible thing war is today with its vast number of guns and high explosives. Really no earthquake could possibly have wrecked more completely a town.

2Lt Arthur H. Lamb, 1st Lancashire Fusiliers, 10 August 1916

Settling down to inactive trench life, we soon discovered what a miserable state we were in. Most of the original men had left their spare kits and overcoats at Le Cateau, as we had received orders there to attack in fighting kit. We were in the front line at Houplines twenty-nine days at one stretch. I for one had neither shirt not overcoat. My shirt had been discarded at the Aisne, being alive with vermin. Beards were common, and our toilet generally consisted of rubbing our beards to clear them of dried mud. Our trenches were generally enlarged dry ditches, where we dug in when our advance was stopped. Sandbags were very scarce, and when it rained the sides of the ditches fell in.

Pte R.G. Hill, 1st Royal Warwickshire Regiment, 1914

We equip ourselves to march off to the trenches. To combat the lice each soldier gets a neck pouch which contains an evil smelling substance. In the evening we march out. As my feet are still giving me trouble I am allowed to load my gear and backpack onto the company's baggage cart. Just behind Courcy it is the first time I get to see our foremost trenches. They are extremely well built, wide and deep with strong parapets, embrasures and loopholed steel plates behind which a rifleman can find cover. In daylight these loopholes afford a safe and excellent view across the terrain in front of the trench. At night the small holes are quite useless and you have to use sacks of sand as footsteps to be able to look over the edge of the trench. On the backside of the foremost trench there are various types of dug-outs. Some are virtually proof against artillery shells as they have been cut deep into the chalk ground. Larger ones, being able to shelter 8 to 10 men are roofed with massive wooden planks supported by iron beams. They won't resist a direct hit, but afford protection against shell splinters and shrapnel balls. The ground inside these dug-outs is covered with straw and they are furnished with a table, benches or chairs and have a window opening on the backside which is blocked with straw when it is cold outside. When there is no daylight, candles are used for illumination.

Our company gets allotted to a section called the 'Hindenburg' trench, which is only about 200 metres away from the enemy trenches. It's part of a protruding section of our line known as the '*Friesennase*'. It's named that way because it looks like a nose on the map and because it has been manned by Friesians since September. Me and six men of my group move into a nice dug-out, the other two men are billeted in the dug-out next to us. At night-time each group has to have four men on watch inside the trench while the others are allowed to sleep. The guards are relieved every 2 or 3 hours. Another group has to supply men for the so-called *Horchposten* [listening post]. These men lie down under the barbed wire, about 30 to 40 metres in front of our trench. Access to this exposed position is through a deep and narrow trench which affords cover against infantry weapons and which is also equipped with loopholed steel plates. Our position is well equipped with weapons like machine guns (including a Belgian and an English one), revolving cannon and lots of hand grenades. In case of an enemy barrage narrow and deep artillery trenches lead towards the rear affording the men with plenty of cover.

UFFZ. FRANZ SEEGERS, RESERVE-INFANTERIE-REGIMENT NR. 73,
29 MARCH 1915

At all times, artillery was king, from the sharp retort of a quick-firing field gun through to a slower, but more powerful howitzer shell or mortar, packing a punch. Men would be on the lookout for threat:

Yesterday I came under effective shellfire for the first time. I have of course had shells uncomfortably close but the Germans have never had the exact range of our trenches before. Yesterday they first of all put a shell in my trench about ten yards from me, seriously wounding one poor chap. They then put eight more in, killing six and wounding four. However we got the men out of the trench along the communicating trench and the Germans did no further damage though they continued to shell the empty trench. A bullet is a kind wound compared to a shell, we have had quite a few casualties of course with bullets since I have been out here but as I said before this was the first time I had seen the effect of a shell. Afterwards I went round and collected some of the pieces which I am sending you along with three buttons, two Belgian and one German, the latter is the flat one, the two former are the ones rather like marbles. From one of the pieces of shell you can gather what the Germans are putting into them.

2Lt Arthur R. Stanley-Clarke, 1st Dorsetshire Regiment,
5 December 1914

I just sent you a hurried Post Card as the Post was just going out. I am afraid it was rather disjointed as the Germans were sending us a few cards in the form of 'Jack Johnsons' and while I sit here the shells keep on passing over. You have no idea how very cheery we all are. I don't wonder people want to get back, this beats big game shooting all hollow. We have no lack of news here as we receive the Official Reports but we do not have much from England.

2Lt Arthur R. Stanley-Clarke, 1st Dorsetshire Regiment,
1 November 1914

During the night the shells came whizzing over and we could not get much rest. Well the night rolled on and when the morning came round they were still shelling.

Pte Philip Whitehead, 3rd Royal Welsh Fusiliers, 1918

As the British extended southwards from Ypres and Artois, the Germans experienced a difference in approach from the French – despite their much vaunted 75mm field gun:

The only unpleasant change came in the form of the English artillery. It was better, having a longer range and using heavier calibres. And different from the French, it kept targeting the villages in our rear, regardless of the French civilians living there. From our observation posts we could see that they expelled the civilians from every village they occupied. For them it is a necessity of war, when German troops did the same in Belgium they were called Barbarians.

HAUPTMANN FREIHERR GEORG VON HOLTZ, RESERVE-INFANTERIE-
REGIMENT NR. 121

Shells bursting in the trenches were a constant threat; many soldiers had to give thanks for the traverses and bays that acted to prevent shell blasts travelling along the trench:

> A shell burst in our trench the other day and the new draft were frightened out of their lives. One cannot make them understand the importance of keeping out of view, they will show themselves and hence the terrific losses.
>
> 2LT ARTHUR R. STANLEY-CLARKE, 1ST DORSETSHIRE REGIMENT,
21 NOVEMBER 1914

As the war progressed, the static lines of front, second and reserve line trenches developed and evolved. At the beginning of the trench war, the ditches themselves were shallow and hurriedly dug, but the lines were soon strengthened into almost impregnable fortress positions that required terrible engines of war to destroy them – with the inevitability that men would have to rise from them in order to take the enemy by force. All too often, the intervening no-man's-land – which swelled and narrowed according to topography and the fortunes of war – would get close enough for the men to hear their enemies, even smell them as they went about their daily business:

> We are just out again and with any luck shall not go in again for about a month. We have done a month in and out of the trenches, this last time we were in for 9 days – 4 days in support and 5 days in the firing line. I wish I could tell you where it was but I shall only get the letter torn up by Old Man Censor! Anyway it was a very well known place and a very hot corner and I am glad to say I got through this time without having any more casualties in the platoon. It was really a most astounding thing as the company we relieved had lost a good many. In one place the Huns were only about 80 yds away and they were also holding a small crater in front of their line the front edge of which was only about 35 or 40 yds distant from us. We were fairly safe from shells as the lines were so close together but there was a tremendous lot of sniping and any amount of rifle grenades flying about so one had to be most awfully careful. The best part of a rifle grenade is the fact that you can see it coming and it often lies on the ground so as a

German trench at
Lievillers, 1916.

rule one has plenty of time to get round the nearest traverse. At night it's
rather a strain on the nerves as one can't see them but one can hear them
coming quite plainly, the only thing to do is stand absolutely still and listen
to it fall then after you have heard the thud of its fall – if it's anywhere near
– down you get as low as possible waiting for it to burst. One afternoon
one fell right into our trench but everyone saw it and nobody was hurt,
it blew a hole about 18 in deep through the foot board! The second night
we were in they sent about 80 rifle grenades at us before we spotted where
they were coming from and then my rifle grenade men got started and the
third we sent off did the trick, it landed right into the little crater where
the Old Hun was and apparently wiped them out as we weren't bothered
again that night.

SGT OSWALD S. BLENCOWE, 18TH ROYAL FUSILIERS, 26 JANUARY 1916

84

British soldiers in a reserve trench in *c.* 1915.

At times, the battlefield became more fluid – with strong points to break up any attack:

> A strange life, this life of 'Strong Posts', cut off from the world during the light; unable to move for bullets from enfilading machine guns and snipers, one sleeps in one's dug-out. By night, however, a different and more dreadful story. Aerial darts and whiz-bangs concentrate on the only means of approach to the dug-out, and so it's a case of all on top all night. Sometimes the night passes quietly, sometimes not.
>
> CAPT. G.M. BROWN, 9TH SUFFOLK REGIMENT, 1916

The static nature of the conflict was such that it sponsored the actions of those men whose skill at arms and nerve was sufficiently true that

German soldier on guard in a forward sap, protected by loopholed armour plates and supplied with extra ammunition carried in a cloth bandolier.

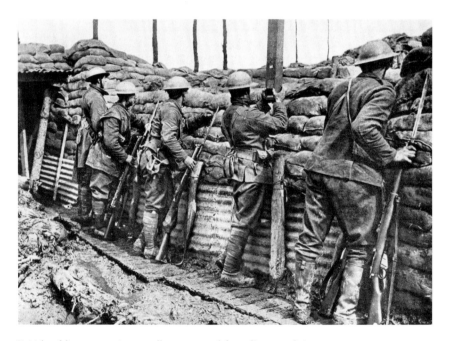

British soldiers occupying a well-constructed front-line trench in *c.* 1917.

they would take on their enemy by stealth. Snipers were these men, often focused on weak points in the trench parapet, or those areas prone to congregation of men, such as latrines. Unsuspecting or unfortunate men would be their targets:

I had a lovely view of two Boches this morning about 5.30am. It was on my tour of duty that at one part of the trench I looked over, I saw two Boches standing in their trench. I seized a rifle from one of the sentries and had a pot shot at one of them, who moved quickly but unhurt. Needless to say I got one back that was a bit too near my head to be pleasant.

2LT ARTHUR H. LAMB, 1ST LANCASHIRE FUSILIERS, 28 AUGUST 1916

The English snipers are very good so we have to be on guard all the time. We already suffered some casualties through headshots. The weather is awful. Our feet are freezing but the rest is kept warm by hard work. We are terribly dirty, but dirt keeps warm.

LEUTNANT STURHAN, INFANTERIE-REGIMENT NR. 53

Since I am the best shot in my company I was issued with a special rifle which mounts a telescopic sight! Both rifle and optics are of similar quality to that on my old Simson, but here I hunt a different prey. Each morning I choose my deerstand, which has to offer a good view of the English positions and wait. When a cap appears over the parapet or I see movement through a loophole I pull the trigger. Sadly I rarely have the chance to confirm my success, but it is interesting and exciting work!

GEFR. HERMANN KIESER, RESERVE-INFANTERIE-REGIMENT NR. 248,

23 JANUARY 1915

After this and several very exciting moments one arrives at ones destination and here are the snipers (as a rule) a lot is said of the bad shooting of the Germans but one acknowledges to ones cost that their snipers are of a different class and considering the really wonderful escapes some of us have from these men at night it is marvellous that we have such few casualties – of course they come often (the bullets) uncomfortably close.

2LT ARTHUR R. STANLEY-CLARKE, 1ST DORSETSHIRE REGIMENT,

18 NOVEMBER 1914

Besides I have been assigned a wonderful job. I am now a sniper and do a lot of observing work. Whenever I feel like it I walk to the observing post

British sniper and his spotter in a front-line trench in 1915.

where there is so called 'scissor' telescopes through which I can observe everything that is going on on the English side. When I spot an Englishman who is bold enough to raise his nose, it is my duty and obligation to shoot him. I do not need to do any sentry duty and am allowed to sleep at night and that while everyone else is on their feet. I feel like I am in heaven!

GEFR. IGNAZ HAUTUMM, RESERVE-INFANTERIE-REG. NR. 236,

21 APRIL 1916

The action of snipers became almost matter-of-fact:

Jacobs No.4 shot in head. Shelled heavily in afternoon, blew in part of trench.

PTE M. WILLIAMS, 11TH WELSH REGIMENT, 4 OCTOBER 1915

German sniper of Reserve-Infanterie-Regiment Nr. 68.

Trench Life

With so many men experiencing the hardships and boredom of the trenches, it was imperative to keep them occupied. In most cases, officers were aware of the potential for problems to arise if men were left idle or under-employed. Improvement of trench positions was carried out by most in an attempt to both improve the lot of the average soldier and also keep his mind off the awful conditions:

Our trenches possessed few of the desiderata carefully laid down in the Field Service pocketbook. The parapet was far from bullet-proof, the bright yellow clay against the green must have been visible for more than a mile, and the average depth of trench was not more than a foot.

Lt Malcom V. Hay, 1st Gordon Highlanders, 1914

In trench with Devons, fine chaps, dug latrines in morning for 1 hour, on sentry in trench, watch artillery bombarding enemy trenches with shrapnel in afternoon. On duty all night. Big scrap somewhere on our left. Hear French have advanced.

Pte M. Williams, 11th Welsh Regiment, 15 September 1915

Trench work all morning, very unlucky, more shelling in afternoon, one or two come over. Stand to at 7 o'clock and leave trenches, march to billets, very tired.

Pte M. Williams, 11th Welsh Regiment, 16 September 1915

The constant digging was a challenge to the average soldier's conception of what it was like to serve in the front line:

Am I a soldier? I still feel like a recruit, an earth worker, a cheap labourer who does not eat much and who is always ready to do his duty. That might change one day, but for now I am what I am. Every night I am on guard duty for 2 hours, followed by another 2–3 hours in daytime. Every day I am digging trenches and dug-outs, I sweep the duckboards, eat what is available and sleep on old hay in a stinking, dark dug-out. I provide the lice with plenty of food and watch the rats and mice eat mine. The sound of their gnawing and chewing is a constant companion, but it fails to make me forget the fact that dirt and sweat form a thick layer on my body, which I will hopefully be able to remove once I am allowed to leave the trenches. This is basically what my life here looks like; day and night, in sunshine and in rain. Next time I will write about life in the peaceful rear at Peronne, which usually is not peaceful at all. But I will not complain, after all there is war going on. Peace will and must come soon, hopefully before 1916.

Soldat Nikolaus Seitz, Königlich Bayerisches 12. Infanterie-
Regiment, 28 August 1915

Well my love we shall have no sleep for the next three nights now as we have to be on the watch all the time keeping the Germans back and there is no dug out where we are going into this time. So I suppose we shall be working most of the time in the day making them. Dug out means a place dug out in the earth and sand bags put all over the top and all around it so as to keep the shells out.

Pte Robert W. Price, 10th Welsh Regiment, January 1916

In the aftermath of battle shell holes would be joined up to provide the necessary cover in that part of ground that had been captured. Getting the trenches into the regulation form to protect life and limb was a significant task; empty sandbags carried into battle were a valuable asset:

We were between 'two lines' and clear of both. We 'stood to' until it was properly day-light, but he didn't send his infantry over to us. We now started digging again, joining the holes up to make one continuous trench. We worked through to each other from the holes dug during darkness and so we kept under cover. We gave each other direction by holding a spade or a pick up. We worked hard till near dinner time (or what should have been dinner time) got the narrow trench joined up, then started widening the top and leaving a fire step about 18 inches from the bottom. We filled sandbags, which we put in front leaving loop holes and rests for our rifles. When finished the sandbags raised us above the level of the ground, therefore giving us a wider vision, and it was necessary to stand on the fire step to fire over the bags, and so leaving a clear road for any one to walk in the trench bottom and be well under cover.

Pte John H. Benn, Loyal North Lancashire Regiment, June 1917

Improving the wire entanglements in no-man's-land was one of the most important tasks; the wire acted as a barrier to German advances and kept the defenders relatively safe; cutting the wire in any attack was one of the most formidable tasks of any infantryman. Maintaining the wire was a complex job:

I was allotted a nice job. My Section Sergeant, coming to me just after dark, said: 'I've a nice little job for you.' ... 'Do you know anything about barbed wire?' says he; 'just twisting it around stakes?' ... 'well, out in front about forty yards,' says this Sergeant, 'You will find a lot of stakes and two reels of barbed wire. Now you go out and I'll send another fellow to knock in the stakes while you can twist the wire round them and make some entanglements. I can't say I liked the job, because I didn't! The enemy lay only a few hundred yards away, and I had to go out there attracting attention by knocking in stakes and twisting barbed wire around them, a thing the enemy would be sure to try their best to prevent.

Pte Frederick Bolwell, Loyal North Lancashire Regiment, 1914

Well my dear I was out last night working putting barb wire down until 12 midnight so you see I have not got much rest we are on the go night and day out hear [sic] I wish it would soon come to an end.

Pte Robert W. Price, 10th Welsh Regiment, 15 March 1916

But working in no-man's-land could be a nerve-racking experience for the sentries peering out into the night from their trenches:

Later on a terrible accident occurred. A platoon of our pioneers sent to repair damage to the barbed wire entanglements was taken under fire by the men of our listening post. The men had not been informed about the repairs and were under strict orders to shoot as soon as they noticed anything suspicious. Expecting an enemy patrol they opened fire and killed one pioneer instantly. Another pioneer was shot through the head, he was still alive when he was recovered but he will be dying soon. How terrible it is to be killed by your own side.

Uffz. Franz Seegers, Reserve-Infanterie-Reg. Nr. 73, 30 March 1915

Wire entanglements became increasingly complex as the war progressed, with explosives, alarms, and a host of other materials designed to hold back the enemy and trap him in time to allow the sentries to defend the trenches. And the role of the sentry was significant, guarding against infiltration of trenches by 'lone wolf' actions or larger raids, watching out for gas or mortar fire, or noting any unusual actions. The conditions made most men jumpy – sometimes with unfortunate results:

A few days ago an older *Landwehrmann* in our unit, who was on guard duty in the trench during the night, mistook our Leutnant for an Englishman and shot him in the face. The Leutnant had not been wearing his helmet, only a soft cap. The *Landwehrmann* was not punished for his mistake.

Unidentified soldier, Könglich Bayerisches 2. Reserve-Infanterie-Regiment, 13 November 1914

German '08/15' light machine gun and crew, 1917.

With noise from no-man's-land causing alarm, both sides would take the chance to fire star shells and Very lights high into the night sky in order to try and illuminate the enemy on the skyline, presenting a suitable target for a traversing machine gun or a skilful sniper:

> Meanwhile the firing continues. Every minute an illumination flare is fired which spends enough light to check the terrain in front of us. No enemy in sight. The same on our left, where all the firing is coming from. Then, as suddenly as it started, the firing dies down. A few more rifle shots ring through the night, then it is quiet.
>
> UFFZ. FRANZ SEEGERS, RESERVE-INFANTERIE-REG. NR. 73, 4 APRIL 1915

British soldiers firing a machine gun close to the front line in *c.* 1917.

I have been in the trenches for the last three weeks and lately I have been up every night entrenching (for the last three nights) it is perhaps the most exciting work which we have here, when it gets dark we move off, the road is generally full of 'Johnson' holes and these full of water so if you don't look out one has a bath, then one marches long up comes a star shell lighting up the whole country and we lie flat hardly breathing for three or four minutes – then up and on generally with a few stray shells over us just reaching the country and they generally light on the road!! But then one gets an expert and when you hear them coming one can generally tell if to the right or left or at one and then ditch or any cover available. The only ones which do are the little 18 lb field gun which come at such a terrific velocity that it is practically impossible to get away from them.

2Lt Arthur R. Stanley-Clarke, 1st Dorsetshire Regiment,
18 November 1914

At 9 pm, in beastly weather me and eight men of 5. *Kompanie* climbed out of the trench. The darkness allowed us to cover most of the distance to the enemy position walking upright, but every time a starshell went up we had to stand still like stakes. If it was exceptionally bright there were nine splashes and we went prone into the muddy soup that surrounded us. The rain came down relentlessly. We continued and machine-gun fire went harmlessly over our heads. Soon we had crossed the Chaussee which led from Ferme-Deband to Wieltje. Full cover! From now on we had to crawl and orders were whispered only. On the elbows, crawling and sliding our patrol moved forward. Now we were about 70 metres away from the enemy trench. Me and a comrade now continued alone leaving the rest of the men behind to cover our advance. We pulled ourselves forward on the elbows, a hand grenade in one hand, without using the legs or knees as every sound could have betrayed our presence to the enemy …

'Whoosh' – another starshell goes up and my head goes nose first into the water. For a moment you stop breathing, there is no feelings only a tremendous sense of tension and suspense. We are surrounded by a huge, glistening sea of light. Will they see us? When the flare has burned out it seems to be even darker than before, but inside I am glowing with joy. I continue alone and manage to reach the enemy wire. I check a length of about 100 metres but I am not able to find any mines. The work is most exhausting. When a flare goes up now I will be a sitting duck. Like a crab I crawl backwards, face to the enemy and soon I have reached my comrade. We covered the first 20 metres in a crawl … there was no doubt that the enemy would hear us soon! Only a bold approach could help us now. We got up … when flares went up or machine guns fired, we went prone. When we had reached the chaussee we had lost all sense of direction. Where were the enemy lines and where were ours? He had changed directions so often that we had got ourselves lost. To make things worse we were suddenly stuck in a wire entanglement. God only knows how this got there. We cut ourselves through. On the way I stumbled a few times and fell into water-filled shell craters and destroyed trenches a few times

… when I returned to our trench my hands were cut to pieces and my
trousers were torn.

LTN. KÖRDING, RESERVE-INFANTERIE-REGIMENT NR. 236,

FEBRUARY 1916

In winter conditions, in the low-lying country of Flanders, the environ-
ment of the trenches could be extremely trying. Even though a common
myth persists up to this day that the German trenches were much better
than their allied counterparts, this is simplistic. Although the German army
in Flanders occupied much of the high ground and so their trenches were
a bit dryer than those of the British, methods of trench building were
very much dictated by the lay of the land. Here in the wet conditions of
Flanders, the flooded plain, the low-lying land and the clay subsoil made it
quite impossible to dig deep trenches and dugouts. Both sides here raised
their trenches above ground by using a breastwork of sandbags, wood or
corrugated iron. Most NCOs and men lived, fed and slept in the trench
protected by rain capes and small hollows dug into the side of the trench,
just like their British opponents on the other side. The longer the war went
on and due to the defensive stance of the German army, the trenches were
strengthened considerably by the construction of concrete bunkers, strong
points and fortified villages in depth running the length of the Ypres Salient
between Pilkem and Messines within an elaborate defensive network – the
Flandern Linie (or Flanders line):

A week ago we had a real dose of *Daily Mail* trenches up to our waists in
water and mud – it was ripping – and one imagined oneself a child again
– so I made mud pies – it was a clayish mud and it stuck well!

2LT ARTHUR R. STANLEY-CLARKE, 1ST DORSETSHIRE REGIMENT,

17 DECEMBER 1914

The mud out here is pretty awful in places. I was wearing gum boots this
morning and as I was cleaning a trench my feet sank so I had to grip hold
of the end of the boot and pull like anything before I could release myself.
The other day I saw an officer talking to a man, meanwhile sinking deeper
and deeper until he was quite knee deep. It looked so funny to see his legs
seemingly getting shorter and shorter.

RFN WILLIAM C. TAFFS, 1/16TH QUEEN'S WESTMINSTER RIFLES,

20 JANUARY 1916

Suddenly we can hear voices and the sound of men working. The enemy guards are talking to each other, but we cannot understand them as they are too quiet. All of a sudden another sound: 'splash, splash'. The boys on the other side seem to be even deeper in the shit than we are, their trenches are obviously even more flooded than ours. I can hear the 'Gentlemen' swim through their trench. I take a mischievous pleasure in that.

LTN. KÖRDING, RESERVE-INFANTERIE-REGIMENT NR. 236,
FEBRUARY 1916

You have read no doubt like I have of trenches knee-deep in water and taken it like I have with a grain of salt, but it's quite true – I have just spent two days and two nights in a trench knee-deep in parts and waist-deep in others – and instead of being very ill as I should be by rights I am feeling rather fitter than I was before!

2LT ARTHUR R. STANLEY-CLARKE, 1ST DORSETSHIRE REGIMENT,
6 DECEMBER 1914

It was the consistent rainfall of the low-lying parts of France and Flanders that represented the greatest challenge, and the ability of the water to collect in the ditches dug by the troops across them:

The horrible French winters seem to consist of storm, snow and rain, lots of rain.

UNIDENTIFIED GERMAN SOLDIER, 13 JANUARY 1917

We are having some rotten weather just now and hope you are having better at home it has been raining and blowing all week and made it miserable for us as we have had to stop in all day through it being so bad and God help the poor lads that is in the trenches. I am doing A1 just now and hope to be out soon.

DVR PERCY HARTLAND, ROYAL FIELD ARTILLERY, 17 FEBRUARY 1916

The weather here is terrible, but being company runner I do not have to suffer a lot as I spend most of my time in a warm dug out. My poor comrades are not so well off, their coats and clothes are soaking wet and they are freezing in wind and rain.

MUSK. WILHELM SCHLIEPER, INFANTERIE-REG. NR. 157, 18 JANUARY 1916

In the long run there is nothing so exhausting than to stand guard in the trenches. Especially in bad weather, which is something we are suffering from constantly here. No proper winter, but an overcast sky, cold wind and rain. Parapets and dug outs collapse and the trenches are so flooded that I wish I had webbing between my toes. It is not at all comfortable, but rheumatism comes for free!

PIONIER WERNER SCHREIBER, PIONIER-BATAILLON NR. 11, 7 JANUARY 1915

We also have had a good deal of rain and the trenches are in an awful state; in some of them we literally walk through water up to our knees and one gets wet through several times a day. Things have so far been fairly quiet since we have been in the front line except for the day before yesterday, when, about 6 pm the Germans bombarded us for about 1 hour heavily and knocked our trenches about a good deal and caused seven casualties. I must [say] it was awful, the artillery is terrible and but for that the war would be much nicer. But when they start bombarding with High Explosives it is nothing more than Hell. I know it shook me up terribly and I felt good for nothing for some hours.

2LT ARTHUR H. LAMB, 1ST LANCASHIRE FUSILIERS, 20 AUGUST 1916

The situation was a lot different on the chalk regions of the Somme, Artois, Arras and the Champagne. Here the German defences were indeed much stronger. Dugouts could be up to 40ft deep; there were underground strongholds, concrete machine-gun emplacements and many German front-line units had the comfort of electric lighting, piped water supplies and air ventilation systems. In permanent positions like these, plundered household items were often used to furnish dugouts with timber wall panelling, tables, chairs, sofas and even *objets d'art* and carpeted floors. But even here, the weather conspired against their martial inhabitants:

On the 3rd of April heavy rainfall set in which made our residence in the trenches unbearable. The rain turned the hard chalk into a sticky and slippery surface which forced us to cling to the parapet when walking the trench to avoid falling down. On the first day of Easter (4th of April) it was still raining hard, but we found consolation in the fact that the mail brought a lot of presents from home.

UFFZ. FRANZ SEEGERS, RESERVE-INFANTERIE-REGIMENT NR. 73, APRIL 1915

It was necessary for men to guard against exposure and frostbite in the sodden conditions, and the armies issued clothing to try and combat this. More often than not the men of the winter trenches looked like a ragtag army:

> By Jove you would laugh if you could see your little son now looking like an Esquimo more than anything else – in a wonderful fur coat – short so that one can march, they keep one wonderfully warm.
>
> 2Lt Arthur R. Stanley-Clarke, 1st Dorsetshire Regiment,
> 30 November 1914

> I enclose a photograph of your little son trying to wear some of his numerous clothes, at the time this was taken there were German shells bursting about one hundred to one hundred and fifty yards away. I very wisely put the house between myself and them. I have a knitted waistcoat on over my breeches as I could not get it on anywhere else and I had four scarfs around me as well as the fur coat – I have a turnip in my hand, after they had finished taking one I had a very rough ride in my chariot (wheelbarrow). I have a revolver in my right hand …
>
> 2Lt Arthur R. Stanley-Clarke, 1st Dorsetshire Regiment,
> 8 February 1915

Trench foot – caused by constant soaking of feet constrained by ill-fitting boots – was a serious threat to the men of the front line, and early in the war men unable to change their socks or to get relief from the wet ground would fall foul of this condition. Trench foot was not the only threat to men's well-being; lice too were a problem. With so many men in close contact, without the opportunity to get a change of clothes, lice multiplied. This was no simple irritation – lice also led to skin conditions, and even fevers that caused extremes of body temperatures that would see men debilitated and moved out of the line. Combatting the parasites was a significant matter, even in the rear areas:

> Wake up call at Noon followed by Sauerkraut for lunch. In the evening it's cleaning rifles followed by an inspection. After that we are ordered to Courcy to dig trenches there. I stay behind because I have problems with my feet. On Sunday there are no duties except muster in full gear and church service. Only the men that did not take part in trench digging go there. These are the sick men and the ones infested with lice. Lice are a widespread problem, but everything is done to get rid of them. As soon as

someone notices he is infected by lice he has to report himself. He is then put into a bath and gets his uniform cleaned.

UFFZ. FRANZ SEEGERS, RESERVE-INFANTERIE-REG. NR. 73, 27 MARCH 1915

If lice were one part of the problem, the rats multiplying in the dead and getting fat on the refuse and degradation of no-man's-land were another:

The rats in the trenches are too funny for words. Great big things, as big as Gertie, some of them, and as cheeky as anything. They seem absolutely to ignore us and don't think of running away if you come across them. Horrible things they are and one of the vile accompaniments of this infernal war.

2LT ARTHUR H. LAMB, 1ST LANCASHIRE FUSILIERS, 20 AUGUST 1916

For most men at the front, getting below ground was a preferred option; escaping the action of field guns, bursting shrapnel and searching howitzers was a significant reason behind the construction of trench systems. With the German lines largely sitting on the defensive from late 1914, deep dugouts were famously constructed wherever they could be:

I am writing this letter in a so called foxhole, bent down low and dirty like a miner. The dug-outs are in a dreadful condition. Two men share a crude hole that has been scratched into the wall of the trench. When it's raining, and that is nearly always the case, the earthen floor (there are no duckboards yet) of the trench turns into liquid mud with the consistency of dough while the walls on both sides get sticky as if covered with fresh glue. You can imagine what we look like after eight days in the trenches …

PIONIER WERNER SCHREIBER, PIONIER-BATAILLON NR. 11, 11 MARCH 1915

But this was not always possible, and for the British and Germans alike, with in some situations shallow scrapes replaced deep dugouts to protect life and limb:

In the first night we constructed a dug-out. For that you have to dig a man-sized hole into the side of the trench in which you can seek cover if you bend down low. Then we made a roof from wooden beams, covered it with sheet metal hauled it to the trench and covered the hole with it. That is how you make a dug-out. We were lucky as ours was full of ground water so we had to spend half the night putting in wooden floorboards.

Otherwise the water would have run into our boots. Our door is a tent square. For lighting we use candles. All the work has to be done at night, because in daylight the English shoot on anything that moves.

UNIDENTIFIED GERMAN SOLDIER, 22 JANUARY 1915

In Flanders, the British, sitting on or close to the clay plain, were in a position to dig dugout shelters deep into the clay, while the Germans on the high ground were faced, paradoxically, with water-logged sand layers which meant that they were forced to construct concrete fortifications. Picking the right location was an important matter:

Instructions for making a dugout – find a suitable spot, for preference at the bottom of a hill, so that any spare water will run in your direction. Dig a hole 6 ft by 4 ft by 4 ft high and don't be discouraged if it fills with water – bail it out – or invent some means of getting the water to run up hill – next, get a door and lay it across the pit, leaving room enough to get in, bearing in mind however that a Field Officer may want to enter, so allow a little more, otherwise your dugout may be torn to pieces. Next get earth, or if not available, mud and throw it over the door to a depth of about two feet. If a lot of this falls into the dugout, never mind it is the fortune of war! Then get straw, don't bother whether it is wet or dry, the dry soon gets wet and make yourself a floor of this then lie down to look up at the roof you have constructed and count the number of places it leaks in. This if it does not drive you off your head will prove a pleasant afternoon's occupation. At night you can put more earth on top to stop the water and then watch the whole thing cave in. Nobody with a weak heart should try the above.

2LT ARTHUR R. STANLEY-CLARKE, 1ST DORSETSHIRE REGIMENT,
3 FEBRUARY 1915

Let us describe our dug-out: a window frame some three feet square in the chalk in the side of the trench, a steep dark flight of steps, and one reaches the outer tunnel; at the end of which a distant candle reveals my Sergeant-Major, clerk, and gas NCO. From this open little rooms about five feet square where Officers' Orderlies sleep; from this a lower tunnel of the same dimensions, reached by a similar window and shorter flight of steps, and one comes to our living-room; a six by two shelf serves as a table, at which, if one is sitting at it, no other can pass. At the end, the telephone and signallers; an emergency exit, in case the first is blown in, leads to another part of the trench. From our living-room a lower tunnel runs forward into a little sandbagged pit at the top of a flight of stairs; this passage serves as our store, kitchen, larder and everything else we want. Our furniture is crude in the extreme; from nails in the walls hang packs, coats, spare pieces of equipment, post-cards, timetables, orders, fly-papers and tin hats. On the shelf or table is an oil lamp, some bottles, glasses, tinned milk, butter and jam, yesterday's newspapers and all one's possessions that go for a trip into the line. Scattered about the floor are closed stretchers, which, balanced from stairs to table or from petrol tins to pack, form our beds. With Burberry for pillow, or an air pillow sometimes, and fleece lining for covering, we snatch an hour or two's sleep night or day, until our turn for duty comes.

CAPT. G.M. BROWN, 9TH SUFFOLK REGIMENT, 1916

In the harder, drier chalk of France, deep stable dugouts were more possible – and were famously equipped with housewares looted from destroyed homes in the war zone:

The dug-out that has been allotted to me for next week is an old divisional HQ of the German Army, fitted as though it were impregnable, arm-chairs, bureaus, cabinets, framed pictures and electric lights, and upstairs with double and single bedrooms, more like a week-end cottage than a dug-out, but further details later. The main disadvantage is the atmosphere, for the place is littered with German dead.

CAPT. G.M. BROWN, 9TH SUFFOLK REGIMENT, 1916

All too often, dugouts required extra support to maintain their shape and to protect the men from collapse – particularly as the enemy artillery was searching them out:

We have dug ourselves in deep, surrounded with wire entanglements and redoubts and cling to the ground we have conquered. We have dug deep dugouts right next to our guns which offer protection against aerial bombs, steel darts, shells and all kinds of other stuff that both sides throw at each other over here daily without having the intention to actually kill anybody it seems. It has now been 11 days and even though it is comfortable we are eager to finally get to grips with the enemy again, who is only about 1200 metres away from us.

LTN. BERNHARD KORTZFLEISCH, 4. GARDE-FELDARTILLERIE-REGIMENT, 1914

Picture if you can a flight of twenty-four steps leading into the darkness of the underground. At the foot of this is a room, if room it can be called, some thirteen feet by ten by seven high, the walls of tree trunks and railway sleepers, the roof of the corrugated iron resting on railway lines; from this hang stalactites of rust, and large and loathsome insects creep about, above lives a colony of rats; such is our living room, damp with a dampness that reaches one's bones and makes all things clammy to the touch.

CAPT. G.M. BROWN, 9TH SUFFOLK REGIMENT, 1916

Dugouts were of variable size and form; deeper dugouts meant that sleep could be snatched on wire-supported bunks that were erected in rooms and corridors:

This is some twenty feet below ground, six feet wide and six high, and some eighteen feet long; at one end are four bunks in two layers, made of wire-netting, which serve us for beds, and into which we crawl when duty persists.

CAPT. G.M. BROWN, 9TH SUFFOLK REGIMENT, 1916

I am writing this in the inevitable dug out – about 3ft high – and my fellow sufferer has just said this thing will fall on top of us tonight so you may guess it's rather dilapidated. It's a beautiful day here today, just like a spring morning, a circumstance which is rather unfortunate as the artillery is always more active when the air is clearer. As I write I can hear the buzzing of a couple of aeroplanes which are doubtless observing for decent marks. Yesterday we descended into a cellar and had to pump water out of it – the liquid being about 2½ ft deep – with chairs floating about in it.

RFN WILLIAM C. TAFFS, 1/16TH QUEEN'S WESTMINSTER RIFLES,
20 JANUARY 1916

Dugouts were nicknamed by their occupants, who tried as they might to create a 'home-from-home' away from the war raging above ground:

I am writing this in another Dug out or as we rather rudely put it 'Big Hutch' you can tell the mater that we have to get into most of these affairs on hands and knees, and even then it is a tight squeeze. Of course we have to take off our equipment before diving in.

RFN WILLIAM C. TAFFS, 1/16TH QUEEN'S WESTMINSTER RIFLES,
FEBRUARY 1916

Nevertheless, the sounds of the war continued overhead; the temptation to stay in the dugout was something that the High Command was constantly fearful of:

> I wish you could see us sitting in this shelter all laughing and talking by the light of a lamp which we borrowed from a house (no one there) and you would never imagine we were fighting but rather on a picnic, the only disturbing factor is the terrific noise of shells – but I think we would be lost without that, we say it will be funny when we get home and go out shooting. At the first sound of a gun we will fall on our knees and begin to dig ourselves in!
>
> 2Lt Arthur R. Stanley-Clarke, 1st Dorsetshire Regiment,
> 10 November 1914

> The section we are manning now is similar to the one we were in before. My dug-out was a bit smaller and had room for only four men. Between 8 to 9.30 pm I was in charge of the guard. When that period was over I lay down to catch some sleep. An hour later enemy barrage hit a trench section close to ours. Was the enemy planning to attack? Shortly afterwards rifle shots could be heard. The alarm was sounded and all available men armed themselves and prepared to repel an enemy attack. I grabbed my rifle, put on my helmet and joined the men in the trench. The thunder of the guns and the cracking of the rifles was getting more intense every minute. Our own artillery started firing, sending its shells in a low trajectory over our heads. The night is pitch black making it impossible to see anything. When I ask around if everyone has a full supply of ammunition the answer is negative. Me and an officer's assistant open an ammunition storage and hand out all bullets we can find.
>
> Uffz. Franz Seegers, Reserve-Infanterie-Regiment Nr. 73, April 1915

In the gloom of the underground caverns, men would try to engage in day-to-day activities, writing, sleeping, eating:

> I am writing this is in a dug out – not a bad place – by candlelight. We always have to use candles in these affairs as they are abominably dark.
>
> Rfn William C. Taffs, 1/16th Queen's Westminster Rifles,
> 16 January 1916

'Lord Kitchener calls for more men'; Soldiers of RIR236, enjoying a copy of the *Daily Mail* in a trench shelter, Wieltje, Flanders, 1915.

We are all sitting in a dugout here, eight of us all smoking, laughing and talking, laughing at the moments we have passed through. My Sergeant Major has just been telling a story of how he was hung up in a barbed wire fence while a machine gun played on him – two bullets going through his pack, one through his haversack and another his cap (I think with all respect that this is a bit of an exaggeration).

2Lt Arthur R. Stanley-Clarke, 1st Dorsetshire Regiment,

12 November 1914

I am sitting in a dugout and though by no means out of danger I shall be D.V. by about ten this evening, we have had quite an exciting time – a little too exciting to suit me! Beside me there is a brazier burning with a canteen of water which is going to be *well* boiled for my tea. You cannot see the bottom because the mud has been stirred up in it, but before it becomes tea we pretend that it is chocolate. Tell Dad that I have been inoculated so not to bother.

2Lt Arthur R. Stanley-Clarke, 1st Dorsetshire Regiment,

14 February 1915

In some situations, there were more unusual occupants of 'the trenches':

In the last trenches I have just come from there used to be a cat – do you remember seeing in the *Daily Mail* a photograph of a cat as a French mascot – well that is the cat – it wanders impartially between the German lines and ours and was wounded twice. I am sorry to say, however, for the last few days it has been missing and I am afraid it will have to be added to the casualty list.

2Lt Arthur R. Stanley-Clarke, 1st Dorsetshire Regiment,

25 March 1915

Trench Routine

Trench routine meant that soldiers were cycled in and out of the front-line trenches. The time frame varied, but for the most part this meant spending a week in the front line, a week in the reserves ready to reinforce the front when required, and then a week 'out on rest'. This was the ideal; in many cases the spell in the front line would be longer, the men suffering increased fatigue and the increased chance of a careless death. All too often rest periods would mean some degree of hard labour that would bring the troops back into the front line as carrying parties bringing up food, munitions or building materials. This would take them back into the danger zone. The period in the trenches was extremely taxing – little sleep, poor food, the chance that you could lose your life at any time to a shell, mortar or aimed bullet, all conspired to exhaust the front-line soldier. It was no wonder he was often critical of those whose roles meant they were further back in the supply chain, in the rear areas or *Etappe*. It was in the front line that the national distinctions disappeared, and there were more similarities between the German and British soldier than could be imagined by those at home crying for a new offensive. On active fronts, a spell in the front line could be trying:

We spent 10 difficult days in the trenches from where a good number of comrades got carried out wounded or dead. Admittedly the English and their Indian allies are a lot tougher than the French and don't take to their heels so easily. There was hardly a day on which we did not have to attack and even though we were successful most of the time we took unavoidable losses. The enemy is too cautious to attack us in daylight and mostly conducts his raids at night time. So far we managed to repel most of them. We face a capable army with very good shots! I have already treated plenty of casualties and only recently I carried two wounded Indians from the battlefield. The English act and behave like proper sportsmen while the Indians are armed like hunters on the prowl. They are armed with large knifes or daggers which are dangerous weapons. I have been in many a dangerous situation but none was so critical as our last skirmish. We had set up our dressing station 200 metres behind the combat line. On the day after that we were taken under fire because one of our batteries had taken up their positions right next to us. Soon rifle bullets smashed through the windows so we had to take cover in the cellars to avoid taking casualties. Then came the 28 October. We, that means the men of 12th company, had assaulted an enemy position taking 54 men and 3 officers prisoner but at night we heard the shouts of three wounded comrades that were still lying in front of the English trench only 50 metres away from us. We sent stretcher bearers out to fetch them and these were at once taken under enemy fire. Ten of us went out to help them but we were soon taken under fire as well and were pinned down for 1 ½ hours in mud and water before we were able to fetch the wounded men and to carry them back to the safety of our trench. Let's hope this affair will come to an end soon.

UNIDENTIFIED GERMAN SOLDIER, 4 NOVEMBER 1914

We do twelve days in the trenches and four out. We had a fairly hot time last twelve days. The day before yesterday I was standing by opening just like a rabbit.

RFN WILLIAM C. TAFFS, 1/16TH QUEEN'S WESTMINSTER RIFLES,
25 JUNE 1916

Today is our third day in the trenches. Before that we were billeted inside some cellars behind the lines for four days. Due to the lively enemy artillery we do not move in daylight, but tomorrow we will move to the second line into the village of Wingles again. During our last stay in that village an enemy shell came down close to where we were standing. Luckily it turned out to be a dud, otherwise we would all be dead by now. The enemy is about 800 metres away from us. We are facing the English, who up to now appear to be a very jovial lot. At night we can hear them sing, whistle and play their harmonicas. The weather here is generally good; the days are warm, but when I have to spend the night on watch it can get a bit cold …

RICHARD WIENTZEK, RESERVE-INFANTERIE-REGIMENT NR. 11, 27 JULY
1915

Well we stayed there until the 15/4/18, and at midnight got relieved. We marched over no man's land a good while, and then got into some dug out. We stayed in there until morning, when it came daylight old Gerry started to shell heavy again dropping them very near us, in fact he dropped one on one of our dugouts but I don't think he hurt anybody.

PTE PHILIP WHITEHEAD, 3RD ROYAL WELSH FUSILIERS, APRIL 1918

In the front line, the day-to-day running of the trenches did not vary. 'Stand to' at dawn and dusk was meant to ensure the enemy attacks at these critical periods would be futile:

I will just describe to you yesterday's routine. 1st I did 2 hours guard. Stand to at 5.30. At Stand to we put on our equipment and stand in picturesque attitudes leaning on our rifles (in a 'remember Belgium attitude') waiting for an attack which rarely comes. Just before dawn and sunset are the favourite times for attack so we stand to at these times. At 6 we did two hours filling up sandbags and rebuilding the parapet. By this time of course it is light and dangerous to work so we retire to our DO [dugout] and cook our breakfast. All day we lie about sleeping, reading and writing, etc, until the evening stand to.

RFN WILLIAM C. TAFFS, 1/16TH QUEEN'S WESTMINSTER RIFLES,
FEBRUARY 1916

Life was challenging and exhausting for the senses:

Life is very hard in the trenches and very tiring. You get very little sleep and I was so tired last night that I had to move about to prevent myself falling asleep where I stood. I came off duty at 2 am this morning and I was up again at 4. It is continual duty night and day with the additional strain of an almost daily bombardment. I have not had my boots or even my collar off for four days and I am simply caked with mud and then we think how well off we were in England.

It is one consolation to think that one cannot do much more for the old folks at home. The Tommies out here deserve all their country can do for them! Nothing in my opinion can be too good for them when you see what they go through for a miserable 1 [shilling] a day. We have one or two boys about 16, poor kids they ought to be at school instead of here.

2Lt Arthur H. Lamb, 1st Lancashire Fusiliers, 22 August 1916

A spell in the front line was invariably matched by a period in the reserve trenches, before finally being cycled out to rest:

The back trenches have lots of room generally a big dugout where one can rest with comfort and of course a billet is palatial!! Even a billet without a roof. It really adds zest to life living in a house with shells falling near and every time a 'Jack Johnson' comes there is no mistake about it, the whole house seems to rock and windows go poof. I can tell you it makes one sit tight for a minute or two and then we begin to laugh at one another but always with an ear open for the next. 'Jacks' give one lots of time or at all events sufficient to get under cover such as a ditch or trench and one does not move quickly, of course if one is in a trench the only thing is to sit tight.

2Lt Arthur R. Stanley-Clarke, 1st Dorsetshire Regiment,
22 November 1914

On the evening of the 4th we left the trenches to spend the next three days in the village of Courcy which lies only a short distance behind them. Normally the battalion spends six days in the foremost trench, six days in the second line (in and around Courcy) and six days in the third line (Auménancourt le petit) about 12 kilometres behind the front, but as the 92nd Regiment only just left this area, our time in the second line gets reduced as we had to take over some stretches of their former positions.

Uffz. Franz Seegers, Reserve-Infanterie-Reg. Nr. 73, 4 April 1915

I am in the Pink, and have been in the trenches a good deal since we were in the fight on the 15th and I have come out of the firing line further back to reserve trenches, the first named trenches we were quite near the Germans and could hear the whistling and shouting at night time, the few lads in our traverse would start singing old time songs and ragtimes, they would stop firing and listen to us, on the whole I think they are a good lot, it is the men that are over them that make them do what they do, anyway if we get near them again they will not get any mercy. We just remind them about the *Lusitania* and they know what it means.

Pte David Beaver, 4th Loyal North Lancashire Regiment,
16 July 1916

Artillery

Artillery accounted for some 60 per cent of casualties in the war; this was not surprising. Men feared the constant bombardment – which played on their minds. It was difficult to express to the families at home:

> You must not worry about me dearest mummy because I am only trying to do my duty and it is the little bit I can do for you all at home and that is a comfort to me, dear mummy, to think I am doing it for your sake especially and my only desire is to do it well and prove a man, not a coward as it is very hard to be brave in the midst of such *terrible* artillery fire as is being experienced down here.
>
> 2Lt Arthur H. Lamb, 1st Lancashire Fusiliers, 10 October 1916

> Well Dearie you must not get afraid of the Zepps because they are nothing you should hear at times when there is a big Battle going on you would think it was your Birthday you talk about being frightened you should see some of us when the shells start bursting around we run like rabbits to get off the road.
>
> Dvr Percy Hartland, Royal Field Artillery, 17 February 1916

> Finally I am able to send you a sign of life again. The past weeks were not easy, but I am happy to be able to say that everything went well. We have repelled the English soon after their first attack. They had thought that none of us could have survived the 166-hour artillery bombardment, but even the foremost dug-outs survived undamaged. Yesterday I was awarded the silver medal for merit.
>
> Schütze Karl Brenner, German soldier, 28 July 1916

Artillery pieces were surely the modern equivalent of medieval siege engines in a war that pitted two sides against each other in the longest and greatest siege in history. The sheer mass and range of artillery pieces was staggering; men tried to make sense of them by the use of nicknames for the incoming weapons:

> That day witnessed one of the worst battles I have ever experienced, as we were badly equipped with guns, having mostly only eighteen-pounders –'pop-guns,' as the boys called them – whilst it was the first day on which we met the really big guns of the Germans – those promptly dubbed 'Jack Johnsons'.
>
> Pte Frederick Bolwell, Loyal North Lancashire Regiment, 1914

Took the lorry to place called Ploegsteert to pick up gun platforms. While we were doing so we were being heavily shelled with 'coalboxes', coming over two and three at the time. One of them hit a large house that had been used as hospital but luckily it had been cleared out earlier in the day. At another house a young woman was doing her hair near the window and a piece of shell struck her behind the ear and passed out above the eye. There was not a sound window in all the village broken glass, pieces of brick and a shower of broken shell coming down like hailstones. This same day the next village to us namely Armentières was suffering just as bad, one woman getting her head blown off and several other civilians being wounded. Since our battery has been in action here there have been compliments on their splendid work several times. Now we have got a very large gun going close to ours known as a 9-2, the first day it went into action it let go nineteen rounds and accounted for four batteries of German guns.

Pte Henry W. Talbot, Army Service Corps (Motor Transport),
1 November 1914

Often, the two enemies would range on a clear target; a church spire, the Basilica of the Virgin and Child in Albert on the Somme, or a humble village building – in order to catch out the unwary or men intent on ranging artillery fire in their own direction. It was also very unwise to show smoke or light fires – as this was likely to draw the attention of the artillerymen:

A quiet day. In the evening, at 5 o clock, some artillery shells are fired over our heads. The enemy is targeting an old windmill a couple of hundred meters behind our lines, where now and then a heavily smoking fire is lit to draw enemy fire away from other sectors of the front. The fire is lit every day and put out at about 7 pm when everything gets quiet again.

Uffz. Franz Seegers, Reserve-Infanterie-Reg. Nr. 73, 30 March 1915

Bombardments and pre-battle barrages were essential if the enemy trenches and their occupants were to be destroyed and the infantry do their job. Hanns Schäfer observed the barrage at the Somme first hand:

Artillery barrage. The English are trying again. This time at Thiepval. From my observer's position in a tree an eerily beautiful sight. A glorious summer morning with a magnificent red sky. There are actually birds singing near our battery. Thiepval is covered in firey black detonation clouds rising up and falling down. I can't help thinking: Poor chaps that have to withstand that. A few hours later we get shelled as well. The bunk in my dug-out is shaking ... rocking me to sleep ... dreams of childhood.

KAN. HANNS SCHÄFER, RESERVE-FELDARTILLERIE-REGIMENT NR. 263,
JULY 1916

The slightest alarm could trigger a barrage – or invite assault by other weapons. Sergeant Mason, of the Oxfordshire and Buckinghamshire Light Infantry, recorded a typical spell in the Ypres Salient:

Friday 11. Left Poperinghe for line. Rained all day and we arrived wet through. SOS about 4 in morning.

Saturday 12. Germans attacked. Spent an awful night.

Sunday 13. Germans shelled all day.

Tuesday 15. Went into trenches again.

Wednesday 16. Zep passed over lines.

Thursday 17. Planes and Zep passed over lines.

Friday 18. Aeroplanes bombed Poperinghe.

Saturday 19. Germans again strafed heavily and made small bombing attack.

Sunday 20. Artillery very active and trench mortars.

Monday 21. Trench Mortars again very busy. Germans made bombing attack about 20 coming over 9 being killed.

Tuesday 22. Heavy Bombardments on both sides SOS at night. Snow nearly all day. Went up to transport at night.

Wednesday 23. Germans made small bombing attack, coming over in British uniforms.

Thursday 24. Came out of trenches again going back to camp near Poperinghe. Walked about 3 miles and trained the rest.

Friday 25. A lot more snow fell. Aeroplane again dropped bomb.

SGT H.N.T. MASON, 6TH OXFORDSHIRE AND BUCKINGHAMSHIRE LIGHT
INFANTRY, FEBRUARY 1916

Expressively, Germans called the effect of a bombardment *Trommelfeur* – drumfire:

All of a sudden a *Trommelfeuer* started that was so severe that it was quite impossible to keep standing. In the night it made sleeping impossible as the whole ground was shaking and trembling. It is customary that this announces an imminent English attack.

NORBERT LÜGKE, GERMAN SOLDIER, 12 SEPTEMBER 1917

Even in the reserve trenches, just behind the firing line, the artillery fire was merciless:

> We are in reserve trenches and oh! My goodness mummy dear, the cold! In the early morning, it is intense and for three miserable nights I have shivered in a shell hole with a bit of cover put up by ourselves. The guns are roaring right and every now and again our own bombardment reaches an intensity that surpasses anything one could conceive. It is awful, simply awful and it almost gets over one at times, I know it does over me!
>
> 2Lt Arthur H. Lamb, 1st Lancashire Fusiliers, 22 October 1916

Mortars – with their ability to lob high-explosive shells a short distance from one trench to another, creating inordinate damage – were feared by both sides. For the British, the ungainly flight of the German *Minenwerfer* shell, in three calibres, was viewed with trepidation:

> Bombarded with trench mortars and some shrapnel, the latter very close when proceeding to lookout post. Quiet night, Mathews, C.Coy., Dogfield St killed.
>
> Pte M. Williams, 11th Welsh Regiment, 15 October 1915

> The Bosche treated us to a 'Minnie' display, quite the worst thing I have yet been up against. Starting on our right, it was a wonderful thing to watch. One saw these engines of destruction creeping through the air like red-hot airships, leaving their trail of sparks and smoke; one saw the light, heard the dull rending sound that is their characteristic noise, and felt the blast of their explosion, and the shaking earth.
>
> Capt. G.M. Brown, 9th Suffolk Regiment, 1916

All too often sentries would be placed to give warning of the impending arrival of these munitions:

> Outside – or rather up above – a cold drizzle adds to the general discomfort, 'pineapples' drop promiscuously about, but one can hear them coming, save when barrages are about, and the roar of the gun and bursting shell drowns all else.
>
> Capt. G.M. Brown, 9th Suffolk Regiment, 1916

The King's Royal Rifles occupying the front line on the right of the road, nicknamed 'Bomb Alley', on account of its being so near the enemy and continually under bombardment. We used sentries on each traverse to look out for bombs: on seeing one coming and at what position it would be likely to drop, the sentry would yell out 'Bomb right,' or 'Bomb left' as the case might be, when the men would at once clear to the opposite direction.

PTE FREDERICK BOLWELL, LOYAL NORTH LANCASHIRE REGIMENT, 1914

We were on ordinary sentry duty, and the front was fairly quiet, being free from artillery fire. The only thing that troubled us during the day were rifle grenades and trench mortars, we called them 'flying pigs'. The latter were big and made a terrible noise when they exploded, but we could see them coming, so we had a chance to dodge them.

PTE JOHN H. BENN, LOYAL NORTH LANCASHIRE REGIMENT, APRIL 1917

While the men were struggling with the battleground below, aviators flew overhead in order to map out the trench lines, seek out strongpoints and direct the enemy fire:

I am still in Brigade Reserve about 3 miles from the trenches. We had a lovely day yesterday as regards the weather but during the morning we had three Taubes circling over the camp and it was really a fine sight to see the shells from our anti-aircraft guns bursting and five of our own aeroplanes chasing after them. However we paid for it during the night as old Fritz started shelling us with 5.9s and kept it up most of the night. We had no casualties among the men but 11 mules from the transport were knocked out.

It is an awful sensation hearing these shells coming screaming over us one after the other and not knowing where they are going to burst and of course the din is terrific and for the second night in succession I didn't get a wink of sleep. I don't think I am at all cut out for this job, and I don't know how long I shall be able to stick it, but I am far too nervous. Last night I was all in a sweat when those blooming shells came over.

2ND LT ARTHUR H. LAMB, 1ST LANCASHIRE FUSILIERS

Each day enemy aircraft can be seen circling above our positions. They get targeted by our anti-balloon guns. Their shells detonate close to the aircraft without ever bringing one of them down. Most of the time the enemy planes do not drop any bombs. The damage they inflict stands in no relation to the danger the pilot is getting himself into. They are reconnaissance planes, mapping and photographing our positions and trenches.

UFFZ. FRANZ SEEGERS, RESERVE-INFANTERIE-REG. NR. 73, 30 MARCH 1915

Saw aeroplanes fight. The German was the largest biplane in the world but British got above and drove enemy down with machine guns. British plane shelled, machine guns, rifle fire. Great sport? No grub. Quiet. Big attack on left in evening rapid rifle and machine gun fire. Our artillery gave them Hell and they make feeble reply with whiz bangs and shrapnel. Quiet again.

PTE M. WILLIAMS, 11TH WELSH REGIMENT, 21 SEPTEMBER 1915

Counter-battery fire – also directed by aviators – as well as methods of watching the flash of the opposing guns, or ranging the sound of the fired shells, meant that the artillery duel was larger than the trench battlefield itself. Distress rockets fired from the front line would summon a response from the gunners:

One learns to laugh at Fritz's efforts to kill one, and at the appalling waste of money he spends in misplaced shells; one laughs still more when they fall in his own lines from his own guns and frantic cries of distress and protest, in the form of coloured rockets, fill the air.

CAPT. G.M. BROWN, 9TH SUFFOLK REGIMENT, 1916

Fourteen days ago my battery had a black day and was nearly wiped out by enemy artillery. Three guns were disabled by enemy fire and a munition cart received a direct hit and exploded. Shrapnel after shrapnel detonated and after having spent the last of our shells we got the order to abandon the guns and to move into cover until nightfall. A third of the men were killed or wounded. I was put in for the Iron Cross, if I get it is another question, but on the long run I will get one. I did not tell the family about it, it's better to do that when I finally have it. I suppose you have heard that Klose and Kortzfleisch the Elder are dead?

LTN. BERNHARD KORTZFLEISCH, 4. GARDE-FELDARTILLERIE-REGIMENT, 1914

Ensuring that activity in no-man's-land was kept in check was important, and both sides sent out patrols, to test defences, raid the enemy trenches, and gather intelligence. This was carried out by brave men who would cross no-man's-land under direct threat of discovery. It was quite common for enemy patrols to pass each other in the inky darkness of no-man's-land, illuminated in stark relief by flares and star shells:

British officers – from the Scottish Rifles (Cameronians) – in a dugout in Flanders, *c.* 1915.

I am still in the beastly trenches and shall be until Monday night, that is if all goes well and we are not shelled out. The weather continues wet and cold and last night on patrol about 2am it was really bitter. Quite a large party of Huns passed quite near my little patrol of six last night. I heard them talking and got ready for a bit of a scrap, however they did not see us and we were left alone. I dare not fire at them as we should have been so outnumbered, so I let them alone. We were watching about 500 of 'no man's land' so you can see it was not exactly a bed of roses.

2Lt Arthur H. Lamb, 1st Lancashire Fusiliers, 26 August 1916

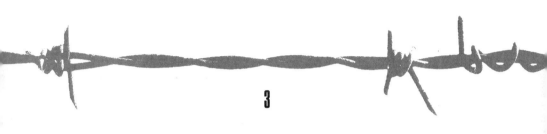

3

Morale/*Die Moral*

I wish the war was over. I don't think it will last more than this summer, it is deafening to hear the guns go off and see the shells fly all about us.
PTE ROBERT W. PRICE, 10TH WELSH REGIMENT, 15 JANUARY 1916

May the war come to an end soon … one gets a bit hung up about it.
GEFR. J. GÖRTEMAKER, FELDARTILLERIE-REGIMENT NR. 503, 1918

Soldiers' opinions on the war varied throughout; from the open warfare of 1914 and 1918 to the trench warfare period, the views of soldiers were conditioned by their immediate experiences. Here, occupying open ditches separated by a few yards of broken ground, British and German troops would go through similar routines and occupy themselves with similar activities. Facing the same conditions throughout the year – from the cold, muddy and damp weather of the trenches of autumn and winter, to the dust and heat of the summer – the morale of the soldiers was subject to some trials.

The soldier's view of his enemy was dependent on the conduct of the war. In both nations, men joined the colours in a time of national emergency, responding to a threat to nation and home. This was as real to the average German, his country facing the vice-like jaws of the Allied nations, as it was to the British soldier – who had gone to war on principle and who was now locked into a war from which there was no immediate escape. The reality of facing the enemy challenged some men to reconsider. Just what was the enemy really like, and what was he fighting for?

Trains loaded with troops, ammunition and forage came in about every 30 minutes … train after train drove past us and often I had the time to speak to some of the passengers. I have made note of a few inscriptions on some of the wagons:'Upon return, parade of tamed Englishmen … Free admission',

'John Bull, we will beat the daylights out of you', 'SMS Albionhunter', 'For sale: Englishmen salted in seawater – U9'.

Gustav Rehnisch, Liege, 5 October 1914

We are a little depressed about the raid on the East Coast and we think that the Navy might look after us and our homes better – if we let the Germans through to Calais there would be no forgiveness for us and our Navy is surely large enough to guard the East Coast, however it is a splendid thing for recruiting and the men for the most part chuckle to think of the seacoast under shell fire though we mean to take it out of the Germans the first opportunity we get and I am afraid the toll of prisoners will be small as the men are a bit savage.

2Lt Arthur R. Stanley-Clarke, 1st Dorsetshire Regiment,
20 December 1914

Nevertheless, the fact that both sides were suffering the same conditions, fighting the same war, started to tell on their attitudes. There was a respect on both sides:

I hope this will be the last war for a very long time because although the life is topping it's beastly work killing other chaps even if they are awful swine, which I really don't believe they are and as Henry says they are very brave men and wonderfully trained. They are doomed for defeat because they chose to fight the whole world, if they had taken us one by one they would have done the trick except England, she they never could have conquered and they were fools to go through Belgium.

2Lt Arthur R. Stanley-Clarke, 1st Dorsetshire Regiment,
5 December 1914

At the same time though we had to recognise that these English soldiers, who before the war many of us had looked down upon with scorn and disrespect, as we did on other soldiers like the Belgians, had in each case fought bravely and stubbornly, which was attested by the losses our German soldiers had to suffer here.

Oberleutnant Heinrich Heubner, Infanterie-Regiment Nr. 20

The Hun, too, is often brave. I heard from a man who saw it – a Gunner Major – of a case of a quiet nerve that served Germany in good stead. Hill

118

No.– had fallen, and the Huns launched a counter attack in seven waves led by an officer on a horse, until the horse fell dead.

CAPT. G.M. BROWN, 9TH SUFFOLK REGIMENT, 1916

The Allemands are drawing off from here a bit to strengthen their line further south so I expect we shall have it quieter. Poor Germans, at times I feel sorry for them as they loved their country very much and now they are surrounded by enemies on every side and new ones keep threatening. Of course they deserve it, but they seem to me like some sturdy child who with the innocence of youth, with the wonderful assurance of a child and the transparent guile of a child has got itself into a very hot corner and does not know in which direction to turn.

2LT ARTHUR R. STANLEY-CLARKE, 1ST DORSETSHIRE REGIMENT,
15 MARCH 1915

Fatalism also appeared in their letters home:

We are back from the trenches now for a few days. I wish it was for good and I know that you do. I hope to be spared to come home again, but we never know one minute when we will get blowed to atoms. I don't take so much notice of it now, as I did I have got used to it but at times when they are shelling near us the place is all under-mined out here. I think myself that the Germans wish it was all over the same as us. I should not like to be out here another winter as I had enough last.

PTE ROBERT W. PRICE, 10TH WELSH REGIMENT, 1916

The exertions and the intense fighting of the last weeks have made us emotionally disturbed. Due to the severe losses all the old faces I once knew have disappeared. One feels lonely and isolated.

UFFZ. HEINRICH BUSEMAYER, INFANTERIE-REGIMENT NR. 168,
8 MAY 1918

I have not moved up to the front line yet but am still in reserve in a large town! We are hourly expecting to move and I can't say how long I shall be here! Anyway I don't want to, because our fellows are having such a hot time nowadays and the Huns are fighting for every inch of ground like tigers! And they have such heaps of artillery! Things have not gone quite as they should lately and it will not be exact truth what you see in the papers! The only thing seems that the war will last indefinitely yet and that our task becomes harder! Oh! That God would bring the horrible insane business to an end!

2Lt Arthur H. Lamb MC, 1st Lancashire Fusiliers, April 1917

Your optimism over my return strikes me very forcible. I most sincerely hope that it is justified, although there is no sign of it at present.

Rfn William C. Taffs, 1/16 Queen's Westminster Rifles, June 1916

Despite the realities of the war, it was usually a heartfelt wish of most soldiers that it would end:

Just letting you know that I am well and I hope the same applies to you. It's been a while since I heard anything of you, did you not receive my card? Here nothing has changed. Hopefully this stupid war will come to an end soon.

Musk. Heinrich Dünker, Infanterie-Regiment Nr. 147,
4 July 1916

The war news appears good and I really think the tide has turned and I daresay that about 12 months from now this horrible business will be a thing of the past. Of course I am certain the Germans will fight desperately to hold on to what they have won and so it is a little too early to think about peace yet.

2Lt Arthur H. Lamb, 1st Lancashire Fusiliers, 14 August 1916

We are having some cold weather out here now; I dread the winter as I had enough last one. I only wish the War was over and I know you do. We keep on driving them back and taken [sic] them prisoners of war and there are a lot killed well you can see by the papers that we are getting a lot killed as well as them.

Pte Robert W. Price, 10th Welsh Regiment, 23 October 1916

With most men's horizon limited to the small area of the front through which they travelled – or even the small view of sky from the confines of their trench – the hope that the war would end soon was often unfounded:

When one comes out here one absolutely longs for anything in dear old England … How we shall enjoy life when this horrid business is over.

Rfn William C. Taffs, 1/16th Queen's Westminster Rifles,
25 December 1915

It can't last much longer. I don't see that it can there are thousands of troops out here now but we are like a machine always on the move we have been camping at one place now for three weeks that is the longest time that we have stayed in one place and we are likely to be here for a long time yet.

PTE ROBERT W. PRICE, 10TH WELSH REGIMENT, 29 AUGUST 1916

This War is beyond all words terribly cruel and hard and horrible and God only knows when it will be over! It is nothing but organised scientific murder.

2LT ARTHUR H. LAMB, 1ST LANCASHIRE FUSILIERS, 19 MAY 1917

I really feel I ought not to write to you like this while this awful War is on, but it might drag on for years I know if you have once made up your mind on this subject you will not change so I feel perhaps it would be best for both of us if we could understand each other. Of course, as we stand now, I could not think of your engaging yourself to me. I might come home with an arm off or something of that sort but if I come home safe and sound when peace comes do not think I could come to you and say 'Gertie I have thought of no one but you in France. I love you now as I have always, since I first saw you' would it give you pleasure or pain. Of course I shall have to start again from the beginning – as you know this War is a dead loss to me but I think I can soon make my way again, especially if I had you to cheer me up and see I did not spend too much on trousers etc.

RFN WILLIAM C. TAFFS, 1/16TH QUEEN'S WESTMINSTER RIFLES,
11 FEBRUARY 1916

The Rear Areas

At last I have a little time at my disposal to write a little. I have been awfully busy the last four days. On Sunday we got up at five and packed up everything. We drew picks and shovels at the stores and marched to a little place about five miles behind the firing line. It is an absolutely different surroundings to Ypres. The shelling was practically nil and there was no sign of any activity except 'umpteen' aeroplanes. Well, when we arrived there we had the job of picking stones out of the claying soil. We carried haversack rations and for lunch we retired to a nice little nook and had quite a peaceful time. Then in the afternoon our officer in charge (an awfully decent chap – one of the best) asked if any of us had brought towels, because if any had, and they wished, they might have a bathe in the stream. Well I had brought mine, so I went. I didn't have a proper ducking as the stream was too shallow so I stripped and dashed the water over myself. My word, it was cold, but I enjoyed it. One of our chaps was laid out by a pick hitting him on the head and it made quite a nasty wound.

Rfn William C. Taffs, 1/16th Queen's Westminster Rifles,
23 May 1916

We live in quite acceptable conditions about 7 kilometres behind the front. So far the enemy has not fired any shells at us here, which is probably because there is still about 700 civilians living here. Before the war our little village must have housed around 3000 inhabitants. There is sturdy, three-storied buildings and a railway station. We occupy a small room with electric lighting and small oven. There is a number of canteens here and also a *Soldatenheim* which has a cinema and a library. A bottle of lemonade costs 10 Pf, but it is quite impossible to buy something to eat.

Uffz. Gustav Behrendt, Infanterie-Reg. Nr. 165, 17 January 1917

After a tour of duty in the front line, on average seven days, a battalion would be relieved. Its destination would be the reserve trenches – less prone to sniping and trench mortars, but still subject to the random vagaries of artillery fire. Men in reserve could be called upon to reinforce the front when under pressure, and would be the main stock or reinforcements when the front was under severe pressure. More welcome was the withdrawal of a battalion out of the line completely, a means of gaining some rest. With the conditions in the front line so trying, with the constant fear of death, the cold and wet of the trenches, the lack of sleep and the tedium of routine, men were only too thankful when they were taken out of the line:

I have just come out of the trenches again for a week's rest and we want it too as we have had a warm time of it since we have been in but thank God that I am still safe up till now. I am feeling very weak as I have not been able to eat anything for three days. I have been suffering with tooth ache I have had to have another one out, one of my front so that don't leave me with many more now, and the food we get won't keep one of my boys alive we are all grumbling about it we get done up on the march with our pack on our back.

Pte Robert W. Price, 10th Welsh Regiment, 15 January 1916

The time in Courcy was wonderful. Most of its inhabitants had left and most houses were shot to pieces, but there were some undamaged houses left which could be used for quarters.

I had the luck to be billeted with my friend Leutnant Reese and because of that I had everything in abundance. I could sleep in a proper bed covered with my coat and a blanket which made it possible to undress at least partially during the nights. The first night a loud crash tore us out of our sleep and we dived into cover as we were thinking that we were targeted by artillery. On the ground I lit a candle and we waited for the next impact. It stayed quiet and in the candlelight I could see that a large oil painting which had been hanging on the wall had fallen down which had resulted in the crash.

We spent the days drawing, reading and writing. The newspapers we had were already three days old, but for us every kind of news was new. The other two days were like being in paradise. Leutnant Reeses's batman, who was billeted in the room next to ours used to serve in an army kitchen and was a master in 'organising' everything we wished for. Ham, cheese, sausages there was nothing he could not get. In his civilian life he had been a soapmaker in Krefeld and he was a great chap who never asked for anything in return.

UFFZ. FRANZ SEEGERS, RESERVE-INFANTERIE-REG. NR. 73, 4 APRIL 1915

For the Germans, removal from the front line meant moving back beyond the range of effective artillery fire to the *Etappe*, the rear areas where there were facilities beyond the expectations of the average soldier at the front:

I feel happy as a pig in muck, because I have ended up in paradise! I have been billeted in the house of two women. One woman's husband is at war, while the other is imprisoned in Holland. I live 'bon'. One does not realise how good this place is. No drumming artillery fire, no shell craters, no danger, sleep in the nights.

GEFR. J. GÖRTEMAKER, FELDARTILLERIE-REGIMENT NR. 503

Here in the *Etappe* one amuses himself by counting cartridges, in the cinema, in the circus or in the casino (with and without table music), but always with lots of champagne. One can read or order books from Germany, enjoy the relaxing properties of a bath in tub or in a shower (too cold to use the outdoor pools) or spend some time on the rifle range. A war fought in cinemas with champagne and pastiches of opera excerpts.

GUSTAV ADOLF HEINZMANN, FELDARTILLERIE-REGIMENT NR. 26, 25 MAY 1917

There is everything. Supply dumps of all kinds, small railway stations for the small narrow-gauge trains that keep bringing up men and supplies to the front, electrical power stations, bath houses, canteens, *Soldatenheime* and libraries. There is little of these comforts at the front where the men live in deep but damp dug-outs.

UFFZ. GUSTAV BEHRENDT, INFANTERIE-REGIMENT NR. 165

Front-line soldiers could also mix with those men in the rear areas – men engaged in vital military tasks within transport and supply, or the medical services. In many cases, the importance of the tasks these men carried out would be overshadowed in the minds of the fighting soldier by the reality of the trenches. Front-line men could easily resent the 'cushy billet' of the soldier of the back areas:

Percy might as well have stayed in England as far the War is concerned. He certainly will be in no greater danger out here than in England! Oh! the A.S.C. have all the fine billets, <u>miles</u> behind the lines, and lovely cars for them to do their work in and they, and this is the horror of it, are about the only beggars who will see this thing thro and go back to England and take all the credit! But still I suppose there will still be the acres and acres of crosses out here to remind anyone who cares to look that there were infantrymen in the Great War!

2LT ARTHUR H. LAMB, 1ST LANCASHIRE FUSILIERS, 16 MAY 1917

You needn't tell Lucie, in fact I shall be awfully wild if you do, but in France at least the RAMC chaps lead gloriously easy and safe lives compared with us chaps in the line. Most of them have more or less permanent quarters while we have none, and this is no small advantage. Then the RM chaps very rarely come in the trenches while we are there practically all the time.

RFN WILLIAM C. TAFFS, 1/16TH QUEEN'S WESTMINSTER RIFLES,
31 JANUARY 1916

For the Germans, the contrast in conditions between the *Frontsschwein*, and those who lived and worked in relative safety in the rear areas, the *Etappenschweine* or *Etappenhengst*, was equally extreme. Such views were reflected in a soldier's poem:

Pigs Behind the Lines (*Etappenschweine*)

These men who strut around all freshly pressed
And can't be fagged to salute at your behest,
And scoff huge sums of regimental dosh;
Heroes in their speech and letters – all bosh.
Who rob us of the best of wines.
They are the pigs behind the lines.

Shit and porridge fills their heads,
They've even won Iron Crosses it's said
Neglect German women to their disgrace
And pursue fancy French dames in their place;
Sluts with whom they nightly combine –
They are the pigs behind the lines.

When shooting begins they pack their bags
And at Joffre's approach, pull down the flags.
They disperse rumours hatched in latrines,
Pour water on our joys and our dreams.
By their pessimistic whines,
They are the pigs behind the lines.

And so listen here you whey-faced rotters,
You puffed-up, spineless touch-me-notters,
We'd rather not sully our proud recall
With your pitiful existence at all.
Love and loyalty have bound us –
While you are behind-the-lines bounders.

A FRONTLINE PIG

Rest camps were set up in rear areas, though often still within range of the largest guns; they could be based in villages, set up in hutted or tented camps, or simply organised in the least dangerous part of the battlezone. In many cases men would be billed in farms and small villages, living alongside their French or Flemish-speaking owners. Finding 'billets' would be assigned to certain officers – both those who were charged with going ahead of the battalion in search of accommodation and those who were placed in charge

British officers relaxing 'in billets'.

of their location, men who were expected to serve men of all ranks in their search for a suitable place to stay. Not always an easy task:

> The CO sent me to a village behind the line to organise billets etc and be responsible for everything that goes on in it. It is a bon job. My command (!) is a small village but with all the inhabitants I have to put in some thousands of men and numerous officers. My job is to be ready at all hours of the day and night to arrange for board and lodging for everything that may roll up from a drummer-boy to a field marshal and in numbers in three or fours to thousands. The rest of my job and the biggest part is, when the people have been accommodated, to hear their complaints and try and calm m'dear Lieut generals who are purple with rage about something. A few examples:-

a) General Cayenne-Pepper K.C.B., O.H., etc is quite prepared to sleep in a room 10ft by 6ft together with a Major, but he objected to having to climb over the orderlies who slept on the stairs to get to bed.

b) 2Lt Smith finds his bed on the door-mat comfortable, but very draughty.

c) 1010101 Pte Smith, T. does not mind sleeping on four of his pals, but does not like to sleep on 3 dirty cooks who get up at 3 am and on his sanitary.

d) Farmer M'sier Pichot complains in very voluble Patois that his best pig has disappeared.

e) 10472 Pte Jones A, under arrest and looking very well fed says the pig must have fallen into the river and been drowned.

2Lt Kenneth D. Keay, 9 Scottish Rifles (Cameronians), 1917

Men were billeted with people grimly holding on to their existence with varying success and varying standards of accommodation: lice-ridden straw-strewn barns, broken-down farm buildings, or, if men were lucky, farms with welcoming kitchens and sprung beds. It was the luck of the draw in many cases. Most men would have no choice in the matter – though try as they might they would work to get the best possible billets for them and their immediate 'mates':

Billeted in barn. Snow. Still hear very heavy firing. Men pinched farmers' eggs.

Sgt Frederick J. Compton, 16th Cheshire Regiment,
21 February 1916

Barns brought with them attendant problems:

We are having rather exciting times lately in the barn 'strafing' rats. There are quite a lot knocking around and they come out at night time. The other evening one came strolling in the door, and we all went for it, some with bayonets and some with knobkerries. We had a most fierce and bloodthirsty five minutes – about 20 chaps all struggling to destroy this one rat, but the beggar escaped them all, only to be 'done in' a half-an-hour later by a solitary chap who stayed in that evening. My corner of the barn seems quite a favourite one for them – so I find them, rather a trouble. I am afraid that this is a rather strange topic to write on when a chap is writing to the prettiest little girl he knows but really there is absolutely nothing else to talk about.

Rfn William C. Taffs, 1/16th Queen's Westminster Rifles,
25 April 1916

Dear Sister, I have the pleasure to write a few lines just to let you know I am keeping in very good Health, trusting this finds you the same as we are still doing training in a small B. village behind the line, so that we are out of any danger and that is one good consolation, only it is the same practically over and over again, the food as well. Not much luxuries the same as being at home, no such thing here as going in the pantry and getting what you want a bit of good currant loaf or something like that. At present we are not receiving good rations by a long way and you know I can eat a good deal when I start, that is the only difficulty.

PTE WILLIAM HORROCKS, 1/4TH EAST LANCASHIRE REGIMENT,
20 NOVEMBER 1917

Many thanks for the newspapers. Finally, after an exhausting and exciting period, we have been granted some rest. The town we are billeted in reminds me of Wald. We took it from the English 14 days ago. Most houses are uninhabited and shot to pieces, but we have settled in as good as possible and can now rest our weary bones in soft straw.

UNIDENTIFIED GERMAN SOLDIER, 4 NOVEMBER 1914

I'll just describe to you the place I am writing this in. It's a funny little room an offshoot of the Farm. I am sitting on a box with my feet towards a wood fire. There is a long table in the room where ten of our chaps are gambling away for dear life at Vingt-et-un. Others are reading and others like myself writing. The latter may be writing to very nice girls but I don't think they can be anything near so nice as the one I am writing to.

RFN WILLIAM C. TAFFS, 1/16TH QUEEN'S WESTMINSTER RIFLES,
26 FEBRUARY 1916

Slept reasonably well under a warm blanket, washed myself and had sausage and bread for breakfast. No coffee. At 8:50 am I leave. In the mess I buy soap, a torchlight and some batteries. In one of the houses there is a Cafe where we drink hot chocolate and obtain some cigars and chocolate bars. There are German newspapers which are about eight days old. The latest news we get from placards on the walls which look similar to postal telegrams. From one of them I learn that the fortress Przemywl has surrendered to the Russians. Me, Leutnant Reese and another Leutnant empty a bottle of Champagne and at 2pm we march off to St. Etienne.

UFFZ. FRIEDRICH SEEGER, RESERVE-INFANTERIE-REGIMENT NR. 73,
25 MARCH 1915

Dear Sister, I have the pleasure to write a few lines to let you know I am going on in the best of Health and hope this finds you the same, for I like to write when we can make time, at present we are doing a bit more in the line but the weather is not so bad that is one good consolation. We have been staying in a small village for the last few days not a bad place at all I had the pleasure of going to church which I know you will be glad to hear about. I have had a parcel from home and it was a very good one too so that I had a good feed which you know I would do my duty to it.

Pte William Horrocks, 1/4th East Lancashire Regiment,
5 February 1918

You will be amused to see us when we dig in for the night in this barn. It's about 14ft square. In it are 18 of us, so you see it's a bit of a squeeze. Last night I slept with my boots on my pack, the latter being just on the right of my head. When I awoke one boot had just topped over and very soon would have fallen on my head. We were just like sardines. Just about 12 o'clock one chap complained that another fellow would wriggle his toes – the aforesaid toes being against the complainants back. Immediately everybody began to grouse at each other for about ten minutes. It was funny. I was lying awake thinking I was the only one awake and then pandemonium.

Rfn William C. Taffs, 1/16th Queen's Westminster Rifles,
1 March 1916

In my time off-duty I read two books by Courths-Mahler, which I will send to you soon. You know my darling, I need to distract myself here as otherwise I will turn mad. The food is good, duty is not so hard and I miss nothing except you. A couple of days ago I and a few comrades used an old trench to practise throwing live grenades. That was very interesting. We are quartered in Hatrize, a small village which we occupied in 1914. Everything here is in German hands. The citizens are allowed to use 1–2 rooms of their houses and the kitchen. The rest has been requisitioned by the army. Supplies and daily necessities are also supplied by the military. The Belgians keep the roads clean and most of the able bodied citizens have to work for the commandant's office. I am billeted in Madame Bouche's house, together with 24 men and 4 NCOs. On quiet nights we can hear the thunder and growling of the guns. It's then I pray for you and I thank God that this horrible and wicked war is not fought in our beloved fatherland. But now I have to come to an end. Do not worry about me.

Gustav Dintelmann, Feld-Art. Rekruten-Depot Nr. 27, 26 July 1917

We are now billeted in a little farmhouse – waiting. We are rather in clover – pro-tem as there is a gramophone in our room filling the air with melody – so as to speak.

RFN WILLIAM C. TAFFS, 1/16TH QUEEN'S WESTMINSTER RIFLES,
29 JUNE 1916

We are back in billets and there is a beauty about billets which belongs to no other part of the Campaign – it is not the solid luxury of a bed or straw – no apart from this there is a charm – it's the News Centre of the War. One meets everyone and everyone has a new story – delightful little fairy tales improved by each teller and at the end of the day one is quite willing to bet that the war will end by the end of the month; but these are not the charm of the Billet, far from it, the charm lies in the telling the Battalion marching out what the new trenches they are going to are like. Today a certain Battalion marched through this place going out to our old trenches, our men lined the road, walked beside the newcomers and told them spicy little bits which came in through my broken window, from which I can admire a couple of acres of wonderful clay very nearly knee-deep. 'You are going to the trenches at xxxx, dear oh lor! That's where poor Bill 'ad 'is face blowed off – You ain't going to the xxxx trenches, good lor they are terrible – knee-deep and dead men all around them – What you are going by xxxx, my but that road is shelled something cruel, they got the xxxx Regiment on it poor devils – and the Batt'n marched on with even the galloping Major going a bit flat (that's a song) … I chuckled to myself as I sat there for they were the quietest trenches I had been in and really quite dry in comparison to some I've read of in the paper. Still there is the humour of the British Tommy which is sometimes rather twisted but most always to the front.

2LT ARTHUR R. STANLEY-CLARKE, 1ST DORSETSHIRE REGIMENT,
24 JANUARY 1915

As at the front, a routine was developed within the rest areas. Even though men were on rest, military duties still prevailed: training, lectures, fatigues, but contemporary diarists all record the sense of relief obtained from being set free from the random slaughter of the front line, if only for a short interval of time:

As you like to know something of what I am doing I will describe to you the doings in our so called rest. The first day up at 7, washed and shaved (first time for 14 days) cleaned ammunition, sword and rifle. Rifle inspection.

Smoke helmet drill (marking time and firing etc with respirators on – a pretty awful business). Swept up billet yard with another chap. After dinner writing letters and in the evening went up to a debate 'Should Parsons fight'. That is a fairly easy day.

RFN WILLIAM C. TAFFS, 1/16TH QUEEN'S WESTMINSTER RIFLES,
29 JANUARY 1916

After being in the trenches and suffering the worst of the conditions and seen sights that would be difficult to erase, it was hard to return to the old ways of 'bull', discipline and parades – particularly for the citizen-soldiers of the British army:

The heads that be in our lot have just noticed a certain slackness in our saluting so we all had to pass before our Capt this afternoon solemnly saluting. It seems to me rather a funny thing for chaps who have been fourteen months in the trenches to have to do.

RFN WILLIAM C. TAFFS, 1/16TH QUEEN'S WESTMINSTER RIFLES,
1 MARCH 1916

The weather will be better now we have had a nice day today the best since I have been out here and I hope it will keep nice so as to dry up the water and mud we had a General inspection yesterday we had to clean our buttons for the first time I could do with a change of clothes as I am fairly walking I expect to get a bath tomorrow so that will be better.

PTE ROBERT W. PRICE, 10TH WELSH REGIMENT,
1 APRIL 1916

On rest. We have rather a stiff morning here. Up at 7, Physical drill at 7.5. Breakfast at 8. Parade at 9 when we have squad, company and respirator drill until 12 then we have an hour's route march and dinner at 1.15. The Respirator drill is the most hated. We have done exercises with them on – a pretty awful business.

RFN WILLIAM C. TAFFS, 1/16TH QUEEN'S WESTMINSTER RIFLES,
16 FEBRUARY 1916

There was also the chance that parties of men would be required to work, both in improving the military situation in the rear areas and also taking rations, ammunition and military materiel up to the front line, or the reserve trenches at least:

Had fine sleep, cleaned up rifle and mess tin. Paraded at 6 and marched off for trench digging behind line under fire all the time, get back about 1.30.

PTE M. WILLIAMS, 11TH WELSH REGIMENT, 17 SEPTEMBER 1915

We have had a most lively job here the last two days. The roads here are somewhat narrow with thick mud each side, and in some places ditches each side. We have been shovelling the mud away and making ditches (where they exist) drain the road. Where they do not exist we make them. Whatever you do though don't go and make a mistake and address a letter to me as if I were in the Navvy's Batt. I am still in the Queen's.

RFN WILLIAM C. TAFFS, 1/16TH QUEEN'S WESTMINSTER RIFLES, 22 MARCH 1916

We have now moved to the rear to form a regimental reserve and are billeted in a forest camp. The first day was used to clean our bodies and equipment. There was lot of work necessary to remove seven days of dirt. Now the battalion is tasked to do labour service. The companies being on rotating duty in day- and night-time. Our work consists of disposing of the rubbish, digging of communication trenches, construction of latrines. At night we move forward and carry material, munitions, etc, into the positions. While the daily work is quite peaceful, working at night can be quite dangerous as the working parties are often targeted by the enemy artillery.

UFFZ. PAUL HILGER, LANDWEHR-INFANTERIE-REGIMENT NR. 106, 15 OCTOBER 1915

Working parties could be targeted by shellfire or gas, especially if they had to move up the line at night:

We came out here for a rest but you cannot call it much of a rest when you have to spend whole nights up in the firing line digging trenches. We left here last night to dig at 7.15 and returned this morning at 4 o'clock. The Germans attacked with gas last night while we were working and we had to wear our helmets for over an hour. It was an anxious time as the men dread gas so and get very nervy, also there was a terrific bombardment going on! In very truth this war is absolute HELL.

2LT ARTHUR H. LAMB, 1ST LANCASHIRE FUSILIERS, 3 SEPTEMBER 1916

Despite this, rest provided an opportunity for the average soldier to gain some mental freedom – washing, speaking to locals, buying trinkets – as well as engaging women in hopeful conversations:

> Trying to speak French. A splendid failure. Can hear guns plain. Am watching our airmen trying to catch a German aeroplane. Am put on special guard.
> SGT FREDERICK J. COMPTON, 16TH CHESHIRE REGIMENT, 5 FEBRUARY 1916

> In the farm where we are billeted live a couple of women. One of the chaps told them that I was married and nothing I can say can induce them to believe I am not. Yesterday for the twentieth time I should think they asked me 'Etes vous marie' I said 'Non, Mesdames' in my best manner. Then they looked dubious and said 'your wife must be very bad'. Rather a funny way of looking at it, don't you think?
> RFN WILLIAM C. TAFFS, 1/16 QUEEN'S WESTMINSTER RIFLES, 5 APRIL 1916

Paid in the local currency, this buying power could be put to work on the purchase of alcohol – often of lamentable quality – and to indulge in other vices normally frowned upon at home: gambling, fraternisation with women of 'ill repute', visits to brothels. There was some freedom to make simple purchases, souvenirs, postcards and the sustenance from those civilians brave enough to remain – though there were complaints of 'profiteering':

> I am writing this in a farmyard kitchen waiting meanwhile the lady of the farm makes a ripping bowl of café au lait. She makes awfully fine coffee with boiling milk – practically all milk in fact.
> RFN WILLIAM C. TAFFS, 1/16TH QUEEN'S WESTMINSTER RIFLES,
> 26 MARCH 1916

> On the streets there is a lively traffic and I was surprised that one is still able to buy everything here. Only the tobacco is a rip-off, the French charge us 2,50 for a pack that would cost you 40–50 Pfennigs in Germany.
> HORNIST WILLI BRÜLLS, INFANTERIE-REGIMENT NR. 178.,
> 12 NOVEMBER 1916

Moving back to the line was not usually a welcome proposition:

> We are moving tomorrow further north and in a day or two I expect we shall take over a line of trenches. That is the time I dread and I know

I shall be as nervous as the dickens because I know how I felt when the Boche was putting those 5.9s over us at the other place. By jove! I shall be pleased if I get out of this and back home. I am hoping for the best but it is pretty hopeless.

2Lt Arthur H. Lamb, 1st Lancashire Fusiliers, 20 July 1916

Baths

For the men of the trenches, getting clean was one of the most significant attributes of getting to the rear area. Baths would be set up in breweries, tanneries and collieries that were equipped with vats and tubs; otherwise temporary set ups were constructed by the medical corps and other ancillary staff:

On the 15th we marched to Estree Blanche, where we stayed until the 18th; the second day we were paraded and taken to the Colliery Baths. We were very much surprised to find a woman attendant. Had a good bath alright, but had to put our dirty underclothes on again. We had plenty of live-stock about us and without a clean change, it was making game of the job.

Pte John H. Benn, Loyal North Lancashire Regiment,
18 March 1917

Uniforms were fumigated, underclothes exchanged; this would allow the men to escape, albeit briefly, from the merciless irritations of the ubiquitous body louse:

To every man new clothes and underlinen were issued; and we all had a bath – an amusing affair, that took place in a rag-shop. A canvas bath had been rigged up, and each Company took it in turn to bathe, the water being fetched by the cooks in dixies. We had about four of these dixies filled with about twenty quarts of water to each bath, with some disinfect-ant put in it. About one hundred men would bathe to each bath, the last dozen or so revelling in pea soup. Every one had to go in – as at that time we had plenty of live stock crawling over us.

Pte Frederick Bolwell, Loyal North Lancashire Regiment, 1914

We have just (that is this morning) had a glorious bath. I have had the awful job of washing my clothes this afternoon. The water was too cold

German delousing tent in northern France, 1916.

to wash them properly, so I put them in a tub of water, put some sunlight soap in with them and stirred vigorously with a club and hanged them about generally. Then I let them soak for 4 hours, wrung them out and I am now waiting for a bit of sun to dry them. As it rains here for ever and ever I believe the war will come before these affairs are dried. I hope I don't catch cold only unfortunately I haven't got anything to put on in place of them.

RFN WILLIAM C. TAFFS, 1/16TH QUEEN'S WESTMINSTER RIFLES,
18 FEBRUARY 1916

Huts provided by the YMCA, Church Army or similar continued the good works of these organisations abroad; 'dry' canteens they were, but such huts, provided using money raised through 'flag days' and the like, created a means for men to gather, drink tea, eat sandwiches, and write letters home on the paper provided, to kill time before their return to the trenches and in between the military duties that still persisted 'out on rest':

I spent an hour and a half yesterday serving out tea in the YMCA tent. The johnnie in charge thought it would be a good idea to have an urn on the grass outside the tent and as I was reading near by he collared me for the job. I took about 7 frs in the 1½ hours.

RFN WILLIAM C. TAFFS, 1/16TH QUEEN'S WESTMINSTER RIFLES,
17 MARCH 1916

Monday 28. Went to Poperinghe for bath.
Tuesday 29. Cinema show at YMCA Hut. Wet night. Had a parcel from Paignton. German aeroplanes very busy.

SGT H.N.T. MASON, 6TH OXFORDSHIRE AND BUCKINGHAMSHIRE LIGHT
INFANTRY, MARCH 1916

For the British, there were also Expeditionary Force Canteens (EFC) – army-run establishments that provided a means of purchasing necessaries: soap and candles, paper, pencils, food and sauces that would make the ubiquitous bully beef of the trenches more palatable. The German soldier was catered for through the *Soldatenheime*, soldiers' homes, where they could gather, relax and get some home comforts. Like the British equivalents, these were intended to keep the average soldier out of the bars and brothels, and out of trouble:

Nearly every town occupied by the military has at least one house which has been turned into a *Soldatenheime*. They have heated rooms, a library and a mess which sells cheap goods. Soldiers can buy food like potato salad and coffee for a few Pfennigs, there is newspapers and often you can get free cigars. Most have a piano as well. Here soldiers find a comfortable home and they are not forced to spend their free time in bars or brothels. Here there is also a bath house which incorporates a barber's shop.

WERNER VOSSDELLEN, 21 FEBRUARY 1917

Three weeks ago a *Soldatenheime* was opened here. It enables every soldier to spend some quality time without having to spend any money. There the soldier has access to the major German newspapers, magazines and to a small library. The fact that it is very hard to find an empty chair in the reading room is proof of the success of this new institution.

GUSTAV WEIDENHAUPT, 2 MARCH 1916

Soldatenheime, offering home comforts to the soldiers at the front.

I am getting along for money first rate here. Since last Sunday I have only spent 1d – a coffee. I shall have heaps over when I return and then won't I enjoy myself. By the way will you put in a few candles with most parcels (that is in the odd corners). They are the only illuminant we have here and it makes all the difference. You should have seen our dugout in the firing line – about 3 feet high, 5ft wide, 6 feet long. Door about 1ft x 2.0 – a puddle just in the door just where I have to kneel; when entering. Some hostelry.

RFN WILLIAM C. TAFFS, 1/16TH QUEEN'S WESTMINSTER RIFLES,
26 DECEMBER 1915

British soldiers enjoying Christmas dinner in a hut behind the lines.

Religion

In the German army, each division had one Lutheran chaplain and one Catholic priest who administered spiritual guidance and performed their duties down to battalion level. These duties included everything from funeral and field services to comforting the wounded and the dying in the field hospitals. There were also at least thirty *Feldrabbiner* serving on a voluntary basis seeing to the spiritual needs of the Jewish soldiers in the German army:

> Here in the trenches all soldiers start praying, even if they haven't said a prayer for 10 or 15 years before the war.
> SOLD. FRIEDRICH BECKER, INFANTERIE-REGIMENT NR. 57, 18 JANUARY 1915

May the good Lord set an end to this war soon. I, for my part, consider this murder to be great sin and I sincerely hope that our dear God will forgive me should one of my bullets ever hit an enemy.

EMIL GREMLER, 2. ERSATZ-BATAILLON RES.-INF.-RGT. NR. 46, 2 MAY 1915

A glorious Sunday morning in May. Behind Annoeullin we halted, took off rifles and backpacks and, forming a circle, laid down in the grass. 600 of us surrounding the divisional chaplain and the regimental band. 'Helmets off for prayer'. The band played '*Wir treten zum Beten*' and we sang to it. It was a most moving service in the divinity of nature. When the chaplain preached to us from horseback it was 11am and I thought that you would be in church now as well, praying for me.

SOLD. FRIEDRICH BECKER, INFANTERIE-REGIMENT NR. 57, 22 MARCH 1915

Good Friday we celebrated Holy Mass where the chaplain preached a beautiful sermon. It is a wonderful sight to see the church filled with praying soldiers. The French locals say the same. With such soldiers we have to win. Service was held in the ruins of the village church. The chaplain delivered a sermon the like of which I have never heard before. We should have no sympathy for the enemy and should offer him no mercy. We must be merciless, especially towards the English.

ANONYMOUS GERMAN LETTER, 10 FEBRUARY 1915

In the British army, on joining, all men had to specify a religion; some declined, but most indicated their faith and their church, temple or synagogue. Finding solace and spiritual comfort in religion was often the only place a man could turn for consolation; though even this was sorely tried in the battlezone:

It makes me happier knowing you all pray for me and it gives me comfort under fire and God will do according to his wisdom – for the best. One never knows what life holds in store for one and God in his mercy acts for the best. Pray also for our enemies for they need all our prayers, even more than for us as theirs is the war.

2LT ARTHUR R. STANLEY-CLARKE, 1ST DORSETSHIRE REGIMENT,

22 NOVEMBER 1914

Oh! Mummy dear, I dread the future in a way and yet I feel if I pray to God that He will give me strength and help when I most need it so that

I may behave as a man and face all the untold horrors. I know we have to go through as an Englishman. Also I pray with all my heart and soul that my Father in Heaven may be pleased soon to take me back to you, my own dearest mummy. Anyway I trust absolutely in Him and more than that I cannot do. He alone can do it.

2LT ARTHUR H. LAMB, 1ST LANCASHIRE FUSILIERS, 9 OCTOBER 1916

When one is in the midst of danger and hardships and say on Guard at night alone, with the bullets zipping around, one feels what a small place a priest takes in one's life. If one had to go to another man for any sort of spiritual help or guidance out here, he would find his God and his religion of little use.

RFN WILLIAM C. TAFFS, 1/16TH QUEEN'S WESTMINSTER RIFLES,
7 FEBRUARY 1916

Some felt the need to reward providence:

Dear Mother when you are writing again you need not send the order but will you put 1/- in St Anthony's box and the 1/6 in the Sacred Hearts and St Joseph's box. I was in great danger when in the trenches last time so I just said a few prayers and thank God I got out safely.

PTE JAMES HEALY, 8TH ROYAL DUBLIN FUSILIERS, 22 JUNE 1916

Many gained closeness with their faith, and religious organisations abounded in the rear areas, supplying rest huts and local cheer, as well as services. At the front, chaplains would accompany their flock and tend to the wounded at dressing stations, or even in no-man's-land – there were many brave men amongst them:

I have just returned from a ripping service in a field. It's the first one I have been to for five weeks so you may guess I have enjoyed it some. We had quite a number of chaps there, and of course that made it all the better. Our chaplain (Mr Tiplady) is going to provide us with a communion service tomorrow evening at seven and all being well I hope to get to that too.

RFN WILLIAM C. TAFFS, 1/16TH QUEEN'S WESTMINSTER RIFLES,
26 JUNE 1916

Today is Sunday and I have just been to a small prayer given by our Chaplain in the church Army Hut close by our billet so you see we get

British soldiers attending a Roman Catholic service before proceeding overseas.

German soldiers of the *4. Garde-Regiment zu Fuß* engaged in a field service, 1915.

a chance occasionally to have service. The weather is very changeable at present still we can stand practically anything during the day so long as we get a good night's rest and sleep.

Pte William Horrocks, 1/4th East Lancashire Regiment,
3 March 1918

We had a really nice communion service last evening. I do enjoy these little services so. Everybody who comes of course is keen and that ensures a good meeting. I suppose you have heard time and time again how religion out here is absolutely practical and helpful. I assure you if it were not so, I shudder to think how this war would leave me. We are probably going into action very shortly now. We are quite hopeful of success but as you know success nearly always has to be paid for. If I get hit at all (of course it's a jolly good chance I shall not be) but one never knows, I should like to tell you again what a darling you have been to me all these months. Ever since you wrote to me as 'dearest' I have looked at dear old England in a different light and I have thought of what a ripping time we shall have when this is all over. You cannot conceive what a hope this has been to me dear, but when I do come I will be sure to enlighten you as to how I have felt and done over here. You must excuse any blotches on the page at this juncture only I am writing this in a somewhat ruined barn with a perforated roof – the while it's raining like blazes.

Rfn William C. Taffs, 1/16th Queen's Westminster Rifles,
27 June 1916

For other soldiers, comfort was to be obtained from possessing a New Testament, and the army obliged by issuing a small volume; other organisations produced similar pocket versions for distribution. Many were sent to soldiers from home, a comfort at the front:

I think it is time that you send me a prayer book. Out here one's only salvation is prayer, there is not much else to do when the terrible shell splinters come swishing towards you. Every second you can be hit. The only defence against it is prayer. A comrade always hangs a rosary next to the loophole he is manning. It's as close to him as his rifle.

Johann Wierich, Infanterie-Regiment Nr. 29

The Bible you sent me has a smell of home even through the mud which covers everything wonder how much longer the Kaiser will persist in continuing this terrible war for he and the rest of educated Germany must know with God's help we are winning.

2Lt Arthur R. Stanley-Clarke, 1st Dorsetshire Regiment,

27 November 1914

Leave

On average, and if they were lucky, ordinary soldiers – British and German – were to return home on leave once a year. Officers fared better, with a leave granted at around four months, but it was still a rare commodity:

At present am not allowed to even think about going on leave. Mainly because of the long ban. Others were more lucky than I was. I have now been a soldier for 3 ¼ years and I am currently waiting for my third period of leave.

Hornist Willy Brülls, Infanterie-Regiment Nr. 178, 22 July 1918

Detailed direct from the front line, the men would have to find their way back on the long, laborious trail home – and if home was in the more remote corners of the British Isles, this could be a trek indeed. Nevertheless, it must have been frustrating for some families, waiting at home, observing the arrival of their loved ones while others tramped down their home street, still carrying the 'mud of the trenches'. For Private Robert Price of the Welsh Regiment, getting home to see his family was his first priority – especially as he feared he might be killed or 'napoo' in soldier's slang – from *il n'ya plus*, it is no more:

I got your letter and parcel on Thursday Jan 20th the day before my Birthday. I suppose you must have forgotten it was my Birthday but never mind as long as I can see many more. We was just getting ready for the trenches again, we are going in for 4 days now and I hope I shall come out safe again it is a miserable place where we are going into this time plenty of water and rats, and then we come out again for a week and then in again and so on till all the Division has been in, and then we shall have a Divisional rest that means 6 weeks rest and then we might get a pass but you must not make up your mind to see me on pass and then you won't be disappointed but I shall do my best to come to you. Know that the distance is no object to me as long as I can come and see you and my boys.

Pte Robert W. Price, 10th Welsh Regiment, January 1916

I don't know when we shall be able to come home yet it is all the talk about when we shall get leaf [sic] I wish I was coming for good I can tell you I have been out of the trenches for a few days now but we have no rest working all the time now nearer the line I expect we shall be in the trenches again on Sun night I would not care if we had finished.

PTE ROBERT W. PRICE, 10TH WELSH REGIMENT, 1 APRIL 1916

I hope that you and the boys are quite well. I don't know when I shall get to come home as there are only two out of our Bttn and one of them is an officer. I only wish that the War was over so as I could come home for good. I have been lucky lately not having to go into the trenches as I don't want [to] as I have had enough fighting and have been lucky to come through and I might go in next time, and be nappoo but hope not.

PTE ROBERT W. PRICE, 10TH WELSH REGIMENT, 1 NOVEMBER 1916

You seem to think that I can come home if I liked I only wish I had the chance. I can tell you there is only one man going at a time in our Battalion as we are mining under the R.E. arrangements, but you know that I can't put in a letter what I should like to. I wish I was coming, we keep on hearing that they are going to start leave but of course we are looking forward for it I can tell you. I keeps on giving up hopes but I dare say I shall come home some time that is if God spares my life, which I hope he will.

PTE ROBERT W. PRICE, 10TH WELSH REGIMENT, 23 OCTOBER 1917

The desire of Pte Price and his family was shared with many others:

I wish I was only home for a few days which I expect very soon it will be over 12 months since I saw you last and it seems years to me and I do not know what it seems to you but never mind Dear. I will see you again some time if God spares me to do so. I am just getting about fed up of it all.

DVR PERCY HARTLAND, ROYAL FIELD ARTILLERY, 17 FEBRUARY 1916

The feeling of isolation and alienation from home felt by some officers and men was by no means shared by all. The route back to the front after leave was often a desolate one:

Started from Poperinghe 4.50 am reached Boulogne about 10 am Left about 6 pm reached Folkestone at 9 (new time) and Victoria about 10.30. Paddington 11 pm. No more trains till morning so stayed at YMCA in

Frances St for night. Left next morning at 5.30 from Paddington, changing at Didcot and reaching Oxford at 7.

SGT H.N.T. MASON, 6TH OXFORDSHIRE AND BUCKINGHAMSHIRE LIGHT INFANTRY, 11 JUNE 1916

With leave awarded so rarely to the men of the front line, continuing the link with home meant the writing of literally millions of letters home – sometimes under the most trying of conditions.

Leave was rare amongst front-line troops; these men hope for a future trip to 'Blighty' – home.

Letters

As children we always dreamed of war and playing soldiers. Hilli and Anton wanted to join the cavalry together … a real war with field battles such as this we would never have dreamed of. What became of Hilli? Where is Anton? They do not write anymore.

GEFR. J. GÖRTEMAKER, FELDARTILLERIE-REG. NR. 503 FRANCE, 5 JUNE 1918

Letters to and from the front were of great importance in maintaining the morale of the troops. The *Feldpost*, the German army postal service, was of immense importance for the German soldier; mostly the only way to stay in connection with family and the *Heimat*. Together with the rarely granted periods of *Fronturlaub* (front-line holiday), it was a significant factor in maintaining morale – a fact the *Oberste Heeresleitung* was well aware of:

The attitude of the army in the field is strongly influenced by the mental connection with the *Heimat*. There is not many things that see the men through danger and hardship more effectively than the long awaited message from home …

OBERSTE HEERESLEITUNG COMMUNIQUÉ, DECEMBER 1914

From 1914 to 1918 the 8,000 soldiers and officials employed by the German *Feldpost* service transported a staggering number of letters, postcards, parcels and newspapers – a total of 28.7 billion shipments of all kind. The majority of those, letters and postcards below 300 grams, were sent post free. Responsibility for the postal traffic lay with the *Feldpostabteilung* (field mail department) of the *Reichspostamt* (Reichs Postal Service), which faced huge organisational problems, especially in the early days of the war:

How are you? Our battalion has not received any mail yet. If you continue writing to 'Jäger Gehner, 2 Kompanie, Jäger 7 Feldbatallion' it should arrive. Please show this letter to Mr Petersen. It is as much for him as it is for you. I do not suppose to have the chance to write such a detailed letter any time again soon. I wish I could be back at home again. How nice it was, sleeping in one's own bed each night and eat from a bountiful table. Here you only talk about war and where to get the next food from. Only at night in bivouac everyone's thought turns to their loved ones at home and they start to sing folk songs. A while ago I dreamt to be in camp, with a warm blanket and there was food aplenty and everyone had sausage and bread as much as he could stomach. It was wonderful. Then I woke up and found myself lying in the mud and under open sky; wet, cold and hungry.

JÄGER GUSTAV WILLY GEHNER, JÄGER BTL. 7, 28 AUGUST 1914

Not every delivery reached its recipient and long delivery times were the norm; in 1914 a survey came to the conclusion that more than one third of all shipments could not be delivered due to incorrect addresses – a matter of great concern to the average German soldier:

Your letter I have received as this time you have included my company number! Christine's letter and the parcel with the money I have NOT received. If it does not arrive there is nothing I can do. You should have added the company number! You have it as it is on all the letters I sent to you! We have at least 20 men named Meyer in my battalion alone! Without it my mail will be passed through all the companies, before it finally reaches me. It is your thoughtlessness that is to blame. You should not have sent money anyway, the risk is way too high.

Let me explain it again. Two parcels have not arrived yet. The one sent by Christine, which has sausage in it and yours. It is your fault because you forgot to write '4. Kompanie' on them and it is totally irrelevant that I had been sick I still get all my post delivered to me! These two parcels did not arrive, you know that I always send you a card when one of your parcels arrives. Johann's sister in law sent me a letter in which she asks me if I have received her parcel. I got nothing! The reason being that she as well forgot to add '4. Kompanie' to the address! Please tell her to use the correct address.

You can't imagine how angry I am that your mail will probably have been delivered to the wrong persons! I ask you why do you find it so difficult to add the company number to the address. You also forgot to put it on the letter in which you asked me if I had received the parcels. The last 20 cards I sent have the company number written on the back and you do not give a rip about it! I am starving and other people get my parcels!

MUSK. KURT MEYER, INFANTERIE-REGIMENT NR. 56, 8 TO 15 MARCH 1915

To counter these problems the top secret *Feldpost-Übersicht* (Field Post Digest) was issued: a book that detailed the army's organisational structure and listed all its units and locations, updated regularly throughout the war. A great many deliveries were lost due to enemy fire or in accidents. In some cases trainloads of mail burned down because parcels sent to the front often contained matches, self-igniting cigars, petrol and ether, while war trophies like shell parts, fuses, detonators, grenades and even small aerial bombs were sent home as souvenirs.

For the British there was the Army Postal Section, a component of the Corps of Royal Engineers set up in 1913. In August 1914, the postal service moved to France with the British Expeditionary Force (BEF). Mail for the BEF from the United Kingdom was collected by the Post Office and sent to France, gathering at Le Havre, where the RE took over. The Army Postal Section was in charge of ensuring these letters reached home safely, and it was their job to ensure that letters and parcels arriving for the troops were delivered – often a difficult task given the movement of troops to and from the trenches, in many different action fronts. Often, poignantly, parcels would arrive for soldiers recently killed. Here the protocol was to share the consumable amongst those less fortunate, and to ensure that the personal items were returned. Letters returned to their sender with the cachet 'killed in action' or 'deceased' were to provide stark reminders of the fortunes of war. Nevertheless, there was a definite excitement to receiving a letter from home:

> I have an additional thrill when letters arrive. When the orderly Corporal dishes out the letters I can see them upside down in his hand. It's extraordinary what a lot of handwriting is like yours upside down, though of course to me there is nothing to equal yours the right side up. When I see a letter which looks like yours my heart leaps, but when the OC says Rfn Brown or whoever it is my heart goes down in my boots. Thanks to your goodness though, I am not often disappointed, in fact I nearly always get one, when I expect one.
>
> RFN WILLIAM C. TAFFS, 1/16TH QUEEN'S WESTMINSTER RIFLES,
> 18 FEBRUARY 1916

Actually writing the letters could be a challenge in the conditions of the front-line trenches:

> You must excuse both the writing and the state of the paper but this is written in the trenches and as we have had twelve hours rain things are not quite comfy. I am living at present in a little nitch cut in the side just big enough to curl up in and I smiled as I tucked myself up last night – soaking wet – as I thought of the very bad cold I would have had in England. But I was in luxury last night as I had a blanket. We all think out here that the

war will not last much longer and I pray that this may be so for although the life agrees with me, the shells and bullets make it a bit unhealthy.

I am very sorry that I have not been able to write during the past few days but I have been in the Trenches which makes it impossible. Even while I write this, shells come screaming over – however nothing but a Jack Johnson can get as far down as I am now and I believe they have moved it now.

2Lt Arthur R. Stanley-Clarke, 1st Dorsetshire Regiment,
14 November 1914

If you notice any signs of grime on this paper, and as I write it is quite apparent, you must know that it comes off my hands. I have been digging trenches and in the rush from them to the cellar I have come over a cropper in the mud. The note paper I am afraid is not quite up to scratch as it is an old note book I picked up whilst cleaning up a dug out.

Rfn William C. Taffs, 1/16th Queen's Westminster Rifles,
21 January 1916

The British censorship system was efficient – but meant that every letter was open to considerable scrutiny. Each letter would be opened by the relevant officer, who would append his signature to say that he had read its contents, and who would strike through offending passages with a blue pencil. Typical 'offences' – expressly forbidden in the army's *Field Service Regulations* – would be reference to current location, defences, offensives or casualties. A further random check could be made once the letter was in transit – as in the envelope 'opened by censor':

Yesterday my letter was very short as in the middle an orderly came in with letters for one to censor as one has over a hundred a day it takes a bit of doing and also a lot of the time.

2Lt Arthur R. Stanley-Clarke, 1st Dorsetshire Regiment,
13 December 1914

For some men, this was a source of embarrassment. To combat this, and to provide some form of privacy, 'Green envelopes' were provided as a special concession, their contents not routinely read or censored by officers. 'Greenies' were an opportunity for the soldier to share his intimate feelings with loved ones, or to deal with family matters. Once sealed, the sender had to sign a declaration that the letter contained no matters of military importance; these would only be subject to scrutiny at the base:

As I have at last got one of these green johnnies I am giving you the first one, yet it is an extraordinary think that when I came to my small stock of ordinary envelopes I find them all stuck down with the damp so I should have had to enclose this in a green one willy nilly.

RFN WILLIAM C. TAFFS, 1/16TH QUEEN'S WESTMINSTER RIFLES, 19 DECEMBER 1915

I think I told you about the Green envelope they opens them all at the base now I think you will know that when you get this letter you must let me know if they open this one you will be able to tell if they don't.

PTE ROBERT W. PRICE, 10TH WELSH REGIMENT, 9 MARCH 1916

I am afraid if I write to you as often as I want to my supply of green envelopes will run short, so I shall have to write letters to you which will have to be censored. Of course I shall not be able to write as I should like to then, but of course you will understand.

RFN WILLIAM C. TAFFS, 1/16TH QUEEN'S WESTMINSTER RIFLES, 23 FEBRUARY 1916

There is a marked contrast between German and British letters of the time. With the German system overloaded, censorship was desultory, and consequently letters are packed with detail. British letters, particularly from other ranks, tend to be shorter, lacking in detail, and cautious. No doubt this was because British letters were subject to a considerable degree of scrutiny, often by the officers that served with them – though there is a suggestion that the standard of education of the average German soldier was higher than that of the average working class Briton. Nevertheless, it was the quickly written, empty-phrased, field postcard which made up the bulk of mailings sent from the front. But, in contrast to the British, many German soldiers also sent multiple paged, detailed accounts of their experiences at the front, which they illustrated with photographs and hand-drawn maps. Letters were checked and censored on a sample basis, and even though censorship rules became more strict the further the war progressed, the sheer amount of letters sent made tight control impossible and most *Feldpost* was not controlled at all:

Well Dearie I am very sorry that I could not write this because I have hurt my wrist so I asked my chum Jack to write it for me so excuse the writing because he is a good lad and we intend to stick together till the finish he has been out here about 15 month and got fed up of it the same as me. So

now I will close it as it is near lights out so good night and God Bless you
till we meet again.

DVR PERCY HARTLAND, ROYAL FIELD ARTILLERY, 17 FEBRUARY 1916

My dear little friend Ruby

Now to pencil you a few loving lines hoping you and all at home are enjoying the best of health. I hope you will like the P.C. enclosed it is of a French
soldier charging and their sons playing at soldier at home. Well dear little
friend I shall be glad, when the war is over then I will come home and you
shall come and have tea with me your Soldier Boy friend.

GNR VICTOR HUNTING, ROYAL GARRISON ARTILLERY, 1918

Food

Food was a major issue in maintaining morale in the trenches, yet its supply
was a challenge. Cold food derived from tins was often all that was available at
times of pressure. For the British, 'bully beef' – ration corned beef – became
repetitive at the very least, and this was supplied with bread, bacon, tea, sugar
and other groceries, very often brought up to the front line in a jumble.
Corned beef was imported then as now from South America, and was vari-
ously received:

> I had my first meal of bully beef today, and it was very good. We are fright-
> fully cheery and one would never believe we were off to a fight. We have
> not the slightest idea where we are going and we live in expectation.
>
>
>
> 2LT ARTHUR R. STANLEY-CLARKE, 1ST DORSETSHIRE REGIMENT,
> 26 OCTOBER 1914
>

Late in the war, captured stocks were prized by the Germans. Other tinned
food staples included 'pork and beans' – tinned beans with a small cube of
pork fat at the bottom of the tin – and the universal Maconochie ration
– a tinned vegetable and meat concoction that at least served to break
the monotony of bully beef. Jam – 'pozzy' in soldier's slang – was another
welcome ration, but was most often Tickler's Plum and Apple. Fresh rations
– meat, bacon, vegetables – would also be supplied, brought to the front in
the ubiquitous sandbag.

German supplies were similarly unedifying. The *Kriegsration* (war ration)
was the daily allowance of victuals to each German soldier. It consisted

Food 'in the trenches' was usually a simple affair, cold rations with some limited opportunity for hot rations being brought up by ration parties. Here a soldier prepares a meal while his comrade 'takes aim', *c.* 1915.

mostly of cold food – which meant that it was independent of elaborate cooking facilities. The *Kriegsration* consisted usually of bread, sausage, fresh and tinned meat, vegetables and a small amount of sugar, salt, tea or coffee. Getting hot food to the trenches to revive the spirits and warm the bones of chilled men was a significant undertaking. Villages close to the front were sometimes a boon:

> Three times a day some men are sent back to Courcy to fetch coffee and food. A communication trench is leading to the village and without it, it would be impossible to reach the village in daylight. The food is generally terrible, only sometimes when it contains Sauerkraut or green beans it's a bit better. There is plenty of bread and sometimes cheese, sausages and butter.
>
> Uffz. Franz Seegers, Reserve-Infanterie-Reg. Nr. 73, 30 March 1915

Ration parties would bring up rations at night, usually by men 'out at rest' detailed for work up the line who returned to their rest camps at night. With increasing sophistication, hot rations in specially designed ration carriers modelled on the thermos principle were brought up the line; negotiating long communication trenches in the dark meant that this was often an arduous duty, but one much appreciated by the front-line troops all the same:

> Footsteps coming in our rear, we halted them and got the pass-word alright, and were delighted to find that they had brought us hot soup. We were told to take what we could as it would be the last hot meal we would have until the night. These hot soups were sent from the Cookers in containers. They were made on the flask system and would keep anything hot for hours, and were made to strap on the back.
>
> Pte John H. Benn, Loyal North Lancashire Regiment,
> 29 January 1917

All other rations would be brought up in sand bags, often in a hopeless jumble of loose tea, sugar, bread, bacon and tinned rations, intended for a forty-eight-hour period. This was matched by the German *Kriegsration*, usually bread, sausage, fresh and tinned meat, vegetables and small amounts of sugar, salt, tea or coffee. The absence of warm food told on the troops:

> I doubt you will be able to understand what we went through here in the last weeks. Only 2–3 hours of sleep day after day, being without warm food for five days in a row as there was no time for cooking and we did not have any field kitchens. Add to that the scorching heat, the fact that my job as gun commander does not allow for any rest and that I have a bastard of a *Hauptmann* who does everything in his power to make life a misery and

you will have an idea on how horrible this time was for me. Still I have successfully led my comrades through a number of engagements and my promotion to *Vizewachtmeister* came as a release. My future will be filled with culinary delights as I now dine with the officers and otherwise there is not much to do. The nature of this battle of the millions is that you spend a lot of time in one place waiting, which means that supplies come in a lot easier and rations get a lot better. Also the mail arrives on time and things get a lot more comfortable.

LTN. BERNHARD KORTZFLEISCH, 4. GARDE-FELDARTILLERIE-REGIMENT, 1914

Each soldier also carried an *Eiserne Portion* – directly comparable to the British iron ration:

About four miles from Mauberge we could hear a distant boom of a gun, and all lines of communication had been cut. A halt was called in the centre of Mauberge for one hour, and we were told that no man was to eat his 'iron ration,' i.e. emergency ration, or drink any of the water which he carried in his water-bottle, as we were expecting to go into action and probably should not get the supplies up for two days.

PTE FREDERICK BOLWELL, LOYAL NORTH LANCASHIRE REGIMENT, 1914

In both cases these emergency rations were deemed to last two days. The German version contained a small amount of hard tack, salt, coffee, tinned meat and vegetables. Again in direct comparison with the British, the *Eiserne Portion* could only be consumed by order of the unit commander. During the early phases of the war, when not every unit had its own mobile field kitchen or when the available ones could not keep up with the quickly advancing units, soldiers took it upon themselves to eat the *Eiserne Portion*. To counter this problem the consumption of this ration soon became a punishable offence. Another basis of supplying the army came from the purchase and requisitioning of food in occupied territory. Requisitioning was only allowed in times of hardship and under control and accountability of an officer.

In any case, food supply was challenging – and often men would have to make do with what they had – or what could be brought up from the rear areas, often under the most trying conditions. With the diet so mundane, often unpalatable, trying to maintain some form of appetite was difficult. This kind of victualling could easily lead to all-out plundering and quite often the term 'hardship' was widely interpreted:

A few days we enjoyed a roast goose, which helped us to forget that we had not received any food for three days. It was quite wonderful and I still have half of it in my mess tin. The brandy you sent has arrived and it already worked miracles on my freezing feet. We often have to live off the land as our supply lines are overstretched. That means that now and then a number of French chickens and pigs have to be thrown to the wolves. Our main food though is potatoes and more potatoes and there is not a lot of variety in our diet. Jacket potatoes, boiled potatoes, mashed potatoes, salted potatoes (without salt as we are not getting any), fried potatoes and potato fritters.

RES. LUDWIG BARTH, RESERVE-JÄGER-BATAILLON NR. 2 , 11 OCTOBER 1914

We vie with one another to compose dishes. I tried to make some porridge today by chopping some wheat and boiling it but although I boiled it for a good hour it fails to resemble anything as yet. We are on short rations today as last night while our men were carrying up the rations a couple of shells burst nearby and they dropped our bread and fled!! Of course another Regiment picked it up and so we have none!! But biscuits and jam dished up when one is hungry is nearly as good as fillet of beef. I received your parcel today with the belts, air cushion, milk tablets, peppermints, etc – and thanks awfully.

2LT ARTHUR R. STANLEY-CLARKE, 1ST DORSETSHIRE REGIMENT,
10 NOVEMBER 1914

And keeping food away from the myriad rats that were multiplying in the dead zone of the trenches was often impossible:

I had just bought a loaf and gave 9d for it hang it on to a beam for the night on a string the next morning half of it was gone eaten by rats it is nothing to see them where we are now they are walking all over us by night we got to keep kicking them off the brutes I don't like them coming on my face but we have to put up with that.

PTE ROBERT W. PRICE, 10TH WELSH REGIMENT, 1916

Even men in the reserves were called forward more often than not to keep those in the front line supplied:

I was up with a party in the front line last night and I have had no sleep for 24 hours. We expect to take over in the trenches tonight or tomorrow! It's a rotten place this as the Huns have so much artillery and the whole place is blown to smithereens and the stench is awful! Just fancy spending days under such conditions, which I shall do unless I am knocked out, and it does seem marvellous anyone escapes the shells fall so thick and fast.

2Lt Arthur H. Lamb, 1st Lancashire Fusiliers, 19 May 1917

The issue of a rum ration from ceramic jugs labelled 'SRD' – for 'Supply Reserve Depot', a large establishment based in Deptford, London – was a British institution. Rum was issued at dawn and dusk, following 'stand to'; its fiery warmth was intended to dispel some of the ague brought on by the cold, wet and miserable trench conditions. Famously, it was also to be issued to those men about to go 'over the bags', either at dawn with a large-scale attack, or at night prior to a raid. The rum ration was issued by a senior NCO, with an officer in attendance. Given that drunkenness was a serious offence, the ration could not be accumulated and saved for later; poured into mug or mess tin top it was to be drunk in the presence of the officer. Soldiers were otherwise not entitled to alcohol in the trenches – though some had 'taken the pledge' not to drink:

> The rum also came up with the rations and was issued every morning and evening. I was teetotal at this time, because I didn't believe in rum, and only took it when I was either wet or very cold. I had seen the effect it had on some and I didn't want it to have the same on me – I preferred to have my senses at times like this, and any man who exposes himself to the enemy and offers to fight the whole German army, was far from retaining his senses.
>
> Pte John H. Benn, Loyal North Lancashire Regiment, June 1917

Alcohol and tobacco were also given out to German troops, though the issue of hard alcohol (spirits) was initially seen as medically counterproductive, limiting a soldier's physical abilities. Doctors in the *Heimat* warned that the use of alcohol could lead to 'coarsening and disinhibition'; nevertheless a certain amount of alcohol was issued in the trenches when weather conditions demanded it. This amounted to a maximum per day per head of 0.1 litres of brandy in most cases, an amount that was halved by the end of 1917:

> Each Morning me and the other officers in the hospital meet to throw the dice. We gamble for 'typhus drops'. It is forbidden to buy Schnaps here, but

here in hospital and in the aforementioned guise it can be prescribed in gallons by our trusty Dr Husen.

LTN. PAUL GELLER, FELDARTILLERIE-REGIMENT NR. 37

Beer, on the other hand, was seen as an 'essential semi-luxury' in the German armies, each man receiving an allotment of 6 litres per month early in the war, supplied directly from the major breweries across Germany. By 1916, the procurement of beer for the German army became a serious business, centralised in the new department of beer acquisition, the *Biereinkaufszentrale*, part of the war ministry (British soldiers could only dream of such luxury). However, the amount issued fell steadily through the war. Some regiments were more lucky than others, however; the troopers of the *Königlich Bayerisches 2. Ulanen-Regiment 'König'* rarely had to suffer from lack of beer. Having a number of wealthy Munich brewery owners in its ranks, beer was always available, so much so that the regiment was known in the army as the *Bier-Ulanen* (Beer Uhlans).

The German army also opened breweries in occupied territory; by the end of 1917, fifteen of them operated on the Western Front with a total output of 23,000 hectolitres. Extra food and drink could be bought in the army from *Marketender* (sutlers) stores that were set up everywhere behind the lines. Here soldiers could buy anything from beer and schnapps to sausages and writing paper:

This evening we got issued with tea, marmalade, butter, cigarettes, cigars and tobacco. Now the whole company is enjoying the free time, some men are cleaning their kit, others write letters and postcards. Just in this moment a lovely little donkey cart drives and a bit further to the left the Prussians play a game of football. From the right I can hear the sound of military music. I enjoy a cold beer. There is no lack of that here as there is a German brewery in the city.

HANS, A GERMAN SOLDIER IN FRANCE, 25 SEPTEMBER 1916

Thank you for sending me the money. Yesterday a cart brought beer which we could buy a litre for 52 Pf. There is no canteen proprietor here in the field, that is something you find in the Etappe only. There you can even buy artificial honey, cigarettes, soap and shoepolish. Food is getting rarer, there is mostly marmalade of all kinds, lard and herrings.

MUSK. PETER RAUSCH, INFANTERIE-REGIMENT NR. 28

'Prost dear brother, clink the glasses, drink it up. May come what may, we will stick it out.'
Beer was issued to German troops and was seen as a necessary luxury.

Tobacco

In the British army, cigarettes came up with the rations, and everyone was issued with a fair share – but it didn't stop men requesting more from home. W.D. and H.O. Wills of Bristol was to produce many of the favoured brands – 'Gold Flake' and 'Woodbines' being common. Smoking was a means of killing time, of filling the void between meals and routine. It was also a means of combating both the stench of the war, and of deterring the plagues of flies. During the early stages of the war, pipes were common, but as the war developed the 'fag' would quickly supplant it. With tobacco and cigarettes being in such plentiful supply, chain-smoking was an inevitable consequence:

> Tobacco here is very cheap 3d instead of 7d. Quite surprising to get value like that. When you get any change here you get a funny collection. French and English money all mixed and any amount of variety in notes. You have to go to the back and work it all out.
>
> Rfn William C. Taffs, 1/16th Queen's Westminster Rifles,
> 12 December 1915

In the German army tobacco was equally important. Snuff or pipe tobacco, cigars or cigarettes were issued, but the amounts stayed so low that it was virtually impossible for a smoker to satisfy his daily needs from the issued tobacco alone. From February 1915 a *Tabakportion* became part of the ration consisting of two cigars, two cigarettes, 30g of tobacco or 5g snuff. From May 1916 onwards officers, military officials, and some NCO ranks were excluded from tobacco rationing; they had to buy their tobacco in sutler's stores and canteens. From February 1918 one cigar was replaced with two cigarettes due to a lack of cigars:

> A couple of days ago I received another parcel with good cigars. Smoking them is a pleasure, which is not the case with the ones we usually get and which force you to close both eyes to be able to smoke them.
>
> Gustav Stichert, German soldier, 6 June 1916

A total failure was the invention of the so-called '*Kriegstabakmischung*' (war tobacco blend) that consisted of eighty-five beech leaves and just 15 per cent tobacco and which was issued to the army in March 1918. Due to complaints from the troops and the medical departments it was withdrawn shortly afterwards.

Parcels from Home

Parcels from home were particularly welcomed by the men at the front. The postal service was surprisingly good to and from the trenches, and parcels could be received relatively quickly – and still intact – from home. Typically, this would include cakes and tasty morsels in tins that could be opened to relieve the unrelenting boredom of front-line food, sardines and meat pastes being typical. For the British soldiers, condiments of all kinds were welcome – some of the troops had become used to the rich spices of India that had begun to creep into their food through chutneys and sauces, so items such as Worcestershire Sauce, 'HP' and 'OK' sauces were particularly in demand as they could be mixed with corned beef to make it more palatable. Hearty and warming drinks could be gained from meat extracts such as the liquid Bovril and the solid OXO cubes. Manufacturers of both products were quick to press the message home that the 'man at the front' would prefer to see these meat extracts in their parcels from home:

> I received your parcel today of cream, butter chocolate, tobacco, pipe lighter, cocoa, milk and knife, thanks most awfully darling – you are good to me all of you and I hope that god willing I shall be home to bother you all!!!
>
> 2Lt Arthur R. Stanley-Clarke, 1st Dorsetshire Regiment,
> 17 December 1914

> In one of the parcels could you put enough for 2 breakfast cups of coffee into a little linen bag together with sugar, so I can make some of your coffee for a change. I want them in a porous wrapper so I can make it without being troubled by the grounds.
>
> Rfn William C. Taffs, 1/16th Queen's Westminster Rifles,
> 26 January 1916

> Next time you send any parcel please include a bottle of Liptons Coffee and Chicory Essence. Put on the outside 'Contents eatables'. It always passes and if it doesn't through breakage it only gets taken out but I believe it is allowed. Anyway Postal Corporal tells me that is usual way of stating contents and parcels are never opened unless something radically wrong such as liquid leakage or matches smouldering.
>
> Pte Vivian V. Stevens, Army Service Corps (Motor Transport),
> 14 March 1916

Any tinned things are welcome also candles a thing we are very short of – just a moment's stop as I have a cup full of water and I am going to shave! (first time for four days). I have finished with the most disastrous result – I am clean where I have shaved – almost white – and brown and black round my neck and cheekbones.

> 2Lt Arthur R. Stanley-Clarke, 1st Dorsetshire Regiment,
> 27 November 1914

Cigarettes and tobacco were also popular:

I seem to have been cut off from all in England since I came out here and your letter is so welcome. You ask me do I want anything? Well! Mummy one of the chief things I would like is cigs. It is awfully difficult to get them in these French towns. Also choc or any little bits of stuff like that. You know we live almost entirely on tinned stuff here, tinned butter, fish, meat and above all <u>fruit</u>. We are not allowed even to buy fruit let alone steal it. It does seem utterly absurd as the country is full of fruit and vegetables but never a bit do we see.

> 2Lt Arthur H. Lamb, 1st Lancashire Fusiliers, 20 July 1916

Please send some tobacco, sausage, chocolate, writing paper and postcards, cigarettes, a battery for my torchlight.

> Kriegsfreiwilliger Wilhelm Herwig, Reserve-Infanterie-Regiment
> Nr. 233, 10 October 1914

Supply of these essential goods was helped along by funds like that set up by *Weekly Despatch* newspaper, which organised tobacco 'comforts' for British soldiers, or in gifts from German cities to the troops for Christmas:

I have just received your second supply of tobacco and PC thanks very much for same. I have just received a PC dated 18th Sept from you but not written by you it is very good and made me very happy to know that all at home are proud of us we are doing well and hope to have it soon finished what a tale I will have to tell you when I get back … you will see in the papers since I left we get two ounces of tobacco per week here … you know that wouldn't do for three days so you see the bit you sent me just pulls me through but it is a strug-gle to get a match so if you could manage some matches for me they would be very welcome if I get my allotment remember me all I know I would?

> Pte Jeremiah Daly, 2nd Leinster Regiment, 20 October 1914

On 7 January we received the Christmas presents sent to us by the city of Aachen. They contained a lot of good things which we were very pleased about. An additional allowance of the finest cigarettes and cigars gave us the chance to do a bit of bragging in town later in the evening. Sadly all the *Estaminets* [bars] are closing at 7pm.

Hornist Willi Brülls, Infanterie-Regiment Nr. 178, 7 January 1917

Parcels and other mail was often distributed to soldiers after they had come out of the line, sometimes after experiencing battle first hand. With casualties an inevitability, it was understood that parcels of the fallen would be distributed between those living:

We had a good breakfast, as nearly all had a parcel, and there were also parcels addressed to the lads who were not with us now. We divided into twos and threes and these spare parcels were divided out, without being opened, as evenly as possible, so we took our chance as to what their contents were. Our only job this day, was to make ourselves respectable, which was no easy job, as we were chalk and clay from head to foot.

Pte John H. Benn, Loyal North Lancashire Regiment, June 1917

For German soldiers, the desire to supplement their food resources with supplies from home was equal to that of the British. Food and drink obtained locally could be equally unpalatable, and while the British felt that the locals were in the habit of watering down their beer, the Germans thought it 'disgusting':

There is plenty of beer, but it tastes terrible – a sour and quite disgusting brew. There is also a local Schnapps which tastes a bit like strong wine. This is quite nice and I have already emptied a few bottles of it. There are plenty of fugitives from western Belgium on the roads. Some of them carry all their worldly goods on a small cart, it is a sad sight. The signs on the roads have been painted black to hide the place names from us.

Kriegsfreiwilliger Wilhelm Herwig, Reserve-Infanterie-Regiment Nr. 233, 10 October 1914

Half a pound of flour and some fat would also be nice as we have to cook our food. The field kitchens do not reach us here as the roads have been destroyed by the constant shellfire. Some men receive tins which are sealed by using a rubber band and a spring. In it there is roast meat, goulasch, sausage and vegetables; briefly speaking everything that's on the menu at home. These tins just have to be put into boiling water for ten minutes. Much cheaper than the meat tins you have to buy and it is even possible to send the tins back home to use them again.

Karl Lindner, Königlich Bayerisches 12. Infanterie-Regiment,
12 May 1916

Early so-called *Liebesgabenpakete* (Gift of love parcels) were sent to the front in huge numbers, filled with tobacco, food and warm clothing, putting a massive strain on the postal system. Newspapers in Germany appealed to the population to send more and more gifts to the front:

> Please stop sending me butter! Firstly you need it much more than I do and secondly I only get 3/4 pounds of bread each day anyway, I cannot eat the butter without bread! Send lard or chocolate. The lard has many uses and chocolate I can eat on its own. You can also send cigarettes, Kaiser and Salem Aleikum are good. Do not send cigars!
>
> Musk. Kurt Meyer, Infanterie-Regiment Nr. 56

Even though they proved to be invaluable in the winter of 1914, the continuous flow of parcels and goods to the front soon became a burden to the units receiving them:

> This is the final request to all enlisted men to pack up all unnecessary stuff and everything that would be a hindrance on the march and to send it back home immediately! There will be one more cart going to Aachen soon, so all parcels have to be handed by Tuesday evening before 6pm. All parcels arriving later and all parcels arriving from the *Heimat* thereafter will be thrown into the Meuse!
>
> Daily orders, 4. Kompanie, 9. Landsturmbataillon (Ansbach),
18 January 1915

Newspapers were also sent to the front; for some soldiers, this was a chance to get to grips with the wider news; for others, it was simply a hindrance:

> Many thanks for your lovely letters, the newspapers and the parcels. Everything arrived. You do not need to send me newspapers. We are not cut off from all kinds of culture here, only this morning we got the morning edition of the *Frankfurter Zeitung* from July 26.
>
> Ltn. G. Dintelmann, Feld-Art. Rekruten-Depot Nr. 27, 26 July 1917

16 April 1915. Why do you never send me any newspapers. Most comrades get some, but you never send me any. It is not difficult and they do not weigh much.

23 April 1915. I really do not know what you are thinking. Aunt Paula sent me a number of editions of 'The Christian Family'! What are you thinking? Do you miss the gravity of my situation completely? Send me some useful newspapers, we do not get to hear a lot of news here.

MUSK. KURT MEYER, INFANTERIE-REGIMENT NR. 56

The flow of parcels was not only one way, however; during the Spring Offensive of 1918, German forces captured huge stocks of food. After having satisfied their own needs, the soldiers took the opportunity to supply their starving families at home with food like butter and sausages, items that most Germans had not seen for years. Due to this, the number of parcels sent to the Fatherland reached numbers that could not be handled by the *Feldpost* offices anymore, resulting in a ten-day mail ban that was imposed on 10 June 1918:

> In the parcel you will find a few tins of meat and some cigarettes which we have taken from the English during the latest offensive. The meat is very nice, I will send more as soon as I can.
>
> UNIDENTIFIED GERMAN SOLDIER, FRANCE, 12 APRIL 1918

> I'd very much like to participate in another small offensive. There's plenty of stuff to inherit. I have captured a nice piece of 'Sunlight' soap, shoes and leather.
>
> GEFR. J. GÖRTEMAKER, FELDARTILLERIE-REGIMENT NR. 503, 13 APRIL 1918

Souvenirs

Many soldiers were inveterate souvenir hunters, and many battle souvenirs would be parcelled off home or carried back when on leave. In many cases these items could be sold to the 'base-wallahs' and non-front-line troops – enough to fund the desire for extra cigarettes, cheap 'vin rouge' and thin beer when out on rest. The 'flotsam of battle' was collected – shell nose-caps, grenades, German *Pickelhauben*, belt plates, cap cockades and British cap badges, weapons, gloves and boots:

I am sending with this the Christmas card I received from HM the King and HM the Queen, they sent one to every Officer and man in the Army and I shall be given HRH Princess Mary's present shortly.

2Lt Arthur R. Stanley-Clarke, 1st Dorsetshire Regiment,
25 December 1914

There must have been some heavy fighting here judging by the German guns, waggons and dead horses there all about the fields including a Maxim with millions of rounds of ammunition. Most of our chaps have been out souvenir hunting and got some very good finds. I myself getting a German equipment, including haversack with drinking cup and some spoons and fork & a water bottle 2 pouches full of cartridges (which I have had to dump) belt and a proper murderous Bayonet, which I had got permission before I could keep it.

Pte Henry W. Talbot, Army Service Corps (Motor Transport),
September 1914

I could bring back any number of souvenirs, but as we are not allowed to send any home by post and we have to carry them about with us until we return home I have not collected anything at all, except two small pieces of shrapnel with a small history to each of them. I suppose I shall end up losing them, at the last minute.

Rfn William C. Taffs, 1/16th Queen's Westminster Rifles,
February 1916

Germans, too, were not averse to 'souveniring':

Soon Leutnant Strelow will go on leave, so I will tell him to take a parcel for you with him. It contains:
1. A collection of field newspapers
2. An English revolver
3. An aerial dart
4. A Gurkha's knife
5. An English steel helmet
6. A selection of English regimental cockades and buttons
Please take good care of it all. I love and kiss you,

Ltn. Karl Assmann, Reserve-Infanterie-Regiment Nr. 234

Other souvenirs were made by the locals. Amongst British troops, silk post-cards were popular, made by local artisans. Each card was produced as part of a cottage industry which saw mostly women engaged in intricate designs being hand embroidered onto strips of silk mesh, before being sent to a factory for cutting and mounting as postcards and greetings cards:

> Nan I am not in a place now where I can get any more cards or else I would try and get 2 for the boys but they are dear don't you think there are some that costs a Frank that is 10d we have only had 4 pays since we have been out here yet but what there is to come it will come all in a lump we have to have so much money before we can come on pass.
>
> PTE ROBERT W. PRICE, 10TH WELSH REGIMENT, 28 JANUARY 1916

Photography

The phenomenon of the *Schützengraben-Fotograf*, the amateur trench pho-tographer, was widespread in the German army – in sharp contrast to the British. Cameras had been banned from the front line in 1915, in the fear that such photographs could fall into enemy hands, supplying evidence of trench conditions that they would not be able to see through aerial photographs and trench raids. Such fears were less widely held by the Germans, and up to the end of the war there were few restrictions relating to photography and the use of cameras at the front line in the German army:

> I hastily attached the Kodak to my belt, still holding a huge piece of Christmas cake … grabbed my rifle, shouldered my backpack and off I went.
>
> MARTIN MÜLLER, GERMAN SOLDIER, 1 DECEMBER 1914

> Just to let you know, the film has arrived. A few of my plates are still missing it seems, which is a shame because I am on at least two of them. We occupy a position in a forest of which I will send you some photos soon. The cloud of smoke you see on one of the last photos I sent was taken during a flame attack. Please have five copies of that made and send them to me.
>
> KARL LINDNER, KÖNIGLICH BAYERISCHES 12. INFANTERIE-REGIMENT,
>
> 12 MAY 1916

The German High Command even *actively* encouraged the use of cameras, believing their use preserved the will of the soldiers to remain there, and

The trench photographer. In the German army taking photographs was encouraged as it was thought to preserve the will and the morale of the soldiers at the front.

actively enhanced the morale of the soldiers at the front. Sensible precautions were taken, however, and special permission to use cameras had to be sought from commanding officers or regimental staff – but it was usually granted. This permission came with the proviso that the soldier make sure that his photographs did not include anything that might be used by the enemy in case of capture:

Only rarely did I see a professional photographer taking pictures for German newspapers and magazines. Much more common were comrades armed with cameras. The 'trench-photographer', as we called him, was an amateur who knew exactly what kind of photograph his comrades wanted. When I look into my own album from the Champagne, I see images just like you can find them in albums all over Germany taken and in trenches all over the front.

Doing the laundry, at the barbers, sunbathing in a shell hole, playing cards in a dug-out, my foxhole, eating, being on guard, our trench 15 metres away from the enemy, digging trenches, sitting on the latrine. The trench-photographer's field of activity seems to be endless, but there is two kinds of photograph that always are of even greater interest: images showing funny situations and those that can tell the people at home about the dangers and horrors we are facing. A simple dug out acts as the perfect dark room for the field-grey photographer even if he has to cover his acid bowls with a light and waterproof tent-square. True, supplying a usable form of lighting for the dark-room always causes trouble as he has only limited room in his kit and there are changes of position, but soldiers are an inventive lot and every trench-photographer has his own solution to this problem.

Any kind of photography in the field is subjected to a wise censorship, so the photographer needs a permission of his superior authority and rightly so! You are sitting somewhere behind the lines and celebrate to be reunited with old comrades, the perfect occasion for a photographic memento. There is nothing to it, isn't it? But only days afterwards one of those involved is unlucky and is taken prisoner by the enemy who immediately finds the photograph. Lucky for the enemy they spot an inconspicuous street name on a house in the background. By enlarging it, it is soon found out that the regimental headquarters is situated there ... a valuable target for an aerial attack or an artillery strike.

HANS WALDE, PRESS OFFICE OF THE SAXON MINISTRY OF WAR

Soon after the start of the war the first snapshots taken by the soldiers themselves found their way into magazines and newspapers, and it did not take long before the German photographic industry recognised the opportunity, starting major marketing campaigns advertising the value of robust and light-weight '*Feldkameras*' or '*Waffenrock Kameras*' (field or uniform jacket cameras). Specialist magazines published detailed articles that advised the soldier how to achieve the perfect war photograph, and even went so far as to advise on the camera of choice:

Today the *Feldkamera* or *Waffenrock-Kamera* has become an important tool in this war which has been forced upon us.

DAS ARBEITEN MIT KLEINEN KAMERAS, *PHOTOGRAPHISCHE RUNDSCHAU*,
BERLIN, 1915

Photos from the front were immensely popular, and were often sent home as postcards. Millions of them ended up in households all over Germany, and played a big part in easing the fears and worries of the families the soldiers had left behind. Good photographs were also copied, traded, and swapped. So great was the demand for photographic depictions of life at the front, that an ingenious soldier-photographer could also turn a good profit from his occupation:

> My neighbour (in the military hospital) is an amateur photographer. For two completely blurred photographs he receives two pounds of butter, a large cheese and enough compressed leather for 12 pairs of soles; and only for supplying the gentlemen of the rear echelons with some photos from the frontline.
> ANONYMOUS GERMAN SOLDIER, 21 NOVEMBER 1917

With British soldiers banned from taking front-line photographs in 1915, they had to make do with studio images. As a consequence, photographers in the rear areas did a roaring trade in providing soldiers with photographic images of themselves as a souvenir of their service. Often these were posed in studios – but the ruins of Belgium, France and other places were also popular. Sad to say, many of these photographs were never collected – their owners having been claimed as casualties of war.

Entertainment

In order to keep the average soldier's mind off gambling, drinking and other vices, and to maintain morale in general, it was understood at a very early stage that suitable entertainments would be a benefit. There is no doubt that for men starved of entertainment, and particularly entertainment that might involve women, this form of release would be valuable. As early as 1914, British concert parties were being created from those servicemen who had a theatrical bent, and almost every major unit of the British army was to have its own brand of concert party. Often, female roles would be convincingly played by young, slim, men:

> On 6th April, we marched to Carnarvon Camp, Reninghelst, and were billeted in huts. There were many camps in and about this village, and it had a Theatre, Supper Room and Canteen. One Divisional Concert Party called 'The Trumps' had the Theatre taken, and they were very good.
> PTE JOHN H. BENN, LOYAL NORTH LANCASHIRE REGIMENT, APRIL 1917

Royal Artillery concert party. Many such 'pierrot troupes' were organised by the British army, and by groups such as the YMCA, in the rear areas.

Some officers relished the opportunity:

I am having absolutely the time of my life, I am fit and radiantly happy and singing the live-long day. I have been frantically busy and have not had a minute to write. I am with my battalion again and have been doing Assistant Town Major and OC recreations for the battalion and I seem to have just fallen on my feet. It is practically YMCA work and I enjoy it immensely. You have heard me speak of Dr Francis. I asked our CO if he would like to have for a lecture as he was near. He came and we had absolutely the finest lecture I have ever heard. So our CO said and everyone was bucked to the skys with it. Then Cameron is always near at hand and I have great times with him. Then I arranged a great concert which was a great success. I say

and told stories and recited ruthless rhymes to everyone in the Bn from the
CO downwards (I'm coming on) I'll give you some examples

Oh! Graham he's our Dr fine

He doles out beaucoup No 9

Whether you're well or whether you're ill

You'll always get that same damn'd pill.

(NB: No 9 pill is a standing joke in the Army it is composed mostly of
calomel!)

Again a parody on 'Gilbert the Filbert'

I'm Collyer the Sergeant, the Hermaville knut,

The pride of Rue de Tilloy, bully of the lot,

Oh! Hades, the mamselles that leave estaminets,

Collyer of B Coy, best of the lot.

Today we marched to another village further away from guns and danger
and we are in for a bon time. We are settling down in a French farm home
and I have been 'parlering' here and making friends and they are going to
give us French coffee and coal and generally anything we want. Oh it's a
great life! I have had ripping letters from so many people. I never knew
I had so many friends, and of course regular and most touching letters from
M.A. who is now quite fit again and walking 10 miles per day and working
hard with the lambs on the farm.

2LT KENNETH D. KEAY, 9TH SCOTTISH RIFLES (CAMERONIANS),

2 MARCH 1917

Cinemas were also popular on both sides of the line, and men could escape
with the latest comedies from Hollywood – or locally produced. Such places of
entertainment were run by the army directly, particularly in the German army:

The division now operates a cinema. When it opened it was completely
full, even the General of Division attended. I was in it yesterday as it is quite
nice. It is funny when images of the war in the foremost lines are shown.
More amusing than the best of comedies.

ADOLF TREHBE, KÖNIGLICH BAYERISCHES 23. INFANTERIE-REGIMENT,

13 DECEMBER 1915

The cinema is the best place to kill time. There always is plenty of
Landsturm comrades there and it is a cheap amusement for only 10 Pfennig.

FRITZ NETT, WÜRTTEMBERGISCHES LANDSTURM-INFANTERIE-REGIMENT

NR. 13, 13 JUNE 1916

German soldiers at rest with a gramophone in a *Soldatenheim*.

I have become an avid cinema enthusiast. I go there 2 or 3 times a week. There is not much else for evening entertainment.

SOLD. WERNER FRIEDE, INFANTERIE-REGIMENT NR. 71, 17 SEPTEMBER 1917

Awards

Medals, orders and decorations played an important role in the life of the German soldier. The endeavour to get an award, particularly the coveted *Eisernes Kreuz* or Iron Cross, features prominently in letters and diaries. The Iron Cross was instituted originally in 1813, during the wars against Napoleon, and was reinstituted only in times when there was a 'declared danger for the Fatherland', as in August 1914:

We, Wilhelm, by the grace of God, King of Prussia, etc … in view of the serious position in which our beloved fatherland has been put, by being forced into a war, and in thankful remembrance of our forefathers' heroic

172

achievements during the exciting years of the liberation wars and the struggle for Germany's union, we wish to renew again the Iron Cross donated by my Great Grandfather who is resting with God.

The Iron Cross is to be awarded without exception to all persons of the Army, Navy and the Home Guard, the members of the volunteer nursing units and to all other persons who offered their service to the Army or Navy or are designated as Army or Navy officers. The award will be made for every sacrifice made in the war. Further, all persons who earn it, by serving the needs of the German Empire and their allies at home, may receive the cross.

WILHELM, BERLIN, 5 AUGUST 1914

Even though there were higher awards for bravery and military merit, the Iron Cross had a much deeper meaning. It symbolised the cause: the protection of the Fatherland and the will to shed the last drop of blood for it. Due to this and because of the fact that both classes of the Iron Cross were awarded regardless of rank, it was a coveted and much respected medal:

My Iron Cross
For fearless deeds my Kaiser gave
Me my Cross of Iron.
The greatest thing that I did crave
Of gongs it is the high'un.
This Cross is my most precious thing
And makes me feel so good!
P'raps another day will bring
one hewn from Argonnes wood.
Whatever! We don't all return
Our house and hearth to see.
Yet from every proud lip we learn
Our fathers' heirs are we.

MAX B. VANSELOW, INFANTERIE-REGIMENT NR. 67

The Iron Cross was awarded without regard to rank: unusual in most German states. The First Class, however, was far more likely to be awarded to officers and NCOs than to junior enlisted men. The Grand Cross and the Star of the Grand Cross were reserved for senior general officers. The first NCO to receive an Iron Cross First Class in the war was *Unteroffizier* Oskar Brieger:

Oskar Brieger, a German Jew and the first NCO to be awarded the coveted Iron Cross 1st Class (September 1914).

This is how I earned my Iron Cross Second Class: On August 25, after an exhausting march, we arrived at Hofstade where we were greeted with a withering defensive fire. Even the civilian population, incl. the women, had opened fire on us. Many of my comrades were killed. One of the *Franctireurs* shot the rifle out of my hands and had to seek cover in a barn. From there I could observe a Belgian soldier who was shooting at some wounded comrades lying on a field. I ran up to him and rammed my bayonet into his heart. After having done so I dressed the wounds of my comrades and carried them back to safety.

The Iron Cross First Class I earned thus: From 9 to 13 September 1914 we were in constant action. As we were being targeted by heavy artillery we set up a dressing station in the cellars of a two-storeyed building on the other side of the road, next to the trenches. Even though the building had been clearly marked with a red cross it was targeted by enemy artillery. I carried six wounded comrades there and Dr Leiferstein from Berlin at once treated their wounds. When a shell exploded near the house it collapsed and caught fire burying 32 people alive, including the six I had carried in. I managed to dig myself out of the debris and found a door which I had not noticed before. Using a heavy stone I smashed it in and so made my way into a neighbouring cellar in which I found a cross-barred window facing the road outside. I failed to rip out the metal bars but managed to bend most of them sufficiently to squeeze myself through and to get help from the trench on the opposite side of the road. In that instance a shell exploded nearby, throwing me into our trench and knocking me out. When I regained consciousness, I asked the comrades nearby for help, but the heavy artillery fire made it far too dangerous to get out of the trench. I grabbed a pioneer's axe, jumped out of the trench and ran back to the house. On the way another shell exploded without doing me any harm. Back in the cellars and using the axe I managed to knock a hole into a wall through which I rescued all the comrades trapped inside the cellar, incl. the severely wounded doctor.

UFFZ. OSKAR BRIEGER, INFANTERIE-REGIMENT NR. 48

In the early years of the war, to gain an Iron Cross was the ultimate goal of many German soldiers:

With this letter I send you the wonderful news that I have been made a Knight of the Iron Cross. Since the start of the war this has been my ultimate goal; the only thing I aspired to achieve. When I die now, I go a happier man, for I know the reason why. Enclosed you will find the medal ribbon and the paper wrapper. Please be so kind and keep them for me. Farewell now my beloved ones! There is still a lot of hard work to do for the Fatherland.

UFFZ. OTTO LEIPNER, INFANTERIE REGIMENT NR. 132,
2 OCTOBER 1914

God rewards the brave! Hurrah it has been done! I was put in for the Iron Cross and it won't be long until I will be able to wear this badge of honour with pride! For this symbol and for our fatherland I will continue to venture my life.

GEFR. PETER JAHN, INFANTERIE-REGIMENT NR. 56, 1 NOVEMBER 1914

Today I was awarded with the Iron Cross 2nd Class. It is the happiest moment of my life. May God help me to survive long enough, so that I will be able to show it to you.

HUSAR PETER NÄTER, HUSAREN-REGIMENT NR. 3, 12 SEPTEMBER 1914

A major problem was faced when re-instituting the Iron Cross in 1914. Wilhelm II had placed the rights to bestow them into the hands of his army commanders. During the wars of 1813–15 and 1870–71 this power had rested solely in the hands of the king and awards had been made very sparsely, underlining the importance and value of the award. The decision to change this soon resulted in an excessive number of awards and commendations and soon soldiers who had never seen the front line could be seen parading around with the precious cross on their chest – much to the dismay of the soldier of the line:

> I have read that since the war has started, 38,000 Iron Crosses have been awarded … today the Iron Cross is not a special honour anymore.
> STABSARZT EGON KRONENBERG, 27 SEPTEMBER 1914

> You have no idea how incredibly happy and proud I am. Half of the men and virtually every officer, even quartermasters, army officials and chaplains have by now been decorated with the Iron Cross 2nd Class. The 1st Class though is earned in combat only and by great personal merit. My parents will surely share my joy. Oh how proud will the old man be. My cross is the simple issue version. Its back is flat and made from pure silver, the front is made of black iron. Please do not buy a fancy piece from a jeweller! First they are far too expensive and secondly I do not want to be mistaken for the type of soldier that is commonly seen with that type of Casino-Cross.
> LTN. RICHARD SCHOMBARDT, INFANTERIE-REGIMENT NR. 57

Nevertheless, the Iron Cross was so revered that its depiction in public life was sometimes frowned upon – it was no wonder that the British themselves issued propaganda versions that mocked the German ones. Children wearing simple badges were also criticised on the home front:

> In recent times it has been noticed that children are wearing small Iron Crosses made from tin, which proves that some people have no palate for the gravity of our time. Generations held the Iron Cross in high esteem; it must never be misused as a child's toy. Those men who proudly wear this badge of honour on their breast, those men who are icons of German strength and German bravery have every right to demand that the Iron Cross is not downgraded to a toy for children.
> *RHEINISCHES VOLKSBLATT*, 6 NOVEMBER 1914

By 31 May 1924 (retroactively) 5.2 million Iron Crosses Second Class and approximately 218,000 of the First Class had been awarded. In many cases the award of an Iron Cross automatically resulted in the award of a similar ranking decoration of another German state. That meant that a Bavarian soldier who received an Iron Cross Second class could expect to be awarded the Bavarian Military Merit Cross Third Class, while a soldier from Württemberg had a good chance to get the Military Merit Medal. Late in the war, soldiers would also be awarded wound badges, recognising the sacrifices German soldiers made for the Fatherland:

> Recognising those who were wounded in service of the Fatherland I want to bestow them with an award. The award shall be given to those who shed blood for the Fatherland or who lost their health due to enemy action and have become unfit for duty.
>
> KAISER WILHELM II, 3 MARCH 1918

The badge was awarded in three grades: *schwarz* (black); *silber* or *mattweiß* (silver or tarnished white); and gold or *mattgelb* (gold or tarnished yellow). The colour of the badge indicated the degree of wounding: black for one to two wounds, silver for three to four wounds and gold for five wounds or more. All were worn with pride:

> Please send me a wound badge in black. It costs 1.80 Marks and an Iron Cross 1st class. The Cross should be curved as it's more comfortable to wear. A good quality one will cost 18–25 Marks. Please buy one with a pin, similar to a brooch, not a screwback one. I will send the one I have here home as soon as you send me the new one ....
>
> KARL LINDER, KÖNIGLICH BAYERISCHES 12. INFANTERIE REGIMENT,
> 18 AUGUST 1918

For the British soldier, medals perhaps played a lesser part in their motivation to fight than that of his German counterpart:

> I do assure you I am doing nothing rash. Now I ask you, could you imagine my doing anything rash. I am too keen on seeing you again I assure you. You say 'I don't care a hang for stripes'. I say 'Hang VC's or DCM's. I want to go home.'
>
> RFN WILLIAM C. TAFFS, 1/16TH QUEEN'S WESTMINSTER RIFLES,
> 16 FEBRUARY 1916

Nevertheless, the war saw the award of an unprecedented number of medals for gallantry – a fact that was not without some controversial aspects at the time, with awards of medals for distinguished service in the rear areas. The Victoria Cross, the highest award for gallantry, was open to any men who were deemed suitable, but gaining it was subject to the strictest scrutiny. There were other awards – the Distinguished Service Order (for majors and above) and Distinguished Conduct Medal – but again these were felt to be too specific. What was needed was the chance for the reward of gallant conduct in the field. Initiated by the king on 31 December 1914, the Military Cross (MC) rewarded junior officers, whilst the Military Medal (MM), instigated later in March 1916, was awarded to all other ranks. The Military Cross was awarded 'in recognition of distinguished and meritorious services in time of war', and could therefore be awarded to those not in the thick of action; over 37,000 awards were made, with 3,155 bars (additional awards of the same medal) also granted:

> Just another wee bit of news, mummy dear! I have been awarded the Military Cross for what I did on the 28th Feb in the attack! All I have to say is! I owe everything to my heavenly father and it is entirely owing to His love and mercy I have gained this small decoration! Oh! Mummy darling, no words can express how badly, how terribly badly I want Him to bring me back home to you!
>
> 2Lt Arthur H. Lamb MC, 1st Lancashire Fusiliers, 15 March 1917

The British soldier too would be recognised for his wounds, with a distinctive 'wounding stripe', an award first suggested by influential British writer Sir Arthur Conan Doyle. This strip of braid (or brass equivalent) was worn on the lower left sleeve for each incident of wounding – though not necessarily for each wound. Like the German wound badge, the wounded stripe was the distinction of the front-line soldier, worn with pride.

4

Battle/*Die Schlacht*

To-morrow! At some unearthly hour we go to the trenches and I believe and am very nearly certain we have to attack old Fritz and try to drive him out of his bally trenches! I know that I am one of the two officers to go over and God only knows whether I shall be spared to come back to you! I have prayed I will and do pray every night most fervently that He in His mercy will spare me to come back to you at home!

2Lt Arthur H. Lamb, 1st Lancashire Fusiliers, 19 February 1917

Things are still hot up here. The bastards will not calm down. Quite possibly we will be relieved soon and it is about time. I am still fine, but my nerves are on edge. Received the parcel with almonds, raisins and cigarettes.

Kan. Hanns Schäfer, Reserve-Feldartillerie-Regiment Nr. 26, Somme, 6 July 1916

For Germany, the war had a promising beginning in August 1914. Mobilisation had proceeded smoothly, almost like clockwork – even though more than 20,000 railway transports were necessary to move the troops to the Western Front alone, with most large railway stations seeing trains leaving at ten-minute intervals. But this impetus soon slowed as the Schlieffen Plan was enacted. Advancing through Belgium, there was stiff resistance, and the massive fortresses of the Belgian frontier had to be reduced one by one. Belgian refugees clogged the roads and the supply lines became over-extended. The Belgian city of Antwerp became a pivotal point, holding out until October.

Elsewhere, the British Expeditionary Force had been propelled into their allotted position in the line; soon, though, they were in retreat, as the main French forces retired in the face of the German assault, the German forces in all-out attack along the whole line of the French frontier, with severe battles exacting equally severe casualties. By early September, the first elements of three German armies had reached the Marne, and it was here that the

Schlieffen Plan began to show its deficiencies. Whereas Schlieffen himself had envisaged a strong right wing enveloping Paris from the west, the younger Moltke had reduced the number of Army Corps on that very wing to reinforce the front in the border regions of Alsace-Lorraine. In addition he had moved further troops to East Prussia, to secure the region against an expected Russian offensive. This change of plan not only overstretched the already overextended supply lines, it also massively reduced the fighting power of the German forces concentrated on the Western Front.

These deficiencies weakened the German hammer blows, and along the line of the Marne in front of Paris, French and British troops would enact what became known as 'the Miracle of the Marne'. Faulty operational planning by von Kluck and von Bülow diverted energies from pushing on to Paris; instead, an allegedly beaten enemy was pursued, creating a gap in the line that was exploited by the French commander, Gallieni, who placed the 150,000 Allied troops there. Mobilising all available forces, the German advance was stopped. Standing only 40km in front of Paris the German armies were forced to turn and to retreat towards the Ardennes.

The failure of the German attack at the Marne was a decisive turning point of the war. Von Moltke suffered a nervous breakdown and was replaced by Falkenhayn. A 'race to the sea' followed, as each side attempted to turn the flank of the other. But this war of movement inching towards the Channel coast came to an end during the middle of November 1914; the opponents dug in and created a labyrinth of trenches reaching from the North Sea coast to the borders of Switzerland. With the minute Belgian army grimly holding on to the coastal section along the Yser, the British Expeditionary Force was now anchored to the ancient cloth-trading city of Ypres, extending southwards into French Flanders. Here, in the low lying Flandrian terrain, the winter would be harsh. Facing them were Germans, who for the most part were able to dictate the line of the trenches, and who would occupy the major part of Belgium and the north-east portion of France. Germany was now committed to its worst nightmare: fighting a war on two fronts.

First contact between the British and German troops occurred on 22 August 1914, in and around Mons, Belgium. Regular British cavalryman Sergeant Thomas was one of the first to encounter his enemy and carry out his job:

I could see a German cavalry officer some four hundred yards away standing mounted in full view of me, gesticulating to the left and to the right as he disposed of his dismounted men and ordered them to take up their firing positions to engage us. Immediately I saw him I took aim, pulled

Soldiers of the British Expeditionary Force pass through Flanders in 1914.

the trigger and automatically, almost as it seemed instantaneously, he fell to
the ground, obviously wounded, but whether or not he was killed or not
is a matter that I do not think was ever cleared up or ever became capable
of proof.

    SGT E. THOMAS, 4TH ROYAL IRISH DRAGOON GUARDS, 22 AUGUST 1914

Arriving at Mons on 23 August, the British ran up against their new enemy.
As the Schlieffen Plan was enacted, so the German armies advanced in their
great arc – and at Mons, along the Conde Canal, the British soldiers prepared
as well as they could to meet the onslaught, massed troops in full flow:

August 23rd. We had been marching since 2.30 am and about 11.15 am
an order was passed down for 'A' Company (my company) to deploy to

the right and dig in on the south bank of a railway cutting … We saw the
Germans attack on our left in great masses, but they were beaten back by
the Coldstream Guards.

LCPL BERTRAND J. DERNORE, 1ST ROYAL BERKSHIRE REGIMENT,

23 AUGUST 1914

In good positions, the British did what they were trained to do, and quickly.
Their marksmanship – of fifteen aimed rounds a minute fired into the
advancing ranks – became mythologised and lionised in regimental histories.
Stories of 'plucky soldiers' developed, in which they were firing so rapidly
that the advancing Germans 'thought they were facing machine guns'. The
origin of these stories is difficult to track down, but regimental histories were
notably keen to use them:

About 9 a.m. hostile infantry attacks, supported by heavy artillery fire, began,
enemy movement developing from a north-easterly to a south-westerly
direction. Gradually all around the salient the enemy's troops could be seen
pressing forward to the attack; and, to the utter astonishment of the British
'Tommy,' the Germans advanced in close formation, shoulder to shoulder.
Little they knew that they were advancing against troops whose marksmanship was second to none; for soon there was a roar of 'rapid' rifle fire, and
the machine guns of the Middlesex and Royal Fusiliers began to tear gaps in
the ranks of the intrepid enemy. They were brave fellows, those Germans ….

REGIMENTAL HISTORY, 4TH BATTALION, MIDDLESEX REGIMENT,

23 AUGUST 1914

Various descriptions of the battle of Mons speak of the Germans advancing
like grey clouds covering the earth, of 'massed formation' moving across
the open to within close range of our trenches, to be decimated by 'murderous fire.' On every extended battle line incidents will occur affording
opportunities for picturesque writing, but in the attack and defence of an
open position in the days of pre-trench war, excepting always the noise of
bursting shells, the hum of bullets and the absence of umpires, the whole
affair is a passable imitation of a field-day in peace time.

LT MALCOM V. HAY, 1ST GORDON HIGHLANDERS, 1914

The German view of his enemy was informed by his experience of the
advance through France and Belgium. Having brushed aside the Belgians,
the British were another matter. The battle that followed was challenging:

Finally after many days full of marching and skirmishing we are now able to enjoy some rest. We have received some reinforcements so that the Jäger Batallions finally get some respite. Since last Sunday we have marched an average daily distance of 30 kilometres, the last two days and nights without having a rest at all. Then we had severe battle with the English. We are now in the French province 'Nord', a few kilometres south of the fortress town of Lille. Maybe you would like to look it up on a map.

Today the battle against the English will most probably continue. Yesterday there have been terrible casualties on both sides, there were dead and wounded everywhere. You can thank God that I survived the terrible rain of bullets unscathed. There is only a few of us left. Up until deep in the night the battle raged. You have to know that the English are not as easily beaten as the cowardly Belgians who took to their heels as soon as we arrived on the scene. The English have very brave soldiers!

Yes, war is a wicked thing. Wherever you go you see deserted villages, destroyed houses, dead horses on the roads and dead soldiers on the battle-fields. We are encamped behind a railway embankment. There is an endless stream of wounded soldiers, some get carried here some crawl here on their own. One had lost half an arm, the other half his face, some had holes in their legs. Blood, blood and blood everywhere. At night the sky, illuminated from the fires roaring in the burning villages, is red as if of blood. It is a horrible spectacle to behold. We have to thank god that there is no war in Germany. How lucky are those who do not have to witness these scenes. Otherwise, I am quite well. Only sometimes there are days we suffer from hunger as it is not easy to supply such a fast moving army. We badly needed the rest we are enjoying today. Everybody is worn out and exhausted. It is so bad that that everyone lies down on the ground as soon as there is a halt during the march, even if only for a few minutes and not minding if it's on a cobbled road or in horse dung.

JÄGER GUSTAV WILLY GEHNER, JÄGER BTL. 7, 28 AUGUST 1914

We ran to our firing positions in a pasture which had a width of about 100 metres, at its other end the English had dug long trenches. We had just managed to lay down when there was an uproar, no commands could be given or heard. The enemy artillery rained fire down on us. Shrapnel burst, but our losses were minimal, some men fell when they jumped up to run forward, but this did not stop us, because everyone instinctively looked forward. We got closer and closer up to about 150 metres. Nonetheless, the English could stand it no longer and began to fall back, while we kept up a steady fire, first lying, then kneeling. The English who opposed us suffered heavy casualties. In one trench I counted 40 dead and 25 wounded and even more might have been there earlier.

Uffz. Alwin Gottschlich, Infanterie-Regiment Nr. 76,
23 August 1914

Following the Battle of the Marne in September 1914, the war reversed into stalemate. As the war took to the trenches, the enemy was observed as a target, as an object to shoot at – a move away from the massed ranks encountered earlier in the war. There is a sense that the targets now became men rather that a militaristic army. Lieutenant Gillespie of the King's Own Scottish Borderers, killed two days later at La Bassée, noted this strange phenomenon on 16 October 1914:

We were at the edge of a village and the Germans were entrenched about 200 yards on. One could see heads in the trench sometimes, and sniped at them. There was a large barn door behind one man, a look out, I think. I and a corporal had several shots at him, and later in the day I noticed through my glasses a white cross scratched on the door. It is a grim thought, but you have to think of individual Germans as a type of German militarism even if they are not.

Lt Thomas C. Gillespie, 2nd King's Own Scottish Borderers,
16 October 1914

The enemy, having discovered that we could be dangerous even at 900 yards, then successfully crossed the stubble field in two short rushes without losing a man, and reinforced their men who were advancing through the beetroot fields on our right. They were advancing in short rushes across pasture-land which provided no cover whatever, and they offered a clearly visible target even when lying down. Although our men were nearly all first-class shots, they did not often hit the target. This was owing to the unpleasant fact that the German gunners kept up a steady stream of shrapnel, which burst just in front of our trenches and broke over the top like a wave.

Lt Malcom V. Hay, 1st Gordon Highlanders, 1914

In 1914, the British first became fully aware of the nature of their enemy. With the war stalled, it soon became a siege war, a war of waiting and stealth. Learning the importance of trench warfare meant understanding the routine:

As father said in his last letter the Germans are very brave and magnificent soldiers, of course they are fighting a war for existence, and they thoroughly realise it, in fact they treat the whole affair rather like a picnic though they would be the first to contradict this, but they go on sacrificing their lives for food and fire and one has to tell them time on time again in the trenches that one can range on smoke, to prevent them making terrific fires. This has been the cause of a lot of our losses largely, the other day they put a fire bucket on the top of the trench with the result that we were shelled and six men were killed and four wounded, yet when we go back to the trenches I shall have to speak about it again.

2Lt Arthur R. Stanley-Clarke, 1st Dorsetshire Regiment,
6 December 1914

On 3 August the first glimpse of an English hat could be spotted on the other side. The French had made way for the English! The men were delighted to get rid of the deceitful and devious French who were always up to some mischief. The English were far more honourable, noble and quiet. Their motto was similar to ours: 'Live and let live'.

Hauptmann Freiherr Georg Vom Holtz, Reserve-Infanterie-Regiment Nr. 121

In the west, the German army had enlarged and developed its defensive positions which usually consisted of three lines of defence. Trench warfare changed the face of war and the daily routine of the soldiers in a radical way. In contrast to their German opponents, the British and French could not afford to spend the war waiting in well-secured positions. Public and political opinion demanded that the invaders be driven from French and Belgian soil – and that any threat to the Channel ports, and therefore to Britain, be removed.

The diversity of the British army units and their colonial troops were fascinating to the German soldier:

The English are not imposing at all. They are now employing black eyed Gurkhas and Belutschis with yellow turbans mounted on thoroughbred stallions. Indians, Turkomans, Spasis, Japs we will take care of them.

Leutnant Bernhard Kortzfleisch, 4. Garde-Feldartillerie-Regiment,
1914

My dear parents, it has been a while since I last wrote to you and I am sorry for that. I hardly have the time to settle down to write even a few lines and if I have I am so tired that I can hardly move an arm. The reason for that is the speed of our advance. This is the third week in enemy territory. We have beaten the Belgians and entered Leuven and Brussels before crossing the border into France. In three battles, in which a lot of us fell, we have chased away the English and their Indian allies. On some days we have marched for 16 hours with hardly a rest and without supplies. At Le Cateau we won a great victory but many comrades are now resting under the grass. There is so much to say I can't write it all down.

One night we slept in a barn when suddenly there was a shout from the guard. The English were coming. It was a pitch black night and suddenly there was shooting everywhere. We had to make use of the bayonet and everywhere there was screaming and shouting. Günther has lost a thumb, and our *Leutnant* has a bullet lodged in his shoulder. A man from my company killed three Englishman with an axe. I am still filled with horror when I think about it.

GEFR. WILHELM BLUM, INFANTERIE-REGIMENT NR. 26,
31 AUGUST 1914

With the British Expeditionary Force still small and underequipped, with major deficiencies in the supply of artillery, and with its volunteer citizen army in training, the year 1915 was a challenge. Committed to wars on other fronts, notably Gallipoli, the strains in the supply line were challenging. Spring 1915 saw the British operate according to the wishes of the French commander, and supporting the French offensives in Artois and the Champagne, attack at Neuve-Chapelle, Fromelles and Aubers Ridge. All foundered on the German defences, for the want of artillery and shells.

Gas was first used in modern warfare in the Ypres Salient, when the German *4. Armee* launched a surprise attack on the French on its northern limb on 22 April 1915. The French retired in the wake of the gas, but the line was stabilised; even though the use of this chemical weapon had a tremendous psychological value it failed to bring any operational success:

Even though my time is limited and there is hardly any rest, I want to send you a few lines as it has been a while since you have heard from me. A short while ago I was transferred to a Pionier-Kompanie working with a 'special thing' [gas] with which we have recently caused a lot of trouble for the English and their colourful brothers in arms. The whole enemy front collapsed and just in the right moment. You will probably be interested to know what the enemy's retreat in our sector looked like. Our troops had taken a lot of ground on our right wing leaving the English with two solutions: to retreat even further or to stage a frontal attack on the section held by my regiment. We were well prepared and if they had come they would have bled to death on our wire entanglements. The enemy seemed to know that and did not sally out. And so it came, that during the night of the 4th, between 1 and 3am, he gave us a 'French Farewell', which means he tried to sneak away in secret. In the area where our trenches were closest to those of the English, our guards noticed it first. Immediately our machine guns opened fire to hasten their retreat. They seemed to have left reluctantly for when we entered the English trenches I found a piece of paper on which someone had written in German language: 'It is a shame that we have to leave you, but we will see us again in the field'. On the back he had written 'Gott strafe Deutschland! Long live England!' We had a good laugh about that …

If it continues like that, Ypres will soon be behind us. But the town will not fall without a fight. Even though it has been turned into a pile of rubble, it acts as an important enemy strongpoint … To revenge themselves the English had mined the trench. Two of our men were unlucky and got killed by the mean devices.

Pionier Otto Döhner, Infanterie-Pionier-Kompagnie Nr. 5
'Schmelzer', 6 May 1915

Nevertheless, gas was used by the British four months later on 22 September 1915, when gas was released at Loos, in an attempt to make good the deficiencies of the artillery supply. As at Second Ypres, the use of gas was equivocal; for the British, this offensive in support of the French in the Artois saw the replacement of Field Marshal Sir John French by the 1st Army Commander General Sir Douglas Haig, and set the British army on a long, hard learning curve:

At forty minutes past zero, or 6.30 a.m., every battery lifts its fire from the front line to the second line, and still the furious fire continues. And then suddenly came time zero, bringing with it a scene that could never be forgotten. From the whole length of our front trench, as far as the eye could reach, rose, vertically at first, a grey cloud of smoke and gas, that, impelled by a gentle wind, spread slowly towards the enemy's trenches.

Major C.J.C. Street, Royal Field Artillery, September 1915

British cylinders ready
for the release of cloud
gas prior to the Battle of
Loos in 1915.

After 17 exhausting and hot days we are now able to enjoy some rest. It
came just in time as our nerves are overstrained. We stink as we were not
able to wash or attend matters of bodily hygiene for a long time. We were
in the reserves in Wingles when we were called out. When we reached
Hulluch we were peppered from all sides with machine guns, grenades
and rifle fire. We found cover in a trench, but not before a number of us
were killed and wounded. Fifteen Englishmen advanced towards us, but
soon retreated again. Later in the evening we attacked and I can count
myself lucky to have survived. Being quite unprepared we also suffered
from gas. The next day the English attacked again, but even though they
outnumbered us three to one we gave them a good thrashing and they
suffered heavy casualties. Two of their divisions were wiped out by us.
Their dead lay everywhere in piles. Here behind the lines the situation is
not much better. We are under constant artillery fire and heavy shells are
exploding all around us. We have to take shelter in the cellars and sometimes we can't get out for three or four days. It is astonishing to see what a
human being can endure. The weather is warm and tonight we are tasked

to dig trenches. Wingles has been completely destroyed. I have to finish now because tonight we will have a rifle inspection. Please write soon as receiving mail is the only thing we can look forward to out here. Best wishes from enemy territory,

UNIDENTIFIED GERMAN SOLDIER, 11 OCTOBER 1915

After a gas attack the English attack in dense masses. Five seconds pass before our artillery reacts wreaking havoc in the densely packed ranks. Legs, heads and arms get thrown into the air by our long shells. The enemy retaliates and we draw heavy counter battery fire. The English attacked on the whole length of the front. We lose the Schwaben Redoubt. The guns there are aiming over open sights. In section 71 dead Englishmen are piled so high that they are blocking the field of fire of some of our machine guns ...... By the end of the day the 26. Reserve-Division can proudly claim: we did not let the enemy pass!

KAN. HANNS SCHÄFER, RESERVE-FELDARTILLERIE-REG. 26, 1 JULY 1916

The effectiveness of mass cloud gas releases was equivocal. As the war developed, so gas became more of a tactical weapon; in grenades, limited bombardments or mortars. It became yet one more aspect of the modern battlefield both sides had to contend with:

Fritz gave us the devil of a time last night; things were fairly quiet till 11 p.m., then he gave us twenty minutes in his best style, whiz-bangs and aerial darts fell thickly around us. At 11.20 pm gas shells came for five minutes, and at 11.30 pm for ten minutes. Living as we do at the bottom of a quarry, the place was full of poison, a dark night, men coughing and groping in their respirators, some got the wind up properly.

CAPT. G.M. BROWN, 9TH SUFFOLK REGIMENT, 1916

Gas masks and respirators were soon developed that would negate the principle of gas attacks – that of the clearance of trenches by killing the occupants. Training was essential:

We had a demonstration of a gas attack yesterday afternoon. We put our smoke helmets on and then we went down into a trench which was filled with gas. It was quite a funny experience.

RFN WILLIAM C. TAFFS, 1/16TH QUEEN'S WESTMINSTER RIFLES,
6 MAY 1916

German soldier wearing the M16 *Gasmaske* and *Stahlhelm*, 1917.

No the gas does not have any effect on me at all, the new helmets are quite a protection but of course one feels the heat when they are on, and they make one look very bedraggled, especially the officers who wear their hair long while we have ours clipped off short.

RFN WILLIAM C. TAFFS, 1/16TH QUEEN'S WESTMINSTER RIFLES, 17 MAY 1916

Sometimes there is plenty of artillery fire. Gas is the worst as it is no fun if you can only breathe through a muzzle [*Maulkorb* – gas mask]. Luckily it is not as dangerous as one thinks.

KARL LINDER, KÖNIGLICH BAYERISCHES 12. INFANTERIE-REGIMENT, 18 AUGUST 1918

I did not get to bed until 5 o'clock this morning as I was out with a working party again last night. I had a rotten night as there was another gas attack. I was the last to leave the trenches with my party and about 1 mile from billets I heard the infernal gas alarm going. I did not want to be stranded so I put the pace on and tried to get back to billet as soon as poss. Whenever the Germans attack with gas they always shell heavily and I simply dreaded being caught in the open. About half a mile from home as the alarms were still sounding we put our helmets on and struggled on. It was bally awful they are such suffocating things and you cannot see as the goggles always become steamed. I fell down shell holes and crashed into trees and eventually landed back with half dozen men at the billet. I was utterly done up and tore my helmet off and if there had been any gas I should have gone under but I was just on the point of fainting and couldn't endure it another minute. The helmets are soaked in chemicals and I was perspiring so that it has apparently drawn some of the chemicals out of the helmet and burnt my forehead. I think it will leave a permanent mark as it's horribly sore now. This gives you some slight idea of the minor thrills we enjoy here. Give me old Blighty and peace and quiet and I shall be perfectly happy.

2LT ARTHUR H. LAMB, 1ST LANCASHIRE FUSILIERS, 15 AUGUST 1916

Later on in the war, gas became more of a complex tactical weapon, issued to supplement artillery and catch the infantry off their guard.

The development of siege tactics and the re-emergence of mine warfare – the opportunity to mine beneath the enemy, lay an explosive charge and destroy the enemy defences – were another important strategy. From late

1914, below ground men struggled to lay mines at the end of long tunnels that were simply intended to blow the occupants of trenches and dugouts to kingdom come. Mining was a top-secret activity – even for those infantrymen attached to the engineers for such duties:

> As the English had been tunnelling towards our positions and had been getting dangerously close our pioneers had to blow one of our biggest mine shafts. It was 24 metres deep and ended just in front of the English trenches. The result was spectacular and a giant pillar of earth rose into the air. Never have I experienced anything like it. One has to be sorry for the souls that are affected by such an explosion. The ground beneath your feet slowly begins to move, giving you plenty of time to realise what is happening to you. Then you get thrown into the air before pieces of you come falling down and get covered with earth. Lucky is he who is killed instantly! If you are buried alive a slow and even more horrible death awaits.
>
> RES. W. MUNZ, RESERVE-INFANTERIE-REGIMENT NR. 235

Even in the trenches there is nothing but digging going on. Still this is rather a different sort. I shall be able to tell you quite a lot of interesting details when I come home. I don't like to put them in a green envelope for after all they would not be personal and private.

> RFN WILLIAM C. TAFFS, 1/16TH QUEEN'S WESTMINSTER RIFLES,
> 17 JUNE 1916

Diaries record in matter-of-fact coldness the manner in which the explosion of mines under the trenches dealt out death, almost at random:

> 8 March 1916 Snowing. Very cold. Germans explode mine killing 21 men (Welsh Regiment). Return of fire. Very lively.
> 9 March 1916 Stopped snowing. German sniper fired 5 rounds but misses me. Take party of 30 through danger zone. No one hurt. Tucker, Silbert and Martin wounded. Still lively.
> 10 March 1916 Am very queer, exhausted and bad cold. Snowing again for 2 hours. Germans explode mine 12 killed. Water in trench up to waist. Firing heavy.
>
> SGT FREDERICK J. COMPTON, 16TH CHESHIRE REGIMENT, MARCH 1916

It was not knowing when the next explosion might occur that unnerved the average soldier:

My Dear Nan, I got your letter Monday night and I was glad to hear from you. I am glad to say that I have come out of the Trenches safe again but there are many a poor chap that has not. It is the worst lot of trenches that we have been in plenty of water and mud. We have had to wear long boots to keep us as dry as possible and the Germans have been laying mines and they blowed one up and we lost 26 men out of one company A Coy and they can't find a lot of them. We are going to give them something to go on with just now as we have got a lot of mines nearly ready, the sooner the better to get them out of the way.

PTE ROBERT W. PRICE, 10TH WELSH REGIMENT, 15 MARCH 1916

The strain on the morale of the infantry occupying sectors which are known to be mined is a terrible one, especially if they have no engineers to combat the stealthy attack. For the hundreds who are killed, buried, or injured from enemy mines there are thousands who suffer mental strain from the mere suspicion of their existence.

CAPT. H.D. TROUNCE, 181 TUNNELLING COMPANY, RE

Very often the men working below ground were infantry, attached to the engineers to help them drive the tunnels forward, and to assist in bringing up supplies, and carrying out 'navvying' work. Once laid, the mines would be blown – and the infantry would have to surge forwards in order to take the crater – before the enemy gained this advantage, the crater rim being that much higher on the battlefield. In the best cases, coordinated artillery fire supported the attacks. Some locations were more sought-after than others: Hill 60, a pimple in the Ypres Salient that was just 60m above sea level, was hard fought over:

I shall give you a description of modern battle. All of us knew that there was a mine under the enemy's position (Hill 60) and that it was to be exploded that evening. So all day long there was a sort of restlessness amongst us and firing was continuous till about 6 pm when everything grew quiet. Not a round was fired from our trenches and a few hundred men probably would be blown to eternity and one could not help praying for their souls – then half a minute – quarter of a minute – earth shook once – twice – three times, there was a rush in the air of falling trees and stones, a second's silence and then a terrible roar of rifles, machine guns, hand grenades, rifle grenades, trench mortars, bombs and cannon – the air was full of lead – everyone was firing as hard as he could and my machine guns going like fury. This lasted for nearly two hours – then a quiet and then another burst which continued through the night and all the next day and the next and now once again there is a silence and we occupy a new little bit of trench.

2LT ARTHUR R. STANLEY-CLARKE, 1ST DORSETSHIRE REGIMENT,

22 APRIL 1915

Mines were also subject to underground fighting, as the two enemies broke through into each other's fighting tunnels. The havoc underground must have been truly horrendous. Limited 'camouflet' mines were used to counter such threats, intended to destroy the enemy's gallery, while maintaining your own intact.

I was just working in a main tunnel when one of my pioneers ran up to me and reported that while driving one of the galleries forward they had come upon an enemy tunnel and had broken into it. First I could not believe it because in the hard chalk both sides were usually able to hear each other long before things like that happened, often in ranges of more than 30 metres. I decided to take a look myself and soon I saw it: they had broken into an English tunnel which lay about 80 centimetres below ours. As the entrance hole was not yet big enough to squeeze through we quickly enlarged it before myself and acting *Vizefeldwebel der Reserve* Reber, well-armed with grenades and revolvers, dropped through it to reconnoitre further. We had hastily removed our boots or wrapped empty sacks around them which enabled us to advance about 20 metres into English side gallery undetected. During this exhausting advance we came across a large number of filled sacks of sand, which had been brought there in preparation for an impending detonation. At that point we immediately informed *Oberleutnant* Lehmann by telephone and started to fetch explosive charges from a nearby ammunition dump which we placed near the entrance to the enemy gallery. When our *Oberleutnant* and *Leutnant* Straßer arrived they immediately started to investigate further. Without giving it a long thought it was decided to blow it up. Using a compass our *Oberleutnant* mapped the extension of the gallery. It was 1.25 metres high and about 80 centimetres wide. In contrast to our galleries it was built without a framework and had an arched ceiling.

The gallery was a huge threat for us, as the English were able to blow it up at any time which would cause us great harm. We now brought the sacks of sand, which were piled up in the gallery, further up towards the direction of the English positions and used them to build a wall to tamp the tunnel. When that had been done a large amount of explosive charges was brought up, which myself and *Unteroffizier* Hock piled up behind the sacks of sand after which the wall was sealed.

In these moments our nerves were stretched to the limit. Every now and again we stopped and listened to find out whether the enemy had detected our intrusion. We worked for two hours, disconnected from the world outside, deep inside the earth in the light of an electric torchlight as candles would not burn at a depth of 15 metres.

In addition to myself seven other men had volunteered and we were assisted by *Leutnant* Straßer and *Vizefeldwebel* Reber. Finally the last sack of sand had been placed the tunnel was sealed and an ignition wire had been installed. The circuit tester which was attached to the end of the wire showed that everything was working as planned so we switched on the electric detonating machine and everyone hurried into cover.

Our *Oberleutnant* gave the order: 'Fire!' *Vizefeldwebel* Reber pressed the igniter and – nothing happened. The next few tries failed as well and now we started worrying. Had the English found the charge and cut the cables? Had they attached their own ignition wires and were now planning to use our own charge against us? What were we to do?

Another advance to the charge could mean certain death. We looked at each other and decided to finish what we had set out to do. With our offi-cers at the front we moved silently towards the charge, carefully removed a few sacks added another 500 kilos of explosives to the existing 900 kilos and re-wired everything.

When the dangerous work had been done we hurried out of the tunnel and at 3:10pm we were finally able to blow up the charge. It was obvious that the resulting detonation not only destroyed the English side gallery but also led to a collapse of the enemy's main tunnel. Explosive fumes could be seen rising up from the enemy trench in thick white clouds.

UFFZ. WILHELM ORSCHLER, PIONIER-ABTEILUNG 4. INFANTERIE-DIVISION,
1 APRIL 1916

At 6am I and *Pionier* Jakob Breiner had just arrived in the side gallery to man the listening post there when suddenly there was a terrible blow. The torchlight slipped out of my hand and fell unconscious. When, after a while, I had regained my senses and opened my eyes I was surrounded by darkness. I could hear whimpers of pain from my comrade and instantly realised that we had been buried alive.

GEFR. JOSEPH GUCKERT, PIONIER-ABTEILUNG, 4. INFANTERIE-DIVISION

1916

In 1915, the Allies had flirted with the possibility that other fronts might offer possibilities, but the failure of the Gallipoli landings, and the stalemate in Salonika that followed, suggested otherwise. Though there was a split in the British cabinet between the 'Westerners' committed to France and the 'Easterners' seeking salvation elsewhere, there was no doubt in the mind of General Sir Douglas Haig that the main event was to be fought in France and Belgium against their most determined enemy. For the German High Command, there had rarely been any doubt that the decisive battle that would end the war would have to be fought in the west. It was only on the Western Front that it would be possible to strike the decisive blow that would force France and England to their knees. What was true is that the scale of the battles of 1916 and 1917 – and the resulting casualties – exceeded everything that had been thought possible.

In the autumn of 1915 the German High Command decided that the deadlock, the static trench warfare of the Western Front, needed to be broken. It was planned that Britain would be weakened and forced into capitulation by unrestricted U-boat warfare, while France would be defeated by one swift and hard blow – at Verdun, a garrison town on the Meuse. Verdun was heavily fortified, with a double ring of fortifications set in almost impenetrable hills. The battle was carefully prepared; the Germans moving an enormous amount of men and equipment to the sector: the normal strength of the German *5. Armee*, under command of *Kronprinz* Friedrich of Prussia, was nearly doubled.

The Battle of Verdun was opened by a one-hour artillery barrage on 21 February 1916, followed by the attack of three *korps* of *5. Armee* from the north-east. It took the French by surprise; but even though thousands of guns had been brought to bear, they hardly had any effect on the French defensive positions in the densely forested and undulating terrain. It took the Germans four days to reach Fort Douamont, taken in a *coup de main*. The battle was fought using modern technology – heavy artillery, gas and aerial attacks – but is known for its 'man against man' battle that raged in underground tunnels and narrow trench systems. Every inch of ground was fought for with grim determination. After the final major German attack on 23 June 1916, the Battle of Verdun slowly came to an end; the French still holding their fortress town. The casualties were huge, the Germans losing 330,000, the French 380,000.

Verdun had undoubtedly come as a surprise to the Allies. With the offensives of 1915 showing few signs of breaking the trench warfare deadlock, at a conference in Chantilly the Allies decided that the best way to end the stalemate of trench warfare was to force a breakthrough in 1916, attacking the Germans simultaneously on all fronts. For the British, in 1916 the inadequacies of the 1915 offensives would start to be ironed out. Since ammunition supply had been taken under the control of the Ministry of Munitions, and with the great mass of volunteer soldiers becoming available, the British commander-in-chief, General Sir Douglas Haig was confident that sufficient weight could be brought to bear on the German lines to break through. Meeting the French commander, General Sir Joseph Joffre on 14 February 1916, they decided the location of the largest Anglo-French offensive yet. It would be fought in the rolling hills of Picardy, astride the River Somme, at the junction between the armies of the two nations. From May 1915, the 'New Army' divisions moved into position south of the sector so far held by the British, taking over the line of the French on what was to become known as the Battlefield of the Somme. The French would lead the attack, to be fought in June 1916.

But all plans changed with the German assault at Verdun. Almost as Haig and Joffre had made their decision to attack, the Germans launched their offensive. With casualties heavy, and pressure on the line intense, now the main assault would have to be led by the British, relieving the beleaguered French. Though the German High Command had anticipated an attack by the Allies in northern France to relieve the pressure at Verdun, it was not entirely prepared for a major offensive on this particular sector of the front. Compared with the Verdun sectors there were few guns and little ammunition, and Falkenhayn refused to resupply von Below, commander of *2. Armee* – a mistake, and even worse, a massive underestimation of the British determination to start an offensive in northern France in summer 1916.

The Battle of the Somme opened on 24 June 1916 with a massive bombardment, with 1,537 guns firing an estimated 1.5 million shells at the German lines and defences. Most of these were field guns, however, and the majority of the shells were shrapnel – perfect for anti-personnel work but poor against prepared positions. Target accuracy was limited by heavy rainfall and bad visibility prior to the opening of the infantry assault on 1 July 1916, and the solid construction of the German dugouts and trench systems prevented a complete destruction of their defensive positions. If this wasn't enough, the artillery preparation was to destroy the enemy's wire in a hail of shrapnel bullets. It was a tall order.

On the morning of 1 July 1916, confident that their artillery had sufficiently weakened the German dugouts and machine-gun positions, British

The explosion of a mine beneath Hawthorn Ridge Redoubt on 1 July 1916, the opening of the Battle of the Somme.

and French infantry units climbed out of their trenches to attack the German lines. Committed for the first time en masse were 'New Army' divisions of Kitchener's volunteers, men who had answered the call to join the colours in the early days of the war. With absolute confidence that the artillery would do its job, the British troops expected to advance together in extended formation, crossing no-man's-land as a wave that would take the first line, and which would hope to drive the Germans back. The lines held, the defences too much for the advancing infantry. The result would be described as the bloodiest day in British military history, with total casualties of 57,470 men – 19,240 of whom were killed, while the amount of ground gained was a modest 1.5km deep and about 6km wide. Though French attacks south of the River Somme were more successful, managing to push the German

British 8in howitzer in position during the opening bombardment of the Battle of the Somme.

lines about 5km eastwards, the desired breakthrough had not been achieved. Commencing as a major offensive with a large-scale assault intended to envelop and outflank the German army, it had now descended into a series of small-scale battles for villages, forests and hills.

This second phase of the Battle of the Somme lasted from July to mid-September 1916. The first use of tanks on the battlefield was on 15 September – a spectacular but hardly effective premiere. Thanks to the exchange of worn out units with fresh ones, the constant resupply of ammunition and by reinforcing the German air service's reconnaissance and fighter units, the German army slowly managed to stem the tide. The end of September saw the start of the third and final phase of the Battle of the Somme, a series of countless minor skirmishes and battles, but with the autumn rains slowly turning the battleground into a quagmire in which troops, horses and vehicles could only move with difficulty, the battle came to a halt in November with the taking of the fortified village of Beaumont Hamel.

The Battle of the Somme was one of the costliest and bloodiest battles of the First World War; the German army alone lost nearly 500,000 men killed, wounded, missing and taken prisoner, the Allies some 625,000. By its end, the German lines had been pushed back just 10km, on a length of front at about 35km. But the battle was much more than simply an example of attritional warfare. Though the losses to Britain's inexperienced Kitchener's Army and Territorial divisions was staggering, the battle marked the British resolve to fight an all arms war against the Germans, and would influence subsequent offensives on the Western Front. The battle had entered the conscientiousness of the British forever, and the German army had taken a blow from which it would never fully recover.

For the soldiers on the Western Front, the grand strategy developed by high command came down to their own experiences in front of the enemy trenches. Trench raids were still a significant part of the British strategy – probing enemy defences, taking prisoners, gathering information. Of varying size, they could be as terrifying as a full-scale battle:

> I am sorry to hear about Willie Adams. I know it would set anyone mad to see the terrible sights. I saw the Dublins in a bayonet charge one day last week and they simply cut the Germans up just like paper. All Irishmen in bayonet charges simply go raging mad. You can imagine the roaring of guns and the clashing of bayonets. It is terrible but thank God we are safe and sound. We are in our new place and it is fine. Only the weather is awful wet and terrible cold. I got a touch of frostbite here on Saturday but the Doctor caught it in time to stop it spreading I am alright now.
> PTE JAMES HEALY, 8TH ROYAL DUBLIN FUSILIERS, 11 FEBRUARY 1916

Artillery bombardments were also common, a result of the observation of unusual activity by aircraft or forward artillery spotters:

> Artillery programme carried out. Fritz commenced by heavily shelling Ypres. Then we bombarded German front line and Shrops[hires] and our bombers went over. They took 14 prisoners and inflicted heavy casualties
> SGT H.N.T. MASON, 6TH OXFORDSHIRE AND BUCKINGHAMSHIRE LIGHT
> INFANTRY, 29 JUNE 1916

The Battle of the Somme opened on 1 July 1916:

Many thanks for the numerous gifts. Sadly I was not able to write any earlier, because at the end of June the great English-French offensive started, about which you will have read in the newspapers. The enemy directed his main efforts against our divisional front. We had to fight it out with the English, while the units directly on our left were facing French units. The fighting was severe, a lot of it being close-in combat with hand grenades. Due to the numerical superiority of the enemy our losses were not small, but they pale in comparison to the monumental enemy losses of the English.

HANS CHRISTIAN FEIL, GERMAN SOLDIER, 1 AUGUST 1916

Preparations for the battle, and the build-up of troops, were severe:

Our power in artillery has grown amazingly since the beginning of the year. Every month I have seen many new batteries arrive, with clean harness and yellow straps, and young gunners who were quick to get their targets. We were strong in 'heavies', 12-inches, 9.2's, 8-inches, 4.2's, mostly howitzers, with the long muzzled 60-pounders, terrible in their long range and effectiveness.

PHILIP GIBBS, BRITISH WAR CORRESPONDENT, JUNE 1916

The bombardment was very intense all through the night of June 28 and during the following day. Zero hour was fixed for 7.30 am, July 1. All private correspondence and kit, together with cap badge and numerals were to be left behind. Everyone was fitted out with necessaries for action, such as food, extra ammunition, grenades, etc.

SGT A.H. COOK, 1ST SOMERSET LIGHT INFANTRY, 1916

I am again in the fighting area but owing to our strict precautions as to the movement of troops I cannot disclose my whereabouts. We are now the masters of the Germans, and the Kaiser's doom is finally sealed. Our new army are doing splendid in the field far beyond our expectations. Their spirit is the same whistling and singing in the face of death. Our artillery are doing great work at present pumping shells into the Germans' positions. We are gaining ground steadily and our losses are comparatively small in comparison with the amount of ground gained which means the sacrifice of a few loyal and devoted souls to military duty. I must now conclude but

Reconstructed photograph depicting British troops 'going over the top' in 1916–17.

before doing so I hope my letters may be accepted with best wishes to all. I am writing this as shells and bombs are whizzing all around, this causes my letter to be of a scribbling nature. I now conclude as the noise is deafening.

LCPL LAURENCE DUNNE, 1ST CONNAUGHT RANGERS, 1916

Since I last wrote you I have come up to the firing line and am now only 3 short miles from the trenches. We are under canvas in a wood in a part of the line where the fighting has been very hot and where so far we have been unable to do much. The bally guns are banging away all the time and the bally Germans shell this place quite often.

The preparations for the offensive are enormous but the job is tremendously difficult and division after division has been cut up in the effort to break down the German defences. Well, mummy dear, I will say good night and try to sleep, the guns are making such a devil of a row.

2ND Lt Arthur H. Lamb, 1st Lancashire Fusiliers, 20 July 1916

The 1st Somersets formed part of the 4th Division, facing the strongpoint of Beaumont Hamel, and close to Hawthorn Ridge:

July 1 broke a lovely morning and the birds were singing. Breakfast was at 5.30 am, the men being issued with patent cookers for the occasion. The bombardment was now terrific, the German lines were one cloud of smoke, that it seemed to be impossible for anyone to live in such a hell. It was a wonderful sight. We actually stood on our parapets to get a better view, not a sign of life could we see and still no response from the enemy. We applauded direct hits and rubbed our hands in glee. We were looking forward to 7.30; it looked like a cake-walk.

At 7.20 am, a huge mine was exploded under Hawthorn Redoubt, just on our right front, it made our trenches rock. Punctually at 7.30, the attack was launched, the 1st Rifle Brigade advanced to our front in perfect skirmishing order, and the same applied to all troops, left and right, as far as the eye could see. Everything was working smoothly, not a shot being fired.

The first line had nearly reached the German front line, when all at once machine-guns opened up with a murderous fire, and we were caught in the open, with no shelter; fire was directed on us from both flanks, men were falling like ninepins, my platoon officer fell, he was wounded and captured.

Our guns had made an unholy mess of the German trenches, but very few dead could be seen, owing to the fact they were safely stowed away in dug-outs.

Sgt A.H. Cook, 1st Somerset Light Infantry, 1916

Hanns Schäfer of *Reserve-Feldartillerie-Regiment 26*, experienced the battle first hand:

That things have been really hot up here you will have read about in the army communiques. I suppose it can't be any worse at Verdun. We, that is the 26 Reserve-Division, have held our ground and have repelled the English and inflicted colossal losses. In front of one regiment alone 4000–5000 dead Englishmen were counted. In front of another company lay 700. You see, the English were deadly serious. At O. [Orvillers] a whole division attacked a single German battalion, the commanders leading their men on horseback. The English thought we would be done for, but how wrong they were. Our artillery was still operative and its defensive fire inflicted terrible on the attacking enemy. On our right though, as the army communiques rightly confess, the situation looks much worse. I am not allowed to tell you anymore. Preparations have been made to make sure it does not get any worse. I am still fine, but tired; we are looking forward to getting relieved. It has already calmed down a lot, but now and then the fighting flares up again. I hope this mass murder is 'finis' soon. Send something for refreshment will you?

KAN. HANNS SCHÄFER, RESERVE-FELDARTILLERIE-REGIMENT NR. 26, 1916

By now this damned offensive seems to be slowing down for real. Only now and then there is a brief spell of artillery fire. Putting their tremendous losses and the huge ammunition expenditure into relation the English have gained virtually nothing. At the front there is utter chaos. In some places English corpses are stacked up to 1½ metres high. They attacked with cavalry! And all that now lies unburied. The wind blows from the west, which is a blessing from a military point of view, but with it carries a pestilential stench of decay. The severely wounded do not get evacuated. Briefly said it is horrible and too much for the human mind to bear. If one asks how the English could get that far, there is only one answer. Our flyers bear the guilt. You hardly ever see one of them, they fly up and down the front miles away, waste petrol and cost money. There is an immense amount of anger for these gentlemen here. I hope one of them will cross my path later. Since yesterday it is relatively quiet and I hope it stays that way. I might just make it if it is over on the 17th. If not we could make a boating trip on the Rhine in autumn and drink cold punch, just like we used to do.

KAN. HANNS SCHÄFER, RESERVE-FELDARTILLERIE-REG. 26, 12 JULY 1916

Thank you for your parcels and your letters, that all arrived quite timely. The *Cölnische Zeitung* is only a day old. Our hopes have shifted from the 17th to August 1. If they do not manage to force a breakthrough before that the French will surely ask for an armistice. I do not believe in father's theory that it might last until November. But then you do not have an idea about the ammunition expenditure and the huge losses of the English. It will not last long anymore, that is out of the question. A calm down is already noticeable and the lulls between the fighting get longer. Yesterday and today they have tried their luck at Pozieres and they managed to get into the outskirts. But these are only local operations, a limited final effort. One thing has to be clear though, we have nearly reached the end of the line as well. The reinforcements we are receiving are quite unbelievable.

KAN. HANNS SCHÄFER, RESERVE-FELDARTILLERIE-REG. 26, 23 JULY 1916

Finally what we have wished for with all our heart became true! We have been relieved!! Do you realise what that means? After 30 days of battle it's back to the limbers! Cutting across country, unshaven, unwashed, with long hair, worn out and with my legs nearly failing me I trudged behind one of the gunners. When we marched into the village we heard the peaceful sound of organ music coming from the church. The contrast was nearly too much for me. We are still within artillery range, but tomorrow we will probably go back further into our resting quarters. I suppose we will be deployed further up north where it is more quiet, but at the moment I do not want to think about that. I am just happy that I managed to get out of this mess with my bones intact. It is a miracle that any of us is still alive, but our losses are bad enough as it is. Two officers and NCOs dead and half of the gunners. Enormous for a single battery. Only yesterday I was nearly done for myself, only destiny saved me. I won't even tell you about 1000 other situations where my life was hanging on a thread. Good that I am still alive. After a four week attack the English have finally managed to take Pozieres. Now the pigs sit in our comfortable dugouts, use our gramophone and drink our wine, but as long as I am here, I do not give a damn. I do not want to hear of war anymore.

KAN. HANNS SCHÄFER, RESERVE-FELDARTILLERIE-REG. 26, 24 JULY 1916

On the other side of the lines, Corporal Albert Howard was a Territorial soldier with the 1/9th Battalion King's (Liverpool) Regiment. His battalion had been in action in 1915, taking part in the Battle of Loos, and was moved southwards with the 55th Division to take their part in the Battle of the Somme, as it played out in its second phase. Diary entries record Corporal Howard's part in the battle and its build up – and in particular the attack on the village of Guillemont. His part in the battle commenced with the move southwards:

28 July 1916 Under orders to proceed into line from Mericourt to relieve 1st Gordon Highlanders. Lots of Artillery and ordnance passed through.

Marched 6 miles and rested at camp outside Bray. Bivouacked with heavy firing and bombarding taking place. Many aeroplanes in the sky.

CPL ALBERT HOWARD, 9TH KING'S (LIVERPOOL) REGIMENT, 28 JULY 1916

It wasn't long before Corporal Howard would appear in the Somme trenches, waiting for his turn to attack. In support trenches the battalion observed the hard-fought attack on Guillemont on 5 August, and experienced its own action on the 12th:

4 August 1916 Parade in the morning with afternoon off duty. At 4pm received orders to pack up ready for trenches and await further orders. Moved out at 7pm and arrived in support trenches at 9pm. Several shells overhead stayed overnight and relieved the 8th Irish.

5 August 1916. Still in supports, heavy shelling. Stand to 3am to 5am then breakfast cooked by ourselves, a bit rough. Went around Carnoy, Mametz Wood, Trones Wood and Delville Wood. (Montauban). Left at 4.30pm for line supports under heavy shellfire and got cut off. Heavy bombardment of trenches from 10pm to Midnight, the shelling was horrific a few of the men with the wind up.

6 August 1916. In line supports still trench digging all day, heavy bombard-ment going on and shrapnel flying everywhere. Went out on ration fatigue at 7pm took the rations to the front line and arrived back at 10pm. There was a heavy bombardment overnight.

7 August 1916. In line supports. Heavy bombardment going on, lucky, not much work done. Shelling terrific, Eric H and I buried in our bunk holes by shell, lucky escape. Eric very lucky covered up. 4pm worse than ever (sad). Sangster had half his head blown away by shell and died an hour later. Eric and I detailed to bury him at 9pm task completed (very sad indeed). Got orders to move, heavy shelling still continues. Relieved by 8th Irish [King's Liverpool Regiment] at 10.30pm under heavy fire we managed to get to the reserve trenches at 12.30am and got down for night.

8 August 1916. In reserve trenches doing fatigues, making entanglements. Still being shelled but no damage by our line guns, watched them fire. Bedded down for night, under orders to return to front line again. Never went, Scottish battalion went up.

9 August 1916. Still waiting orders in reserve everything ready for going over the top. Scottish and Irish went over, heavy casualties, Irish cut off trying to capture Guillemont, very heavy fighting going on.

British troops cross no-man's-land at Mametz during the Battle of the Somme.

10 August 1916 Still in reserve under orders to be relieved for rest. Heard from Cochrane that Nip got hit through the leg on the night of the 7th. Cooking our own grub by the batteries of 9.2' and 8' guns. Terrible reports from the front getting shelled again. Cannot get a letter through for home or anywhere too bad altogether. All previous orders cancelled marched off (A Coy) up line and landed in support of 6th Kings at 10pm stayed in support trenches overnight.

11 August 1916. Still in supports, a few shells over, struck with bullet on helmet 10am. Awaiting orders our job unknown to us at present. Heavy bombardment of trenches, worked digging all night.

12 August 1916. Very tired after no sleep for 48 hours. Hard work overnight and heavy shelling. At 7am moved up to line, had a rough passage all day. Got orders at 4pm that we were going over the top at 5.15pm. A Coy men all ready for the job and awaiting order to go. Fierce bombardment commences at 4.30pm one can hardly live under the circumstances. Order to go at 5.15pm boys all over, they are falling on either side, under terrific machine gun, artillery and sniper fire. Heartbreaking to see the boys going down. Just 20 yards from spot when I got blown up by shell and was buried. Lucky escape got fear of God for a while. Lay until it went dusk then cleared myself and made for shell hole, while crawling along got 2 bullets through my haversack, one right through my iron rations. Saw

Morris get hit and went out to dress his wounds under fire, terrible sight he was hit right behind the eyes, both were bulging out. Left him and went for stretcher. On my way back came across B Evans, Eaton and Jackson all wounded. Have not seen Eric Hughes since morning, heard he went over as a batman. Got into trenches at 1.30am much shaken up, the Company had sustained heavy losses. T. Horrocks left out wounded and a lot of the old boys gone. I could only find a dozen of A Company left.

13 August 1916. In front line with C Company and about 20 A Company men. Got orders to move to supports and found more of A Company men at 1pm. A great number of our boys have gone under and wounded, things are in a rotten state, no food for 24 hours or more and no water. At 6pm we were relieved by the Scottish and had a rough passage in supports. Got through alright and down to bivouac camp at 9pm rested for night.

14 August 1916. After a decent night's sleep started on fatigues. At 4pm left camp behind line and marched 8 miles to Ville-Sous-Corbie stayed in barn for night.

CPL ALBERT HOWARD, 9TH KING'S (LIVERPOOL) REGIMENT, 1916

I dare say you can see by the papers that we are doing well in the battle of the Somme it will be a good job when it has finished won't it?

PTE ROBERT W. PRICE, 10TH WELSH REGIMENT, 1916

The Battle of the Somme took its toll on both sides:

This continual offensive is costing us something!! Few people know how much Oh! It is a frightful business and people at home they read about the British troops pushing forward but the realities mother dear, by Gad! Could they but be in the trenches for 10 mins during an ordinary bombardment.

2LT ARTHUR H. LAMB, 1ST LANCASHIRE FUSILIERS, 22 SEPTEMBER 1916

War has caught up with us again. The English are directing a mad amount of fire into Pozieres which we do not occupy anymore! Currently I have made another step towards becoming a *Feldmarschall*. I am acting as assistant group adjutant! Colossal developments don't you think? The other gentleman is on leave and my weak shoulders bear an enormous responsibility. The English have advanced scandalously far in the last days. We were allowed to watch the whole battle through our scissor telescopes. First colossal artillery fire followed by wave after wave of English infantry in thick columns. We can even discern individual features. They jumped quite hard when they were hit by our 15cm calibres. Even though they attacked with 22 divisions they did not break through. The corner stone of Thiepval remains unbroken.

KAN. HANNS SCHÄFER, RESERVE-FELDARTILLERIE-REGIMENT NR. 26,

15 SEPTEMBER 1916

It is a pouring wet day and away in the distance our heavy batteries are pounding away at the German lines. Just near here all is quiet. It's an extraordinary thing to think about that for two long and weary years this same thing has been going on day after day night after night without ceasing, and apparently will go on indefinitely, perhaps for another two years! What fools men are! It is too utterly idiotic to think about! They are making all preparations here for a long winter campaign and as far as the authorities are concerned there is no idea of an end to the war yet. I myself see no chance for many months. The powers that be are so determined on utterly smashing Germany to bits. It is a pity that they don't have to do the smashing, isn't it!!!!!

2LT ARTHUR H. LAMB, 1ST LANCASHIRE FUSILIERS, 4 OCTOBER 1916

The German lines held, the bravery of the British not in question, their tactics, more so – at least from the perspective of their enemies:

During the battle of the Somme, the British army and its many newly raised divisions, was not at its best. The training of its infantry was inferior to that of the German infantry, especially so when it came to the movement of large bodies of troops. Single machine gun crews, patrols, interdicting and hand grenade squads behaved incredibly well. The single, mostly young, strong and well equipped British soldier followed his officer blindly. The officers being honourable, bold and brave men, which set an example to the men, leading them from the front. Due to their superficial training they lacked agility in battle and often failed to act quickly and autonomously. Many times they were unable to adapt to sudden changes in a combat situation. Mass attacks were carried forward in dense and partly disordered rifle chains closely followed by a mass of men in column. It's because of this the English, though outstandingly brave, suffered immense losses.

In small unit actions the English were adept in the use of terrain, moving forward cautiously and stubbornly in small groups, and sometimes with small hand grenade squads only. In defence the English were tenacious and more dangerous. The better trained and more agile French soldier was more competent in attack and also knew how to defend. When without leadership the French soldier knew how to act autonomously and to adapt himself to a change of the situation. The French officers had a strong personal influence on the men and were in general more experienced and cannier than the English officers.

Oberstleutnant Albrecht von Stosch, Infanterie-Regiment Nr. 153

1917

Freed from the requirement of fighting a battle at the junction of the armies of the two premier Allied nations, Sir Douglas Haig was convinced that his main assault should fall in the strategically significant area of Flanders. In 1917, the British commander turned his attentions once more to the significant cities of Ypres in Belgium and Arras in northern France. For their part, the Germans had decided to shorten their line and reduce salient created in the aftermath of the Somme offensive. *Unternehmen Alberich* was a tactical retreat in February 1917 to the heavily fortified *Siegfriedstellung* – known as the Hindenburg Line to the British – which was a system of defences dug deep into the chalky ground, lined with concrete pillboxes and bunkers.

Joffre had been replaced by General Nivelle as commander of the French army in January, and the new commander promised a rapid offensive action against the Germans in Champagne in April 1917, drawing upon his flair for artillery action at Verdun in the preceding year. Once again the British would launch a supporting action in Artois around the city of Arras:

> It was a couple of days after the attack and about 5.30am one morning. The Huns started shelling our trench and kept it up for nearly two hours! We just crouched in the bottom of the frozen trench and waited never knowing from one second to another whether we should be blown to atoms or not! However about 7am they stopped shelling! The sun was just getting up into the sky, when suddenly from in front of our trench, between ourselves and the Germans, a little lark rose up singing gaily and went soaring into the sky! We simply gasped we were so astonished! It was a remarkable sight, mummy dear, and made me think of the terrible pity of it all. It seemed to me though it was a symbol of God's love even amid all that desolation and destruction and death!

2Lt Arthur H. Lamb, 1st Lancashire Fusiliers, 1917

German soldiers in Flanders, 1917.

As you may have guessed from reading the papers I have been pretty busy lately and had little time or inclination for writing letters. We are out now and after a rest and a wash am feeling very fit and happy and content. I was very lucky and had a comparatively easy time but it has been very exciting and a great experience. I came out quite unhurt and have quite recovered from the stress and strain … I slept the night in a German dugout and it was quite fun going over the vast quantities of stuff they had left and tasting black bread etc. I could have got any amount of souvenirs I wanted of any kind whatsoever, but one does not feel in the mood to collect them. I am enclosing a little pamphlet prayer which is interesting and pathetic. Tell Nora that my heart is light once again because the night after the attack I received a large box of shortbread and a Charming letter from MA from which I also gathered that one if not more letters had gone astray. So, you see, I am happy! I expect we will be out for a little bit for a rest.

I am so sorry to bother you but could you let me have a few handkerchiefs, a towel and some trench powder. I will write shortly but perhaps not for a few days as I shall be quite safe but pretty busy.

2Lt KENNETH D. KEAY, 9TH SCOTTISH RIFLES (CAMERONIANS),
16 APRIL 1917

Over Easter we had a difficult time. For four days the English had peppered our forward-most trench with mines and artillery fire. On Easter Saturday at 7:30am an English aeroplane dropped gas and smoke bombs behind us trying to interrupt the communication lines with our rear. Immediately after that their artillery set in for another 15 minutes and when it shifted its fire to the rear the English attacked in three waves, overrunning our first trench in the process. I and four men, that had taken shelter in a dug out, grabbed our rifles and started shooting every Tommy who approached us. In front of our second trench they were greeted with machine gun fire. In front of our dug out we later counted 11 dead Englishmen and I do not think many of them got back to their lines.

GUSTAV MÖSSNER, RESERVE-INFANTERIE-REGIMENT NR. 121, 10 APRIL 1917

In a few days we go up the line again for a bit of a 'do' and I am for it again. I simply dread it because I know what it is and you never can forget or get used to the simply awful shell fire we are subjected to on this front! When there is a bombardment on the earth almost bursts into flame with bursting shells and they fall literally just like hail stones! Of course men and buildings and trees all go up skywards! We took a decent sized village not so long ago and it was left fairly intact. Suddenly the Huns turned their artillery on this village and within half an hour it had gone!! Literally swept off the face of the earth and just a smoking patch was left! It's just incredibly awful this war and insane and idiotic too! I wish and long mummy dearest I could be back with you at home. I loathe every second I am here. May God in His mercy have pity on me and grant me the joy of seeing you soon again my dearest mummy. This I implore and beseech of Him who is indeed my Heavenly Father!

2Lt ARTHUR H. LAMB, 1ST LANCASHIRE FUSILIERS, 12 MAY 1917

Tanks were used in the attack, south of Bullecourt; delayed by weather issues, many were subject to mechanical failure, while others were destroyed. Several were captured by the Germans to be used against the British in future actions:

After 14 days of rest we were hurried to the front at Arras. Sadly that meant spending Easter there. Here the English have tried to overrun our positions a number of times, but failed to achieve success. When attacking our section they came with a number of their new *Panzerkraftwagen*, the majority of which now lie in front of our positions, destroyed and shot to pieces.

Feldwebel Gustav Schmidt, Infanterie-Regiment Nr. 173, 14 April 1917

Though there were some successes, the Battle of Arras came to a conclusion on 16 May 1917. Despite Nivelle's confidence that his attack would be both swift and decisive, the Nivelle offensive ground to a halt. With casualties of 30,000 French soldiers killed, the will of the French to fight on had been temporarily broken, and widespread mutinies followed. The British were to take on more of the burden. The Ypres Salient would be the focus of Haig's attention. Flanders had been identified as the main area for a British offensive since 1915, but Haig's ambitions had been thwarted by the demands of the senior *Entente* partner, France, who had firstly insisted on cooperation with offensives in the Artois and Champagne that were intended to cut off the Noyon Salient and surround and outflank the German defenders. The failure of the Nivelle offensive had paved the way for the carefully prepared Messines offensive, and with the success of this attack in driving the Germans from the ridge to the south of the city, Haig committed General Sir Hubert Gough to continuing the offensive, removing the bulge of the Ypres Salient and driving in the German lines to the north of the *Siegfriedstellung*.

In planning for some two years, the Battle of Messines in June 1917 marked the opening of an offensive that would develop into the costly Third Battle of Ypres. For the Germans, these battles were part of a long-running offensive action in Flanders that had been fought since the first battle in October 1914. Messines was a limited operation that was intended to drive the Germans from the ridge top that ran from Ploegsteert to Hill 60, and was to use a coordination action of carefully sited mines dug beneath German strong points. Nineteen mines were exploded in all, twenty-four had been laid, and up to twice as many again had been planned. The battle was a complete success, and the Germans were driven off the ridge top:

Suddenly, all hell broke loose. It was indescribable. In the pale light it appeared as if the whole enemy line had begun to dance, then, one after another, huge tongues of flame shot hundreds of feet into the air, followed

British 'female' (equipped with machine guns only) Mark V tank.

by dense columns of smoke, which flattened out at the top like gigantic mushrooms. From some craters were discharged tremendous showers of sparks rivalling anything ever conceived in the way of fireworks. The whole scene was majestic in its awfulness. At the same moment, every gun opened up, the din became deafening and then nothing could be seen of the front, but the bursting of our barrage and the distress flares of the enemy.

ANONYMOUS BRITISH TUNNELLER, 250 TUNNELLING COMPANY

It was getting near 3 am now, and everyone was very excited, but trying to keep the fact from his mate. It was still dark so we couldn't see the expression on each other's face, but many a voice had a tremor with it. We had to advance in three waves. One Company forming the first wave had to take the

Destroyed British tank, Herenthage Park, 23 August 1917. The tank has been used as a German strongpoint.

enemy's first line. The Company I was in had to take the second line and the other two Companies formed the third wave and had to take the third line. Everyone who had a watch was looking at it every few seconds, all having been correctly timed the previous day. It was a very weary wait and I for one was hoping for the time to begin, because the suspense is worse than being in action. Someone in our platoon said two minutes to go. Exactly on 3.10 am there was a terrible explosion on our left. It was the blowing up of a mine, which was the signal for everything to start. The next second there was such a war, the like of which I had never heard before or since, and I hope I never hear such a one again. It was caused by the explosion of a further 18 mines and every gun on the front had been standing with a shell in the breach and all were discharged on the second. It is an impossibility for me to describe all that happened. The concussion from the mines and guns was terrible, and the earth trembled under us. I managed to keep on my feet.

PTE JOHN H. BENN, LOYAL NORTH LANCASHIRE REGIMENT, 1917

Messines was the prelude to the British offensive in Flanders, the principal assault on the German lines since the Somme. The Third Battle of Ypres, often known as the Battle of Passchendaele – after the last phase of the offensive – opened on 31 July 1917, some six weeks after the success at Messines. Third Ypres was fought as a series of 'bite and hold' battles that achieved varying degrees of success. Notable for its artillery preparation, the creation of a cratered battlefield topography, the destruction of the drainage ditches on this low-lying ground, and heavy rains combined to give the classic view of a First World War battlefield as a quagmire. This expended the energy of the attacking troops, made the digging of defensive trenches difficult, and rendered supply almost impossible. Going was tough – and faced with a stalled battle, Haig committed tanks to the fray, even though the ground conditions were wholly unsuitable. The battle continued on into the winter of 1917, in the face of political opposition, and once again came to a close in November after a hard fought campaign. The total numbers of casualties is disputed, but both German and British forces lost somewhere between 250,000 and 350,000 men each, gaining 10km of ground but driving the Germans from the ridge tops. The German line once more held, as it had done the year previously after the Battle of the Somme.

J. Görtemaker of *Feldartillerie-Regiment Nr. 503* was on the receiving end of the great attack:

You have to excuse me that I did not write earlier, it just was not possible. In the previous days we have experienced frightful things and exertions. On the 28th we left Cordes and arrived at Moorslede on the Ypres front on the 30th. On the morning of the 31st we were ordered to hitch up as we had been assigned to form an assault battery (*Sturmbatterie*) as part of an assault group (*Sturmgruppe*). First we thought there would be an exercise, but soon we were under fire and could see what was happening. The Tommies were successfully attacking and had to be repelled.

Countless masses of infantry and vehicles covered the roads. Our guns were manoeuvered into position and opened fire, while we took the limbers a few hundred metres further to the rear. At the front gun by gun had been hidden behind shrubs. All throughout the day we received a lively fire and had to flee with the limbers. One particularly naughty enemy flyer circled 100 metres above us and only 5 minutes later the Tommies started to pound us. Finally some of our flyers brought the enemy down in flames. While it was quite warm during the day, it started to rain in the evening. The fighting ebbed down and the enemy had been repelled.

It cost us a lot of blood. Some have horrible wounds and needed to be dragged out. In the village of Zonnebeke the dead are lying in heaps. On the first day already we lost one *Wachtmeister*, two *Unteroffiziere* and four men in addition to a number of wounded. The 6. Batterie has lost 6 drivers and 18 horses. Actually it is a miracle that we got through so well. Ours, gun no. 3, has had no losses yet. Even though it is standing at the very front and is only firing against tanks only of which it has already culled six! Three of our trench lines have been retaken.

GEFR. J. GÖRTEMAKER, FELDARTILLERIE-REGIMENT NR. 503, 3 AUGUST 1917

The ground conditions were awful, too awful for the tanks that were eventually committed to the fray:

The country resembles a sewage-heap more than anything else, pitted with shell holes of every conceivable size, and filled to the brim with green, slimy water, above which a blackened arm or leg might project. I remember a run I had at the beginning of this week – for dear life if you like. Five of us had spent the night patrolling and were returning … when the enemy sighted us and put a barrage along the duckboard track … with a 'run like Hell boys' went off in a devil's race, with shells bursting at our heels, for half a mile, dropping at last in complete exhaustion in a trench out of range.

PTE HUGH QUIGLEY, 12TH ROYAL SCOTS, 17 SEPTEMBER 1917

The depressing effect of rain, rain, rain, day and night, and the postponement of their hopes of driving back the enemy, made the army commanders sullen and embittered. They looked round for a scapegoat, and found it in the numerous tanks stranded on all sides in that desolate swamp.

MAJOR F. MITCHELL, TANK CORPS

The severity of the assault tested the Germans:

You will probably have read about the Battle of Flanders and the 31 July in the Heeresbericht. The Kaiser has sent his compliments to Kronprinz Rupprecht of Bavaria and his valiant troops. The 31 July was the main day and I will not forget it even if it is still bad enough at the moment. They say that the Tommies might try again a bit further towards Ostend and maybe we will be transferred there to chase them away. We have taken a lot of prisoners here, mostly Scots.

GEFR. J. GÖRTEMAKER, FELDARTILLERIE-REG. NR. 503, 6 AUGUST 1917

We were hit by a number of barrages, but such a hell has not yet been experienced. Even the Somme was not that bad. The whole terrain is one chaotic field of craters. Holes so deep you can put a house into them. The roads destroyed. Darkness, fog and mud in which we nearly got stuck. In one place a Bavarian gun was stuck in a mud hole. We had to squeeze by and suddenly me and my horse stumbled and fell, so that I was stuck in the mud up to my belly. I was lucky that the Bavarian gunners could pull me out from underneath the horse … There are no trenches here anymore, only shell holes which afford some cover.

Gefr. J. Görtemaker, Feldartillerie-Reg. Nr. 503, 12 August 1917

Since the 31 July we have lost 40 men. Virtually all of the personnel that has moved out with me from Berlin is gone. On the 21st we received Ersatz. Mainly 18 year olds, 7 weeks of soldier's training in a *Feldrekrutendepot* and now they get thrown into this mess. Only a day later, on the 22nd four of them got killed plus another eight of the old hands. That is 12 men in a day. Our guns have been shot to pieces and the parts spread over the landscape so that we could hardly find anything again. That is not a major problem as we just need to fetch new guns from Roulers so were are quickly back in action in the evening …

Of the last 12 dead only a few could be found. The others had been blown into a thousand pieces, all torn apart into unrecognisable bits …

Every day a huge number is buried. Our chaps get coffins while the infantryman get hastily buried in their tent squares as there are too many of them. Young lads all of them. The infantry suffers a lot more than we do, but the Tommies will not get through. Now and again they get thrown back. Here the Tommy has a special combat tactic. He lays down a smoke screen on two places and into the middle he fires gas. They then advance in the harmless smoke …

Just now a comrade tells me that it is Sunday. We do not usually think about that here, a Sunday is as good for murder as any other day.

Gefr. J. Görtemaker, Feldartillerie-Reg. Nr. 503, 26 August 1917

The idea that the offensive was going to end the war was not taken altogether seriously by some:

This life is getting dreary, every day passes and the same over and over again, the nights longer and cold. According to the papers the war is practically over but I put it down as bluff. Still we have not to look on the black side for better days are to come, but how long are they off. We are still roaming about Belgium, from one place to another up the line and then down as I sit in my dug-out facing a place which is prominent on the war map, as usual it has been battered to the ground by the guns, of course I would give the name of the place to you so that you understand where about I was only it is against army regulations.

Pte William Horrocks, 1/4th East Lancashire Regiment,

26 October 1917

Though tanks were used unsuccessfully at Ypres, they would be used to much greater effect when the British Third Army launched an attack towards Cambrai on 20 November 1917, using the largest number of tanks yet assembled. The massed formations overwhelmed the Germans on good ground, and in taking on the *Siegfriedstellung* – the Hindenburg Line:

> The amazed Germans were completely overwhelmed. As scores of these monsters loomed up out of the mist, with their weird humps on their backs, the defenders of the line fled in panic … The great fascines were released and cast into the bottom of the trench. The snouts of the tanks stretched out over the wide trenches until the point of balance was reached, then dipped down and down until they seemed to be standing on their heads. Then, when they touched the far side, up and up they reared until their tails rested on the fascines … Thus was the famous Hindenburg Line, the much boomed bulwark of the German Army, crossed as easily as a boy jumps over a small stream.
>
> Major F. Mitchell, Tank Corps

Even though the attack began with significant gains on the first day, over half of the tanks were put out of action and as the battle continued, British progress slowed amid intense fighting. By the end of the month the German forces launched a counter-offensive, using intensive artillery fire and modern infantry tactics, forcing the British to retreat and leaving them only with the gains they had made around the villages of Havrincourt, Ribécourt and Flesquières.

1918

The year 1917 had been a tough one for the Allies, and with the German strategy of holding the Western Front successful, it was able to dispatch the ailing Russians and look forward to the possibility that there would be a chance to reinforce their armies in the west. Counter to this was the fact that the German policy of unrestricted submarine warfare had finally committed the United States to the Allied cause in April.

Since the beginning of 1918, thousands of US soldiers had begun arriving in French ports, and the US economy turned to a war footing. Time was running out if the war was to be concluded before the new enemy could fully engage on the Western Front. In January 1918, the German army in the west stood at 5.1 million men, and the focus of the German High Command was to deliver the enemy a single hard and decisive blow, hurting him so much that it would force him to accept a negotiated peace on honourable terms.

The months of January to March 1918 saw a never-before-experienced concentration of German troops and guns. Everywhere behind the lines new *Sturmtruppen* (stormtroop) formations gathered. Trained in tactics that had been in constant development since 1915, dedicated stormtroop units had first seen major action during the opening phases of the Battle of Verdun, while the following year they would punch through the Italian lines at Caporetto and would retake the ground captured by the Allied tank offensive during the Battle of Cambrai. Their attacks began with a short but intensive artillery barrage on a narrow segment on an enemy trench, followed by a rapid onslaught by squads of heavily armed troops who would force a breakthrough at key points, bypassing concentrations of Allied troops and speeding into the enemy rear areas to spread chaos and confusion. The ground thus gained could then be exploited and defended by the regular infantry that followed after them.

The planning for the offensive had already started in November 1917. Finally the *Oberste Heeresleitung* (OHL, the Supreme Army Command) decided that the ideal location to deal the decisive blow was the seam between the British and the French armies in the middle sector of the Somme. Ludendorff was quite sure this join would break under pressure, and the resulting rift would be hard to heal:

> For political and military reasons we decided upon (staging the attack) on the English Front. We expected that England, if it suffered a crushing defeat on French soil, would be more inclined to make peace than its allies the French. In our estimation operational flexibility was less inherent in the English army as in that of France. This achieving success against the English seemed easier and safer.
>
> GENERALFELDMARSCHALL ERICH LUDENDORFF

The breakthrough between St Quentin and Arras would be aimed on the southern wing of the British army in the area between Ham and

German soldier in the front line: he is aiming a *Gewehr 98* mounting a *Grabenmagazin* (trench magazine) giving it an ammunition capacity of twenty rounds.

German 'stormtrooper' hurls a hand grenade on a special training ground at Doncourt, 1917.

Péronne. Once tactical success had been achieved it was planned to 'roll up' the front from there. On the German side 61 divisions, 1.4 million soldiers, stood ready for the *Große Schlacht*, the Great Battle. Never before in the war had such a number of men been amassed. All available manpower had been concentrated for the initial attack. It was a risk, though, as there were hardly any reserves to follow up the advancing troops. At first everything went as planned, motivation and determination were at a peak. Within only a few days the leading divisions had advanced 60km into enemy territory and had reached the area around Amiens. This was up to fifteen times more ground than had been gained with great loss in the great battles of the years 1916 and 1917. Within two weeks 90,000 Allied soldiers – 75,000 of them British – had been taken prisoner, and 1,300 enemy guns had been captured.

The British army had reeled back at the ferocity of the German assault, and there was concern that the British would have to fall back to the Channel Ports. To stem the growing tide, Field Marshal Sir Douglas Haig was forced to issue his famous 'Backs to the Wall' order on 11 April 1918:

> Three weeks ago to-day the enemy began his terrific attacks against us on a fifty-mile front. His objects are to separate us from the French, to take the Channel Ports and destroy the British Army.
>
> In spite of throwing already 106 Divisions into the battle and enduring the most reckless sacrifice of human life, he has as yet made little progress towards his goals.
>
> We owe this to the determined fighting and self-sacrifice of our troops. Words fail me to express the admiration which I feel for the splendid resistance offered by all ranks of our Army under the most trying circumstances. Many amongst us now are tired. To those I would say that Victory will belong to the side which holds out the longest. The French Army is moving rapidly and in great force to our support.
>
> There is no other course open to us but to fight it out. Every position must be held to the last man: there must be no retirement. With our backs to the wall and believing in the justice of our cause each one of us must fight on to the end. The safety of our homes and the Freedom of mankind alike depend upon the conduct of each one of us at this critical moment.
>
> FIELD MARSHAL SIR DOUGLAS HAIG, 11 APRIL 1918

The depth of the advance became a major problem for the German army, however. The battleground they traversed was the same that had seen the

Battle of the Somme of 1916 and the German retreat into the *Siegfriedstellung* in 1917. All infrastructure had been destroyed, making the advance and the upkeep of working supply lines a difficult task. Even though the German army had access to huge numbers of guns of all kind, it hardly had any motorised transport, and the lack of transport and supplies brought the German advance to a standstill. On 5 April 1918, *Operation Michael* was cancelled by the OHL, though April 1918 saw other attacks into a north-western direction towards Bethune, Ypres and Lille (*Operation Georgette*), with *Operation Blücher-Yorck* in May 1918 between Compiegne and Reims and finally, in July 1918, *Operation Marneschutz-Reims* and *Friedenssturm*.

For many German soldiers, the failure to achieve victory in these battles came as a demoralising shock. German losses had been severe and even though during *Operation Michael* alone the French and the British had lost about 212,000 men, the promise of much larger troop concentrations as the Americans arrived in France meant that these losses could be made good. German reserves, however, had virtually been exhausted. This, together with a lack of supplies and the ever-present food shortages, had had a catastrophic effect. German troops that had fallen onto the abandoned British supply dumps often preferred to stay there, rather than to continue their advance into enemy territory. Never before had they seen such a mass of tinned meat and other luxury supplies, and it revealed to them the mass of resources available to the enemy.

For the German army, July 1918 came as a turning point in the war, as for the first time German soldiers began to leave the front lines in large numbers. With the Allies now under central command with Ferdinand Foch as Generalissimo, the time came for the offensive to be resumed against the Germans. On 8 August 1918, a day that Ludendorff had called 'the black day of the German army', the opening of the Battle of Amiens saw the use of an effective 'all arms' cooperative battle in which infantry and artillery coordinated with massed tank formations and aircraft to turn the tide of the war against the Germans. Here, the British and the French in an attack that was supported by over 400 tanks, forced a break through the German lines between Montdidier and Albert. The few German reserves available were unable to stem the tide, and were completely wiped out. On the evening of 8 August the German *2. Armee* had lost 48,000 men, 33,000 of them reported missing, with the Allies reporting 30,000 Germans taken prisoner.

From 8 August the Allied forces would push the Germans back continuously for 100 days in a series of hard-fought engagements that would see young conscripts from both sides fight out the final campaign of the war. From July to September 1918, an estimated 340,000 German soldiers were reported missing by the Germans, and in the final months of the war between 700,000 and a million German soldiers were registered as 'absent'. There was no hope that the German army could ever mount another offensive in this war.

The final Allied push towards the German border began on 17 October 1918. As the British, French and American armies advanced, the alliance between the Central Powers began to collapse. Turkey signed an armistice at the end of October, and Austria–Hungary followed on November 3. On 29 October, faced with the prospect of returning to and most probably dying at sea, the sailors of the German High Seas Fleet in Kiel mutinied. Within a few days, the entire city was in their control and the revolution spread throughout the country. On November 9 the Kaiser abdicated; slipping across the border into the Netherlands and into exile. A German Republic was declared, and peace negotiations were commenced with the Allies. At 5 a.m. on 11 November 1918 an armistice was signed in a railway carriage parked in a French forest at Compiegne, near the front lines. After over four years of terrible conflict, the Great War was at an end.

News of the preparations for the final German offensive of the war was not lost on the British. In March there was a hesitant expectancy in the air, recorded by laconic cavalryman, 2Lt Conyers Bridgewater:

1 March 1918 At Montigny. German offensive expected again.

2 March 1918. At Montigny. Offensive does not seem to materialise.

3 March 1918 At Montigny. General 'Wind Up' all sorts of generals about including Haig.

4 March. At Montigny. Germans don't seem to be in a hurry.

5. March. At Montigny. No attack yet.

6 March. At Montigny. No attack has come off yet.

21 March. At Brie. German Offensive began. Devil of a barrage. Rushed off at 4.30 to Villeselve. Arrived late. Bivouacked in field.

2Lt Conyers Bridgewater, 6th Inniskilling Dragoons, 1918

Lt-Col Rowland Feilding was commanding the Connaught Rangers near Bray when the storm broke:

I have had no opportunity to write during these last three days. As you will have learned, the much advertised offensive crashed upon us last Thursday,

since which we have been fighting a rear-guard action, almost continuously. A retreat was the one possibility that had never occurred to us, and,
unfortunately, it involves a kind of manoeuvring in which we are unversed,
in spite of all our experience. For the time being the enemy has turned the
tables in a manner which is difficult to realise, so great is the contrast with
what would have been possible at any time during the past year.

LT-COL ROWLAND FEILDING, 6TH CONNAUGHT RANGERS,
24 MARCH 1918

The German offensive started full of hope, with huge preparations:

All the roads clogged with one huge, never ending column. Motorcars
and trucks, one big cloud of dust. Every hole in the ground is packed
with ammunition. A thousand rounds every night. This will turn out to
be a wonderful hell. One or two weeks until it starts. The world will be
astonished when the dance begins.

GEFR. J. GÖRTEMAKER, FELDARTILLERIE-REGIMENT NR. 503, 15 MARCH 1918

On the way to Folies we traversed the battlefield of the previous days. They
had not been tidied up yet as there had been no time. The bodies of dead
Englishmen with their conspicuous flat helmets were dotting the ground
in large numbers, between backpacks, ammo boxes, gasmasks and destroyed
carts and wagons. Proof of the precision of our artillery bombardment.

HAUPTMANN GOTTFRIED ESSER, INFANTERIE-REGIMENT NR. 53,
2 APRIL 1918

On 20 March we advanced to the front and took position about 100 metres
away from the English lines. At 4:40am our barrage started which continued up until 10am. The English answered by firing shells and mines. One
of those mines, a huge thing of about two centres, exploded about one
metre behind my foxhole. I was lucky as I was only showered with sand.
I am nearly deaf on my right ear now, but this is getting better. The man
standing next to me had his head torn off. At 10:05am we assaulted the
Tommie's lines and took 80 of them prisoner, the remaining ones fled and
we chased after them. While doing that we captured a number of English
supply depots. You cannot imagine what we found there. Thousands of
meat tins, pineapple preserves, socks, shirts, underpants, soap; briefly said
everything you can imagine was freely available. I still have three pieces of
soap and ten tins of meat in my pack. I would have liked to send you the

soap, but we cannot send any parcels at the moment. Please do not send any food, I have not even opened the last two you sent. This morning one of my men brought 120 eggs, six pounds of butter, twenty bottles of English beer, 5 litres of Cognac and ten tins of pineapple preserves, so we have spent the day eating scrambled eggs.

We have now reached the Ancre and cannot advance any further as the English offer a stiff resistance. You will have read about the general situation in the newspapers …

UFFZ. WILHELM FORST, RESERVE-INFANTERIE REGIMENT NR. 227,
20 MARCH 1918

Finally the Tommy retreats. Our flamethrowers had taken a terrible toll. Darkness sets in and with it comes a lull in the fighting. English white bread, ham and bacon serve us as a welcome dinner. Instead of the usual hot coffee we have cold water collected from shell craters. A good Tommy cigarette forms the dessert.

VIZEFELDWEBEL RICHARD KRÜGER, INFANTERIE-REGIMENT NR. 53,
22 MARCH 1918

The offensive makes good progress. There are victuals of all kinds. We revel in white bread, chocolate, lard, a mass of sugar. A never-ending supply of red and white wine. Carts full of food tins and other stuff. You do not need to worry about me. The battle begins.

GEFR. J. GÖRTEMAKER, FELDARTILLERIE-REG. NR. 503, 27 MARCH 1918

In January 1918, the German High Command had ordered the formation of units equipped with captured British tanks; they formed part of the German offensive:

Our time had arrived! 'Crank up! Both one! (both tracks first gear)'. Slowly our tank '*Käthe*' set into motion. Eerily illuminated by the muzzle flashes of two 21cm mortars, the steel beasts pushed out of the forest, ready to crush resistance wherever it would be offered. English artillery fire was getting weaker and now and then we could hear the impact of enemy shells muffled by the engine sound of our tank. Soon we had reached the first trench and stopped to wait for the attack that was about to be launched in an hour … 4:15am! The signal came! Colourful illumination shells crashed into the English trenches ahead followed by a creeping barrage of our artillery that slowly rolled across the enemy positions.

Again we could hear the command 'Crank up! Both one!' *Käthe* was going into battle! Far ahead of our own infantry we approached the first English trench. I was manning the frontal machine gun. It was dusk and so we had left the two adjoining hatches standing ajar to improve visibility. About 30 metres in front of the enemy trench an unarmed Englishman climbed out with his arms raised and dropped shaking to his knees. I waved to him to tell him to walk towards our positions. As soon as he started walking his comrades started to surrender as well. This way we took about 20 prisoners half of which were wounded. Our tank advanced further, tipped headlong into the trench, pulled itself out again and headed towards the Aisne. Then, all of a sudden, it started. We were met by raging machine gun fire which was getting more intensive by the second. After closing the hatches I trained my gun on an enemy nest of resistance and let fly with everything I had. When I had emptied the first drum magazine I felt a sudden blow, my gun had taken a hit and became useless. A bullet had ricocheted on the spring housing before falling to the floor. Quickly we installed the spare gun, which soon afterwards shared the fate of his predecessor. This time a bullet had hit the barrel from the outside and blocked it. In this situation our unarmoured guns were quite useless. To make a more stable firing platform the commander had halted the tank and the gunners had opened a well aimed fire on the English machine gun nests, destroying them one by one without giving them the chance to retaliate. A plethora of bullets ricocheted off our armoured walls like a hailstorm. I moved to the right gun to support the gunner. Shot after shot was fired. The temperature inside the tank became quite unbearable so we took off our tunics and hitched up our sleeves. Sweat soaked we were soon standing knee-deep in a pile of empty shell cases. Slowly our ears turned deaf from the continuous sound of four firing guns inside the tiny fighting compartment. In situations like this, time stands still. I do not know if the fight lasted one hour or two, but finally the English were broken. They had fought like the devils, but we had forced them to surrender. Later we learned that they had been transferred from Kemmel to this 'quiet' sector for R&R which makes their feat of arms even more impressive. By now *Reserve-Infanterie-Regiment 66* had caught up with us and went into the attack as if there were no tomorrow …

Uffz. Karl Schrever, Sturm-Panzerkraftwagen-Abteilung 11
(Beute), 27 May 1918

There was a belief in the air that the war would finally be won:

From Erquinghem we then marched back towards our command post passing an endless stream of advancing regiments and columns. I would have loved to join them. Everywhere Tommy is on the retreat and hopefully we will throw him into the sea … Today the weather is glorious. In the west the clouds of war show where the enemy is retreating. We will finally win!
LTN. RUDOLF SCHOLDER, FUSSARTILLERIE-BATALLION 37,
11 APRIL 1918

Hopefully there will be better times ahead. The way it looks we will finally be victorious. In Flanders we had some nice successes as well.
GEFR. J. GÖRTEMAKER, FELDARTILLERIE-REG. NR. 503, 12 APRIL 1918

But the euphoria would not last forever:

Dear parents and brethren, pray for me because it is frightening here.
GEFR. J. GÖRTEMAKER, FELDARTILLERIE-REG. NR. 503, 31 MAY 1918

On the 30th we suffered heavy casualties and were nearly wiped out. Many old comrades made off or were killed.
GEFR. J. GÖRTEMAKER, FELDARTILLERIE-REG. NR. 503, 6 JUNE 1918

With the German advances stalled, it was the turn of the Allies to go on the offensive, in August 1918:

Zero hour was timed for 4.20 am; it was now 11.30 pm; so I donned my steel helmet and box respirator … I became more keenly sensitive to the damp mournfulness of the night. What if tomorrow should result in failure? It was only four months since the Hun was swamping us with his tempestuous might!
CAPT. G.H.F. NICHOLS, 18TH DIVISION, ROYAL FIELD ARTILLERY,
7 AUGUST 1918

Tanks formed a significant part of the new, modern battlefield, joined up with new artillery techniques and linked infantry attacks:

The enemy is using an enormous mass of material against us. Tank after tank, metal beasts that have an enormous oppressing effect, followed by wave after wave of attacking infantry. All these attacks are initiated by hour-long artillery barrages. Our infantry allowed the tanks to clank over them where they were met by our artillery and mine throwers. On one day 60 enemy tanks were destroyed in front of our divisional positions. When I was manning the telegraph station at Buochoir I had the chance to witness an enemy tank getting hit by one of our guns after which it burned out completely.

WILHELM HOPPE, GERMAN SOLDIER, 17 SEPTEMBER 1918

Lt-Col Feilding would also experience the change in the tide as the war flowed back towards the German lines, the German offensive stalling as the Allies soaked up the pressure:

We have been at it, hammer and tongs, the last few days, but I got out last night for a breather, having been continuously on my feet – which are very sore – almost continuously for four days and nights. Things have gone well, and there is no doubt in my mind that we are killing a lot of Germans – considerably more than they are killing of us. Besides, we are capturing large numbers of prisoners.

LT-COL ROWLAND FEILDING, 6TH CONNAUGHT RANGERS,
26 AUGUST 1918

We pushed on forward again this afternoon, and I am writing this from what was, on July 1, 1916, the German frontline: a place of desolation; a place where many of our countrymen have died, and where, during the great battle that started that day, I often was. So, it is familiar ground to me … The enemy is moving fast, and is miles away, and will take a bit of catching I fancy.

LT-COL ROWLAND FEILDING, 6TH CONNAUGHT RANGERS,
· 29 AUGUST 1918

On that 29th August, when Major O'Malley-Keyes assumed command, we knew that the campaign had taken a definite turn in our favour, but none of us expected the Boche to be so harried and battered that by November he would be suing for peace.

CAPT. G.H.F. NICHOLS, 18TH DIVISION, ROYAL FIELD ARTILLERY,
7 AUGUST 1918

For the Germans, the experience signalled the impending end of the war, and of defeat:

My dearest,

Thank you for your letter. I am not feeling well. For a frontline soldier retreat means a constant run for one's life. On 8 October we had to run; an infernal artillery fire, Tommies as far as the eyes could see, tanks and aircraft. Right now I am sitting with the baggage train, tasked to write after-action reports. We will have to hold this position for a few days, and when it continues I trust in my luck and my long legs. This is the way it is over here. We have spent the last 14 days at the front, brought forward in trucks which drove us to wherever we were needed, until reaching unconsciousness; mud caked and with a beard like Barbarossa. Then on 8 October at six in the morning the pounding started. Smoke, gas and high-explosive shells were bursting all around us and soon machine guns started thrashing us as well. Fighting and with a strange inner calm I waded through the infernal fire, death and perdition all around me. A shell splinter ripped open the upper part of my shoe and I wish it had taken the foot. Now our feet are sore from running and Tommy is following hard on our heels. There is some comfort in knowing that it cannot last long anymore. When it is over you will be my little bride. Then we will work and build ourselves a cosy nest, just like the swallows do. I know you have always been dreaming to own your own shop. I do not dream, but I often think of you. Too often I think about the loved ones at home and my thoughts turn melancholic. It is hard to dream when you are constantly facing the worst. I am almost the only survivor of our old company and who knows if I will make it through. There won't be a lot of letters from me in the near future; there is nothing I can do about it. A comrade will take this letter with him. I greet and kiss you ....

UNIDENTIFIED GERMAN OFFICER, 20 OCTOBER 1918

5

Wounds and Death/*Verwundung und Tod*

I am sorry to have to inform you that on 20 June 1916 your son had died
a hero's death for his Fatherland. He was shot through the head and died
instantly. He was buried in the field between the villages of Aubers and
Fromelles. In the name of the whole company I offer you my most heartfelt
condolences. With your son the company has lost a dear comrade and an
incredibly loyal and brave *Unteroffizier*. We have avenged him; a hundred
enemies will never return. You can console yourself with the knowledge
that he shed his blood for the greater glory of Kaiser and Fatherland.

HACKEN, OBERLEUTNANT, 22 JUNE 1915

Allow me to offer you my deepest sympathy in these sad moments when
you mourn the death of your son Killed in Action the 18th of this month.
He was killed by shellfire whilst trying to capture a trench held by the
Germans. I buried him myself and at present a large cross marks the spot
where he lies buried. He was a good lad and had Holy Communion and
Absolution ½ hr before we left for the line so he is in heaven above watching over you and praying for us all. Death is always sad, but when it is one
whom we dearly love that is snatched away, does it not seem unbearable.
But God is good. His Blessed Mother will console you in your grief for did
she not lose her son also and consequently she knows how a poor mother
feels in moments like these. I shall continue to pray for him and remember
him at the Altar. I shall also pray for you that God in his mercy may give
you the grace and the strength to bear up under this heavy cross. I return
I shall ask you to say a wee prayer for my lads and myself for we still have
some stiff fighting to go through.

JOHN J. DELANEY, RC CHAPLAIN, 2ND DUBLIN FUSILIERS

Casualties are an inevitable consequence of war, yet in the First World War,
the rate and scale is still breathtaking. It was relatively rare for a soldier

British and German wounded soldiers, 1916.

to survive the war completely unscathed, and wounding was a common experience.

Most soldiers feared wounding, and particularly the chance that they would be maimed, lose a limb, or suffer facial disfigurement. Other wounds were seen as fortunate, serious enough for the soldier to be taken out of the line – and perhaps be returned home – but not so serious that they would be life-changing. With artillery fire being so devastating, wounding from flying shell fragments, or from shrapnel bullets contained in the exploding shells, would be most feared. It is estimated that on average, some 60 per cent of all wounds were caused by artillery fire:

Thanks for your letter dated Sep 12, received last night. I received it during a very exciting night during which I lost 6 men of my platoon, through a bursting of a shell in the trench. I myself was only ten feet away and the shock of the explosion fair stunned me. It was indeed a lively night and one that makes you think our reality brings you face to face with life and death.

2Lt Arthur H. Lamb, 1st Lancashire Fusiliers, 16 September 1916

Death and wounding from shellfire could occur at any time. The opening bombardments during offensive actions were difficult enough, but all too often artillery could range on any suitable target, with inevitable results:

Three shells detonated nearby. I heard screams and felt a terrible, searing pain in my hip. My lower body got lifted into the air while my upper half and my head got smashed into the ground and I blacked out. When pain and cold woke me again I witnessed a scene which I will remember for the rest of my life. It was night-time and the snow on the ground and around the trees seemed to glow. All around me was utter silence. Me and seven other wounded comrades were lying in the snow covered forest. In pairs of two, each pair covered with a blanket. The comrade that shared my blanket, suddenly lay still, I could not hear him breathe anymore. The blanket, which should have covered us both had slipped from him. With difficulty I tried to pull it over his body again and by doing that my hand touched his breast which was sticky and wet, my hand was covered in blood. The comrade was not alive anymore. I could not hold back the tears and rested my head on the knees of his body. Weidlinger, a good-humoured and obliging man, always ready to help. During the advance he had at one time offered to carry my rifle. He took it and hung it over his shoulder with his own. He was a strong man, constantly chatting away and whistling cheerful tunes in the most impossible situations.

Now he was lying next to me, his body broken and his once cheerful eyes dead and expressionless. A few metres away a small fire was burning which was being fed with small branches and wood by a field medic who was sitting next to it. Still everything was silent and still. My wounded side, which had been provisionally dressed, was hurting terribly. The other side of my body, the side which was lying on the ground, was nearly frozen by the cold. I called over to the medic and when he came over I pointed out that Weidlinger had passed away and asked him for something to drink and a smoke. I had just lit the cigar the medic had given me when there was a shrill scream and I witnessed a most blood-curdling scene. Even when I write this, the thought of it still sends shivers down my spine. The fire had nearly gone out and the medic was busy to get it started again. A few metres behind him a wounded man had staggered to his feet. Screaming and moaning he was holding the bandage which he had torn from his blood covered face. The worst aspect though was that instead of eyes his face only had two bloody, gaping holes. A ricochet or a splinter had torn the comrade's eyes from his skull. Before the medic could react the poor man had stumbled into a tree. He had fallen down and had buried his ruined face in the snow, still wailing and shouting: 'What do you want from me! Kill me! Don't torture me anymore! It hurts!' It was such a horrible and distressing spectacle that it made my blood freeze. Pain, fever, hunger and thirst were overpowering. I was feeling terribly alone. What would become of me? How badly had I been wounded? I was thinking about my family home, my mother's loving hands and my brothers and sisters. It was all so very painful and I was losing the will to carry on. I can't find words to describe what I felt that night. It was like a terrible dream. The comrade who had lost his eyes died an agonising death in the morning. Shortly afterwards an ambulance cart arrived and carried us to safety …

ERICH KLEIN, INFANTERIE-REGIMENT NR. 179, 11 JANUARY 1915

The terrible sights and sounds that the average infantryman felt while in the trenches would remain with them for a long time. Not to mention the condition known as neurasthenia – the exhaustion of the central nervous system, a condition that would become known as 'shell shock', or *Nervenschock* to the Germans, from 1915 onwards:

My head seemed to be on fire on the inside and it felt like it was burning. For a long time there was dirt and dust in my eyes which made it difficult to keep my eyes open and I have spent a week in a state of half-consciousness. They have told me that I am suffering from a severe *Nervenschock* and my sense of hearing had suffered as well. I was taken to a Lazarett in Metz where they classed me to be fit for service and released me on the 18 October. Now my regiment is in a nice and quiet area near St. Mihiel. I don't know if I can continue to serve, I do not feel right anymore. In the ears I can constantly hear the sound of *Trommelfeuer*, even though there is hardly any firing here. In the nights I dream the most horrible things and when I wake up I feel dizzy. I will wait for a while and if there is no improvement I will have to see the doctor again.

OTTO KIEFER, INFANTERIE-REGIMENT NR. 87, 20 OCTOBER 1917

In addition to artillery wounds, there was the action of snipers, the spraying of machine gun bullets, the randomness of shots fired across no-man's-land,

and even, when the bullets were reaching the limit of their range. Spent bullets could still cause considerable damage. With men's heads all too often at the level of the trench top in poor trenches, dips in the parapet could put paid to the incautious or unwary as they passed by. The British army medical classification of gun shot wounds (GSW) identified at least twelve major categories of these, revealing their prevalence on the battlefield – up to 40 per cent of typical casualties:

> The bullets began to spray too close to my left ear, and laying my glasses on the parapet I was about to sit down for a few minutes' rest, and indeed had got half-way to the sitting position, when the machine-gun found its target. Recollections of what passed through my mind at that moment are very clear. I knew instantly what had happened. The blow might have come from a sledge-hammer, except that it seemed to carry with it an impression of speed. I saw for one instant in my mind's eye the battlefield at which I had been gazing through my glasses the whole day. Then the vision was hidden by a scarlet circle, and a voice said, 'Mr H. has got it.' Through the red mist of the scarlet circle I looked at my watch (the movement to do so had begun in my mind before I was hit); it was spattered with blood; the hands showed five minutes to four. The voice which had spoken before said, 'Mr H. is killed'.
>
> Lt Malcolm Vivian Hay, 1st Gordon Highlanders, 1914

Facing massed rifles and machine guns was a significant challenge:

> The previous days were generally quiet and passed without any noteworthy incidents. This was a lot different on 29 October. The 11th and 12th company of Regiment 224 had been assembled to advance 200 metres into the direction of the enemy and then to dig in there. Not an easy task, but we did not expect to take heavy casualties; but then our *Leutnant* started advancing further and the *Oberleutnant* followed suit. In front of us was an abandoned farmhouse and our patrols had informed us that there it was not held by the enemy. We were about 600 metres from it when the moonlight started breaking from the clouds and the inferno started. A murderous hail of machine gun and rifle bullets was directed at us, we had run into an ambush. Some of our men surged forward with a shout of Hurrah! But this time we were facing Englishmen and not the French, who usually ran away when the heard our battle cry. All around me men were going down, but those that were not hit surged forwards. I fell down a number of times

and had to drag myself up again. At one time I tried to dig myself in to find protection from the rain of bullets, but I was too exhausted to be successful. When we reached a turnip field in front of the farmhouse we could hear English commands, laughter and the sound of rifles being reloaded. The situation was desperate we were without reserves, but we were lucky as well as most of the English salvoes now went over our heads. The enemy obviously did not expect us to be that close to him. Everywhere around us in the turnip field I could hear the groaning and wailing of the wounded and the dying. Only two men and one NCO of my group had not been wounded. We found some cover behind a fence and soon there were shouts that 12th company was to retreat, so we got up and stumbled back through the turnips. When we arrived at our trench another man had got lost, we never saw him again. We prepared to defend ourselves against an English counter attack, but that never came and in the morning we were relieved by men of Regiment 222.

RES. EDUARD HÖBENER, RESERVE-INFANTERIE-REGIMENT NR. 224,
11 NOVEMBER 1914

Bayonet charges were still very much a feature of the battlefield, despite the seemingly antiquated nature of the weapon – though the actual percentage of wounds by the bayonet was small relative to the explosive power of artillery and the penetrating power of the bullets. Nevertheless, British and German troops were well versed in the use of the bayonet from their initial training. In the heat of battle the bayonet could be used mercilessly:

We walked towards the line, and were within a few yards of it when the company in front got there. It was a mad dash for them and straight in front of me three Germans were standing with their hands up. Two of our lads jumped in amongst them and one buried his bayonet in one German as he dropped into the trench. He pulled his bayonet and done another in, but whether he bayonetted him or shot him, I couldn't say, but the third German jumped over the trench and ran. He ran to my left and into our lines, so he would be picked up by the 'mopping up party'.

PTE JOHN H. BENN, LOYAL NORTH LANCASHIRE REGIMENT, JUNE 1917

The advent of gas warfare in 1915 brought with it the reality that men would suffer the horror of drowning in their own bodily fluids as the lungs struggled to cope with the corruption wrought by chlorine or phosgene gasses. Though respirators were available early on to counter gas attacks, fumbling with them in the confines of the trench, or being unprepared, meant that some men would inevitably inhale gasses that would lead to ill effects. Temporary blindness, bronchial complaints and skin burns from mustard gas were common amongst the men who had served 'in the trenches'. Rifleman Taffs was one such soldier:

> I suppose by this time you are feeling somewhat curious as to my experiences while being sick. Well there is nothing to be alarmed about, just the reverse. Last Sunday as I had extremely sore feet (I had my feet wringing wet for five days and then marched ten miles on them) I thought it would be a good thing to see the Dr. I felt pretty dicky at the time – I must have got a little gas in my lungs. They took my temperature and it was up so they plonked me in hospital, that is an advanced hospital. I slept that night on a stretcher and they transferred me next day to a hospital a little further back – a place that used to be a convent.
>
> RFN WILLIAM C. TAFFS, 1/16 QUEEN'S WESTMINSTER RIFLES,
> 31 DECEMBER 1915

> I was not in a gas attack actually – that took place the day before we went up, but there is always some of it hanging about and I thought I must have got some in me, especially as I had the same symptoms as a couple of chaps who went sick with me. They were classed as suffering from gas poisoning.
>
> RFN WILLIAM C. TAFFS, 1/16TH QUEEN'S WESTMINSTER RIFLES,
> 12 JANUARY 1916

Most men hoped that a 'light dose' of gas would not cause them any major trouble – though might equally get them home:

> This is just a line to say that I am being sent home by the next Red Cross boat. I shall wire when I get up to Town and shall let you know where they are sending me. Now you must not worry about me – the papers talk a lot about one's chest – it's all bunkum except in the case of very badly gassed men and I had a very light dose, just enough to get one back to England and to tell the truth I want a couple of weeks' rest badly as my nerves were getting rather dicky, it becomes a bit of a strain now and again but I'll be as fit as fiddle in a few weeks, I must be as I have a few scores to settle with the Huns.
>
> 2LT ARTHUR R. STANLEY-CLARKE, 1ST DORSETSHIRE REGIMENT,
> 7 MAY 1915

'Blighty wounds' were those that were sufficient to get men home to Britain, away from the trenches, and administered to by the nursing staff. This phenomenon was not limited to British soldiers, of course; the natural and inevitable equivalent for the average German was the *Heimatschuss*:

> Dear Mother, many thanks for your parcel with the cake! I even got an Easter present from Tommy, namely a wonderful wound with the name of 'penetrating shrapnel wound in the right lower leg'. As it looks we will have the pleasure to see each other in the *Heimat* soon!
> UFFZ. JOHANN HERRMAN, 14. KÖNIGLISCH BAYRISCHES RESERVE-
> INFANTERIE-REGIMENT, 11 APRIL 1916

> Dear colleagues, after a long period of silence I take the liberty to send my best wishes from inside our dear Fatherland. On the Somme, on 8 August, the English presented me with a headshot and thus with a ticket to Germany.
> WILHELM THUIR, RESERVE-INFANTERIE-REGIMENT NR. 79, MARCH 1917

Such gifts were a two-way thing:

> George Pike has been sent home, and is now in hospital in Dorset. In a letter he expresses the greatest optimism as to his condition generally. The piece of shrapnel, presented to him by the Boche, is still located somewhere among his ribs, and is, to use his own terms, behaving itself quite nicely.
> *KENTISH INDEPENDENT AND KENTISH MAIL*, 8 JUNE 1917

All too often, men would be envious of those who had received a 'nice' 'cushy' wound; others positively prayed for the chance of a 'Blighty' to get them home:

> Yesterday I was orderly so I had to go to the 'Dump' where our transport people drop our rations and bring them to various trenches. A couple to [sic] poor chaps got shot on this job yesterday and I expect the lucky beggars are on their way to Blighty now perhaps.
> RFN WILLIAM C. TAFFS, 1/16TH QUEEN'S WESTMINSTER RIFLES,
> FEBRUARY 1916

> Nan to tell you the truth I feel done up myself every time I go into the trenches it is a shame that I got to go because there is no rest at all the time we

are in. I only wish I could get out of it but it is not so easy as anyone thinks. Well my dear I suppose I shall have to stick it as long as I can, but I think that the War will come to an end this summer which I hope it will has we are driving them back, but not where we are. We had 35 casualties this last time we was in the trenches, we have just come out again for four days. I only wish I could get a nice Blitie but there is no such luck. I am glad that some one has some luck, but I suppose I must not grumble for what I have been through I should like to see the War through now I have been out so long.

PTE ROBERT W. PRICE, 10TH WELSH REGIMENT, 26 MARCH 1917

Oh! Yes! Mummy dear it is really beyond description out here just now and I am so weary of it all! We were up very close to the front line the night before last digging trenches and the old Hun shelled us steadily for hours! One of our officers got a lovely wound which will take him home to dear old England! Oh! Why can't I get one, mummy dear I am just longing and yearning to see you all again. It does seem hopeless!

2LT ARTHUR H. LAMB, 1ST LANCASHIRE FUSILIERS, 12 MAY 1917

Accidents and illness also contributed towards the flow of casualties from the battlefront; in fact, for the British Expeditionary Force non-battle casualties, including illness and accident, contributed over 60 per cent of all admissions to hospital on the Western Front. Trench fever, trench feet – there were many ailments that originated in the poor conditions of the wet fields of Flanders:

Just a line to let you know I am still here and do not know yet when I leave. My knee is still sore and I cannot walk properly on it yet, but I fear I shall be sent up the line as soon as poss. Anyway I have had a welcome rest and change from the awful mud of the line. The mud was responsible for my accident as I slipped crossing a trench and fell into it on my back and I was almost buried by the foul slime. It took about eight of the men to get me out. My goodness! It is utterly impossible to describe the conditions up there and I dread going back!

2LT ARTHUR H. LAMB, 1ST LANCASHIRE FUSILIERS, 3 NOVEMBER 1916

'Trench feet' was a condition that emerged as a problem early in the war for the British soldier:

It was at this time, the third week of November 1914, that the serious evil known as 'Trench Feet' first made its appearance in the army in France.

239

The cases were first labelled as 'Frost Bite', but as they were subsequently found to occur without any fall in temperature to freezing point, this term was evidently a misnomer.

The condition is caused by prolonged immersion in water, and certainly can occur when the temperature of the water is as high as 50°F. It is seldom caused unless the immersion is as long as 24 hours, but the cooler the water, the less time required to produce it ... Except in slight cases, the men affected are quite unfit for duty in trenches in cold weather. If men are sent back to duty too soon, a short exposure at once brings back all the trouble in an aggravated form ... The only *real* preventative is to arrange that men do not remain deep in mud or cold water for prolonged periods.

FIELD MARSHAL SIR JOHN FRENCH

Trench feet seems, however, to have been less of an issue in the German army; either a function of better sited trenches or the value of the high boots of the German uniform.

Ensuring that men survived their wounds was the responsibility of the army medical services. For the British, it was the Royal Army Medical Corps (RAMC), whose role it was to care for the wounded and to evacuate them efficiently from the front line to, it was hoped by most soldiers, 'Blighty'. The chain was a long one: first to the Regimental Aid Post (RAP), run by a RAMC doctor and a small number of orderlies that was set up close to the front line and adjacent to battalion headquarters (usually in dugouts or ruined buildings). Next in the chain was the Advanced Dressing Station (ADS), set up at the farthest frontwards limit of wheeled transport, and run by the RAMC Field Ambulance, with three such units of men attached to an infantry division. The wounded would be transported from RAP to ADS by a variety of means: on foot, by cart, on a stretcher – the latter with a series of relay posts where there was a considerable distance between the two. Men could then expect to be transported down the line to Main Dressing Stations (MDS), beyond the range of medium artillery fire, Casualty Clearing Stations (CCS), set up beyond the artillery zone, and finally, still within the theatre of operations, General and Stationary Hospitals. From here, Tommy would hope to receive his 'ticket' – a label that marked him for transportation on hospital ships bound for home, 'Blighty'. Though it is estimated that almost 60 per cent of all wounded cases returned to their original theatre of war after treatment.

The German system was, to all intents and purposes, similar to the British. If a man was wounded, and picked up from the battlefield, he was taken to – or made his way to – the first aid posts of the regiment or company (*Truppenverbandplätze*), or directly to the larger divisional first aid posts (*Hauptverbandplätze*). Here the personnel of the divisional *Sanitäts-Kompanie* sorted the walking wounded from the more serious casualties. The walking wounded were sent to the *Leichtkranken-Sammelstelle* and from there to the *Leichtkranken-Abteilung* in the *Etappe*, behind the front lines. The severely wounded were taken to the *Feldlazarette*, where they were sorted into transportable and non-transportable wounded – men who would be likely to suffer if moved:

> On 17 October I was severely wounded and I am now in a *Feldlazarett*. I have a bullet lodged in my neck, so far they are not entirely sure what consequences that will have, but it seems I was lucky. Now that I am fit for transport I will be on the next hospital train to Germany. Writing this is very exhausting for me as I can hardly lift the arm.
>
> UNTEROFFIZIER REINER

Those men who could be moved were then taken to railheads by the *Krankentransport-Abteilungen*, where they were sent by *Lazarettzug* to *Reservelazarette* in Germany. Those who couldn't be moved were treated in field hospitals or *Feldlazarette*. Due to the fact that these field hospitals were required to follow their parent divisions as they moved on the front, the care of their wounded was transferred to the military hospitals (*Kriegslazarette*). The main role of doctors in both hospitals was to ensure quick recovery of the badly wounded soldiers under their care, before they could be transferred to much more comfortable *Reservelazarette* in the German territory. The *Kriegslazarette* functioned as ordinary hospitals in the rear areas, and nursed those soldiers who, under the conditions of mobile warfare, would otherwise be sent to *Reservelazarette* in the Fatherland.

Regimental stretcher-bearers or *Krankenträger* were unarmed infantrymen who worked to gather the wounded on the battlefield and ensure that they were processed through the system. In most cases, these men took their responsibilities seriously – and put men before enmity:

> Then I went over to the right wing of my company. A few days ago the men there noticed a wounded Tommy who was lying inside the wire entanglement and they told me they wanted to help him. First I wanted to deny them this wish as he was lying as close to the English trenches as he was to ours. But then I remembered the Gospel of Luke: 'Of these men,

German prisoners acting as stretcher-bearers.

who do you think was a neighbour to the man who fell into the hands of the bandits?' We were the neighbours of this man. So out they went putting their lives into danger but they did not find him as he was covering himself with his tarpaulin and pretended to be dead. A few hours ago we spotted him again when he was waving to his comrades in the English trenches. It was then when three of my men volunteered to get him. Very carefully, they brought him in just like one carries a sick child. During the whole recovery operation the English held their fire. For nearly seven days this poor chap had been lying in no-man's-land. He was so afraid of us 'Barbarians' that he had not dared to cry for help. Now our regiments' doctors will take care of his wounds which had already turned gangrenous. German Barbarians!

Lt Diekmann, Reserve-Infanterie-Regiment Nr. 55

He offered me a drink from his water-bottle, and pointed to the Red Cross on his arm. I can never hope to convey to any one what a relief it was to see the cross even on the arm of an enemy. The man asked me if I could walk, tried to lift me up, and when he saw I was paralysed said he would go for a stretcher. 'You will go away and leave me here,' I said. 'I am of the Red Cross,' he replied; 'you are therefore my *Kamerad* and I will never leave you.' ... '*Kamerad, Kamerad,* I will come back; never fear, I will come back.'

Lt Malcolm Vivian Hay, 1st Gordon Highlanders, 1914

Unofficial truces to recover the wounded were also a feature of the trench war:

Our dead and many of the wounded still lay out in No Man's Land, and when the fog lifted the German trench became clearly visible. As I stood in the middle of the fire-trench a man came running to me and reported that the enemy had allowed what he called 'an armistice', for the purpose of collecting the wounded who were lying in front of the right extremity of the section.

I hurried along the trench and found that this was literally true. Already parties of men were out dressing the wounded and carrying them back to our line. One of my officers and a German were bending together over a wounded man alongside the enemy wire. The Germans, in considerable numbers, were lolling over and even sitting upon their parapet, watching the proceedings. My own men were doing the same. As the stretcher-bearers started to move the dead the enemy called out to 'leave the dead alone', but no notice was taken of this.

I asked how this extraordinary state of affairs had originated. I was told that the Germans had called out in English, 'send out your stretch-ermen', and that a number of volunteers – stretcher-bearers, real and self-constituted (the latter of course stretcher-less) – had immediately climbed over the parapet.

Lt-Col Rowland Feilding, 6th Connaught Rangers,
20 February 1917

Stretcher-bearers and medical men had to deal with many of the most hor-rific sights the modern battlefield could provide:

Today I had to treat a man with whom I used to share everything, every cigar and every bottle of beer. He got carried to me, his lower jaw had been torn off completely.

ASSISTENZARZT WERNER HEGEMANN

Those men lucky enough to survive wounding on the battlefield could expect to have worked their way through the system to the hospital, and a distinct break from the trials of front-line life:

I am now in a military hospital. I have been wounded. Fist-sized hole in my left lower arm, broken bone, very painful. Nevertheless I can now enjoy some months of well-deserved rest from nine months of constant fighting. Hopefully this terrible war will be over by then.

EDUARD FUNCK, GERMAN SOLDIER, 11 APRIL 1915

This could be either at a base hospital behind the lines in the *Etappe*, or if they were lucky, at home. Here they were met by medical corps orderlies, mostly men not fit enough to go to 'the front'. Forty-year-old medical orderly Ward Muir of the 3rd London General Hospital was typical:

We orderlies meet each convoy at the front door of the hospital. The walking wounded cases are the first to arrive – men who are either not ill enough, or not badly enough wounded, to need to be put on stretchers in ambulances. They come from the station in motor-cars supplied by that indefatigable body, the London ambulance Column. The walking-case alights from his car, is conducted into the receiving hall, and ten minutes later is in the bathroom.

The walking cases are still splashing and dressing in the bathroom when the ambulances with the cot-cases begin to appear. Now is the orderlies' busy time. Each stretcher must be quickly but gently removed from the ambulance and carried into the receiving hall. Four orderlies haul the stretcher from its shelf in the ambulance; two orderlies then take its handles and carry it indoors. The Medical Officer bends over the patient, glances at the label which is attached to him, and assigns him to a ward.

LCPL WARD MUIR, ROYAL ARMY MEDICAL CORPS

Life in hospital was predictably regimented:

In hospital. Get up at 7.30 and wash (using the towel I came out with, which has never been washed yet). Breakfast at 8 (Bread and bacon and

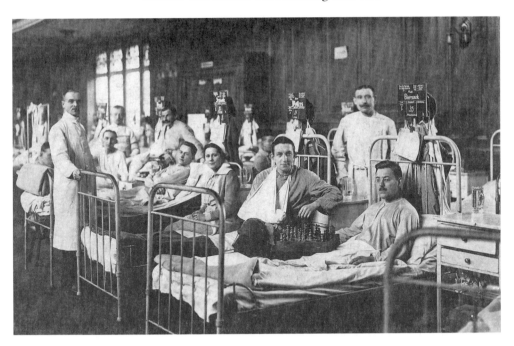

German military hospital in France. Chalk boards display information on the patients.

British military hospital at home; many large private houses and public buildings were used across the length of Britain.

tea). Shave and clean my boots. Then the Dr comes round about 11. Dinner at 12. (meat, gravy, potatoes, bread, sago). Today have been ordered to take exercise which consists of an hour's walk round at 2.30. Tea at 4 – (bread and jam and tea). Supper at 6.30 (soup and bread, or cheese and bread and hot rum). Then we turn in about 9. The intervals I occupy by reading etc. It's a bit of an existence.

Rfn William C. Taffs, 1/16th Queen's Westminster Rifles,

5 January 1916

Missing

In the aftermath of battle, roll-calls would be taken in order to get some idea of the number of casualties: those men who were killed in action, had died of their wounds, or were 'missing' – *vermisst*:

> We assembled behind a wooden barn. Everyone looked worn out and exhausted, our uniforms were torn and most of us had lost equipment, a bayonet, a spade or cartridges. Physically we were all right, we all had received a ration of fat ham and bread when we had returned to the trench and we were well fed and not hungry. We had lost 30 men dead, 35 wounded and 12 men missing. 'Missing' meant they were most probably dead as well. I do not suppose the English took a lot of prisoners.

Eduard Höbener, Reserve-Infanterie-Regiment Nr. 224,

11 November 1914

Many families would spend years during and after the war searching for their loved ones, tracing their every movement, contacting their colleagues:

> As regards men missing, I also have had letters from Last's and Withall's people. Apparently they called at Bunhill Row, failed to obtain any definite information, and were only able to secure our addresses with a view to further enquiries. Of course I knew nothing definite and could only write in an unwontedly optimistic key to the effect that they might be wounded and unreported or prisoners, wounded or otherwise. Personally I fear there's no chance of their having survived.
>
> The other day I heard from Ongley, who gives Lash's name in a list of the killed. I forwarded the letters home and Dad called on Lash's people and wrote to the others who live only a mile or so from home. He has put

the matter in the hands of the Y.M.C.A., which undertakes such enquiries through their French huts, but 'pending their advices' he has not told Lash's people what I fear is the truth. Withall's name Ongley did not mention, but of course you remember him.

The other day I had a letter from a Mr Skinner, whose sons were in 13 Platoon,. Do you remember the poor wretch who had a pick driven into his hand at Ridgwood? (Falsetto voice) That was one of the brothers – not the one missing. To my insanely cheerful reply succeeded another letter clutching at straws, and I have promised to write again to the Battn asking for particulars. But cui bono?

As far as I can remember Ongley's list ran as follows – killed Last and Barney. Wounded Jenner, Stevens, Scarfe, Blake, King and Snelgrove. Missing Maham, Ponting, Woolley and Donaldson. Poor old Last! We used to squabble more with him perhaps than anyone, but you couldn't live with him for twelve months without knowing he had a heart of gold. Certainly he was eccentric but so are most of us. If he and Roberts had known? Barney as well; it turns me sick to think of it, though in his case I never had much hope. All I can say is that if what I know you believe is true, they deserve and their people deserve to earn joy in proportion to sorrows here I <u>know</u> they did not deserve.

Letter to Rfn S. A. Moorat, 1/5th City of London Rifles,

23 November 1916

But missing could mean one of many things – soldiers whose bodies had been literally torn apart by shell explosion, or who had been lost in no-man's-land, wounded and dead in a shell hole. Or it could simply be that soldiers were unidentifiable, or who had no means of identifying them. The German army was the first to issue identity discs to assist with the identification of dead or unconscious soldiers on the battlefield in 1870 – most other nations followed. The absence of an identifying mark meant that soldiers would be buried as 'unknown':

We were all working in our shirtsleeves. One shell claimed three victims in our platoon, two slight and the other badly wounded. The latter was carried away on a stretcher and not till after they had taken him away, did we remember about his tunic with pay-book in pocket. We often wondered what became of him, because he was well liked in the platoon, but we never heard anything about him. Months after when I was in hospital a St Johns Ambulance man came to my bed, asked Batt., Regiment and Coy.

Then he looked in a book, and asked if I knew the chap I have referred to, and if I knew what became of him, as he was posted as 'missing'. I told him what I knew so we surmised that he had died from his wounds at the advanced dressing station, with nothing on his person to identify him, and so be buried as unknown.

PTE JOHN H. BENN, LOYAL NORTH LANCASHIRE REGIMENT, JUNE 1917

Men captured in battle would also be counted as missing, until the military authorities of both sides could communicate the fact to each other through the Red Cross in Geneva, or simply through the expedient of the *Kriegsgefangener* himself sending a notification from a prisoner-of-war camp:

Kriegsgefangenenlager Langensalza

Dear Molly

I was wounded and taken prisoner and I expect I will be alright in about two months my leg is broken. Dear wife I want you to send word around by Nellie to my mother and tell her my address as I won't to be able to write to her as I am only allowed 2 letters a month so you will have to tell her. I can also send 4 PC a month. I hope this won't upset your health as I will be quite safe with God's help. You cannot send any parcels here but if you tell my mother she can send a postal order it will be handy. I will say Goodbye and God Bless yourself Nellie and May and may he keep you safe till I return.

PTE JACK MURPHY, 7TH ROYAL INNISKILLING FUSILIERS, 23 AUGUST 1917

Prisoners were often taken in trench raids, which were particularly designed to create havoc and take men who would be useful in providing information on the opposing troops. The largest were preceded by lightning artillery barrages. They were brutal affairs:

The operation was to be conducted by the 1. Battalion 236, in a manner that each of the four companies was to send out thirty volunteers. After an artillery preparation they were to enter the enemy positions, destroy them and to return to our lines. The trenches were about 400 metres away. We, the thirty volunteers from our company received an exact description of the section we were tasked to take. To do it we were to advance in two waves, about 1 minute apart from each other. On the 19th at 6pm our artillery of all calibres started to sing its iron song, which within two

Scots soldiers captured on the Somme in 1916.

hours had pounded the enemy trench and the five-metre-wide barbed wire entanglement in front of it to pieces.

At 8:15 in the evening the first wave, which included my good self, advanced. Each man was armed with a rifle, five hand grenades and a short dagger (which had been issued to us shortly before). Inside the shot-up trench there were many dead Englishmen lying beside one another, destroyed dugouts with dead or severely wounded Englishmen inside. From one of the dugouts that had remained intact there suddenly came six English soldiers, four of them instantly fell down on their knees pleading and wailing 'German gut, German gut'. The other two tried to get away, but we chased them down and converted them with our rifle butts … we now left the trench behind us to reconnoitre the pile of rubble that remained of Wieltje. Even though they were outnumbering us we could see the English there taking to their heels. In a buried cellar there were about thirty English who had failed to notice our arrival in time and when they finally did they threw out a hand grenade which mortally wounded an Unteroffizier standing nearby. You can imagine that the six of us could not contain our anger, so we approached the cellar and each of us chucked two hand grenades inside. Dear Frieda, you cannot imagine the scene. I only took a quick glance, but there were arms, legs and heads scattered around like cabbages and turnips. Four Englishmen survived and when they crawled out we were just about to stab their lights out, when our *Leutnant* prevented it.

Gefr. Ignaz Hautumm, Reserve-Infanterie-Regiment Nr. 236,
St Julien, 21 April 1916

Often, prisoners were captured when their lines were overrun, or when suddenly faced with their enemy:

Capt. Bell our officer in command seemed to think there was some danger near and I was one of a number of scouts that was sent out to scour the woods to see if we could find out anything but we were unsuccessful. At any rate we left there in the afternoon and drove as far as the cross roads and then for some reason or other we circled round and came back to pull in for another night but it was not to be, for as the captain's car turned the corner he drove into a party of about 80 Uhlans, the other lorries following, who simply blazed away at us. They captured Capt. Bell and Lt. Humphreys who they made prisoners of and a poor motorcyclist they purposely put through it. We also had to abandon a couple of lorries of ammunition but the remainder we managed to get to safety and the men lay in wait for an attack until nearly midnight but they did not come on. There turned out to be about 500 of them including cavalry and artillery and I'm afraid we should have stood a very poor chance if they had done so.

Pte Henry W. Talbot, Army Service Corps (Motor Transport),
September 1914

After I heard the news that the enemy occupying Chateau Wieltje intended to surrender I, accompanied by the regiment's adjutant, betook myself to the frontline where we could observe the English standing in the open, waving to us. Taking Leutnant Lange with me we crossed the bridge and entered the Chateau, where Langer started negotiating with the English. As it seemed without coming to a mutual agreement. We had just returned to our trench when suddenly 60 Englishmen, including three officers, followed us to be taken prisoner. Later we got over again and brought one of their machine guns over.

Oberstleutnant Grimm, Reserve-Infanterie-Regiment Nr. 236

Just behind the front line of German trenches was a house from which we took a number of prisoners … The troops we were fighting there were on the whole very young, and they had new clothing and equipment, and told us that they had left Germany for what they thought would be manoeuvres in Belgium, and did not expect seeing the firing line for some months. I myself really thought the war was over that day, as Germans surrendered from all directions and we overran their trenches everywhere.

PTE FREDERICK BOLWELL, LOYAL NORTH LANCASHIRE REGIMENT, 1914

As luck would have it, I jumped into a part where there wasn't a German, but within a few minutes I saw plenty. I couldn't say for sure how many they numbered, but I estimated about 30, and they came running up to the trench on my left. It is a good job they were in a trench and a narrow one at that – they could only come one at a time. They were unarmed, had their hands up and were shouting 'Kamerad'. I was standing with rifle and bayonet, and I motioned them back over the trench with it.

PTE JOHN H. BENN, LOYAL NORTH LANCASHIRE REGIMENT, JUNE 1917

In some cases, men would give themselves up to escape the conditions of battle, and were curious as to how they might be treated in captivity:

On the morning after our regiment's last assault on the Chateau we observed, from inside our new trench, Englishmen coming out of their trenches and waving to us. They obviously wanted to communicate with us. As I knew the English language my comrades tried to make me go over to them to start negotiations. I was not overly excited about that idea. When I asked them what would happen if the enemy would not let me return to our trenches, Leutnant Ricken, with the consent of my comrades, gave me his promise 'In that case we will attack and get you out of there'. So I removed my belt with the bayonet climbed out of the trench and, curious about how this adventure would end, walked across no-man's-land towards the English lines.

I calmed down when the English received me in a friendly manner, but decided to open the conversation standing well in front of the enemy trench, so as to allow our side to observe the whole affair from their position. I soon realised that these men had lost any will to fight. The only things they were interested in was how they would be treated in German captivity and if they would get sufficient food and drink. After I had given them satisfactory answers they told me that they would come over to us later. After that I returned, undisturbed, to my company.

UFFZ. BRÜCKEN, RESERVE-INFANTERIE-REGIMENT NR. 236

Surrendering was a tricky situation, however; in some cases, prisoners were killed where there was confusion, or where situations got out of hand:

> A few miles from here 14 prisoners were captured and disarmed, a guard being placed over them one of the prisoners had a watch on that the L. Corporal of the guard tried to take from him, in doing so the German hit him one under the chin and sent him to the ground and seized his rifle and killed him and also a private that came to his rescue. They were buried here yesterday. The 14 prisoners were all shot.
>
> PTE HENRY W. TALBOT, ARMY SERVICE CORPS (MOTOR TRANSPORT), 1914

And even in prisoner-of-war camps, death was not too far away – from wounds, overwork, or illness:

Kriegsgefangenenlager Langensalza

Dear Mrs Murphy

It is with deepest regret that I write to inform you of the death of your husband Pte J. Murphy 7th R. Inn. Fusiliers, who passed away on the 18th inst; he had been very ill for the last month with dysentery he also had a very bad wound which of course made him very weak.

Corpl Ross and myself were with him when he died, and it was his wish that I should write to you, he asked me to wish you and his dear children goodbye. I have given his personal effects to Corpl Ross who will take care of them until he comes home. Corporal Ross and I send you our united sympathies to you and your family.

CPL R. DIBBEN, 1ST HAMPSHIRE REGIMENT, 20 DECEMBER 1917

Death

Most men feared death, which could come in an instant:

> At around 7pm a direct hit kills 14 comrades inside the command post, many of them from our regiment. Killed in an eye-blink, there is not even a whimper anymore. All are covered with a thick layer of dust. Something hit me in the back and I was lucky that it was only a piece of brick. The

Dead Scotsmen on the field of battle.

Unteroffizier of our signal squad turns raving mad. It is so bad that we have to tie him down. He slashes around himself and foams at the mouth.

Ltn. Friedrich Kleine, Infanterie-Regiment Nr. 459

The patriotism of the youth of this country has received another demonstration in the case of Private Archibald Laird Gardiner of Eltham … whose death in action on November 5th at the age of 17 years and 4 months was briefly recorded in our last issue. It was his chum's sad duty to convey the sad news of their son's death to his parents, and something of his own grief comes out in the remark, 'I miss him more than you at the time, being with him everyday'. He wrote:

'I am writing this in the trenches. I have just come back from seeing poor old Archie. He was killed by a sniper, this morning at about 10.30 am. He was shot just above the right eye with an explosive bullet, and death was instantaneous. I am sorry there is no mistake about it, but I went and saw him myself.'

Archie Gardner was a true British boy, loving manly games, and not averse to mischief, which distracted nothing from his popularity. He always 'played the game', and he played it to the end.

ELTHAM AND DISTRICT TIMES, 19 NOVEMBER 1915

Receiving an official notification from the military authorities was dreaded by all at home during the war; more often than not it would signify that a loved one had been killed, wounded or taken prisoner. For British families this could be in the form of an official pro forma, 'Army Form B. 104–82', pre-printed with gaps left for the insertion of the unfortunate soldier's name. William Healy was to receive the bald statement of his son's death on the Somme in this manner:

27 September 1916

Sir, It is my painful duty to inform you that a report has this day been received from the War Office notifying the death of (No.) 27221 (Rank) Private (Name) James Healy (Regiment) 8th Bn Royal Dublin Fusiliers which occurred while serving with the 'Expdy Force France' on the 6th day of September 1916, and I am to express to you the sympathy and regret of the Army Council at your loss. The cause of death was Killed in Action.

If any articles of private property left by the deceased are found, they will be forwarded to this office, but some time will probably elapse before their receipt, and when received they cannot be disposed of until authority is received from the War Office.

Application regarding the disposal of any such personal effects, or of any amount that may eventually be found to be due to the late soldier's estate, should be addressed to 'The Secretary, War Office, London SW.,' and marked outside 'Effects.'

I am, Sir, Your obedient Servant

OFFICER IN CHARGE OF RECORDS

In other households, the first inklings of a casualty might be a letter returned home with the brutal and stark message 'Killed in Action' written or stamped as a cachet on its unopened cover; in other cases, letters would be written from the adjutant or chaplain to soften the blow. More often than not these letters would profess that the soldier in question had not suffered, and had died instantly; the truth might be harder to bear. Former miner, Pte Robert Price, had playfully suggested in a letter to his wife that she find 'another boy' if he was 'popped off'. Pte Price was to be killed by shellfire, after so much endurance and suffering:

If I happen to get popped off you must go in and get another boy, but I hope it will be long time yet as I have hardly known you yet eh? Only when you grumble at me but I could do with a pint of beer now, can I go and have one? I won't be long, lend us a tanner there's a dear.

PTE ROBERT W. PRICE, 10TH WELSH REGIMENT, 1916

Dear Mrs Price

I received your letter this evening and you really have no need to apologise for troubling me – because it is no trouble at all. The least I can do is to endeavour to the best of my power to lighten if possible the heavy burden of sorrow which the sad news of your dear husband's death must have thrown on your shoulders.

There was rather a heavy bombardment taking place on the morning of the 30th of March, when your husband and some others were caught by a bursting shell – your husband was not killed outright, but lingered on till he reached the Advanced Dressing Station which was close to the line. He received every possible attention from the doctors – but in spite of all their efforts his wounds were very serious and very shortly afterwards he passed peacefully away.

That same day he was buried at Bard Cottage Cemetery not far from Ypres near the spot he fell. I conducted the service and there he lies in his last resting place with those who died with him. It may be some consolation to you, not now of course but in the future when time has helped to heal the wound – to know that your husband was a good soldier and his loss is deeply felt by Officers and men of the Battalion.

He died also a soldier's death at the altar of duty. Greater love hath no man than that the man should give his life for another. Having been with the battalion through all its hard times, I can assure you we all feel deeply the loss of our brave comrades amongst whom your husband figures prominently. Later on if you would care to have the Photo of the grave – our Pioneers are now at work making the cross – on application to the G.R.U. and E [Graves Registration Unit and Enquiries]

Winchester House, War Office – you will be supplied with one at the earliest convenience.

Again with profoundest sympathy

R. O. LLOYD, APRIL 1917

Writing such letters was the painful duty of all officers, whatever their nationality, who had to find the words to express their sympathy to those families whose loved ones had fallen at the front:

> I have the sad duty to inform you that your husband has fallen. On the 25th of this month he was trying to make his way to the company with the field kitchen when he was hit by a shell splinter. His funeral was conducted by the divisional chaplain on the 26th at 2pm on the military cemetery near Laffaux. Your husband's estate will be sent to you.
>
> With its *Kompaniefeldwebel* the company has lost a shining example of a German soldier and a dear person, whose memory the company will honour. The whole company, myself included, painfully regrets the loss of their *Feldwebel*. Please accept the expression of our deepest sympathy. May the Lord ease the pain that you bear. May he grant you the strength needed to get through this moment in your life. Feel free to get in touch with me should you require any more information.
>
> GLAAB, LEUTNANT AND KOMPANIEFÜHRER, IN THE FIELD, 27 AUGUST 1918

In other cases, hospitals responded to the requests for information about fallen soldiers, putting additional burden on the staff:

> Please excuse my delayed answer. I have only just received your letter. About the deceased Kanonier Arndt I can tell you the following things. When he was brought to the field hospital on 24 November his condition was already so bad that it was clear that he would not survive. The splinter that had hit him a day before had inflicted a massive trauma of bone and tissue of his left and right thigh, he had lost a lot of blood and was suffering from blood poisoning, which is a common occurrence with splinter injuries. Even though the deceased was conscious when he was brought in, he did not speak a word about his family, neither did he ask for anything. It was quite clear that he did not believe that he would succumb to his wound and it would have been cruel to make him believe otherwise. He did not have to suffer pain. He died a hero's death on 22 November 1914. The repatriation of his body to Wesel will

British and Canadian soldiers at a military funeral.

not be possible. Please accept my condolences and the expression of our deepest sympathy.

UNIDENTIFIED GERMAN MEDICAL ORDERLY, 21 JANUARY 1915

Men who died in France and Flanders were buried as close to the point of their death as possible; this meant that in the battlezone, the graves of the soldiers of both countries were all too evident:

There are no towns anywhere near, all open country plough fields, they are sowing their wheat now. The women do the farm work here and plough they work like horses out here as there are not many men as they are all fighting. We have been very lucky, yet we have lost eleven men so they won't see home again. There are hundreds of English graves here, where the poor Tommy has been buried and there are hundreds they can't get to, laying between the two firing lines.

PTE ROBERT W. PRICE, 10TH WELSH REGIMENT, OCTOBER 1916

Everywhere you look you can see graves, cemeteries and single graves in the fields.

PAUL KLEIN, GERMAN SOLDIER IN BELGIUM, 4 SEPTEMBER 1915

Burials were carried out by chaplains, with as much honour as could be countenanced close to the front line. Behind the lines, near hospitals, burials were commonplace – with friend and foe buried in close proximity in death:

There was another regular duty to attend to. The final resting places of the fallen heroes no matter if they were Germans, Englishmen, Canadians or Frenchmen, individual or mass-graves had to be cared for, cleaned and decorated in a dignified manner.

RIR236, REGIMENTAL HISTORY

With so many men killed, repatriation was not possible – particularly as it would have meant considerable disruption to the supply chain, and would also mean that the more well-to-do families would be in more of a position to bring their loved ones home than poorer ones. Fallen German soldiers were not usually repatriated into the *Heimat*, but buried in one of the countless cemeteries at and behind the front:

No repatriation of the bodies of the fallen. At the moment the military administration is receiving countless applications for the repatriation of the bodies of fallen warriors to the *Heimat*. The permission to do so cannot be granted. It is due to the nature of this current war that trains, especially those in the theatre of operations, have to be employed to transport the wounded, prisoners and goods. In true patriotic spirit the next of kin of our fallen warriors will understand that measure even if it means that their wish cannot be fulfilled.

DEUTSCHE REICHS-ZEITUNG, 28 AUGUST 1914

Those who have been killed for their Fatherland find their most honourable resting place in a soldier's grave. Where they fought and where they fell, amidst their comrades, whose peace must not be disturbed for the sake of one single individual. Comrades have created harmonic places on many burial grounds, which have to be retained for the future.

PROCLAMATION OF THE *KRIEGSMINISTERIUM*, 30 JANUARY 1915

Burial of German soldiers by the British army.

The same concept was enshrined in the principles of the Imperial War Graves Commission, embodied in 1917 by Royal Charter to look after the war graves of the Empire. Permanent British war graves in France had been granted by law on 29 December 1915, each one registered under the Graves Registration Units of individual armies. For the Germans, there was the *Kriegsgräberfürsorge der Deutschen Heeresverwaltung* (Department for War Graves in the Ministry of War), which carried the responsibility for the marking and preservation of war graves. Like the British system, each grave was accounted for by a

'*Ich hatt' einen Kameraden*' German soldiers mourning a comrade.

Grave Registration section, or *Gräberaufnahmestelle*. Unlike the British graves, however, the German ones were on enemy territory. This would have impli-cations in post-war France. Burial sites ranged in size from single graves to elaborate comrades' graves with many thousands of burials. Added to this there were thousands of individual or group burial plots in fields, woods, ditches, canal banks and alongside roads:

> Today we have buried my best friend. For eight days we had been praying for his recovery when he suddenly got weaker and died bravely. Today on All Hallow's Day, the day on which we remember all those that we will one day meet again in heaven, we buried him. Tomorrow, on All Souls Day, we will again commemorate our beloved friend and comrade. If we fight as hard and die as bravely as he did we will see him again in heaven. He was solemnly buried. The service was held by the divisional chaplain in the beautiful village church which has lost its spire from English artillery fire. 200 soldiers went to celebrate Holy Communion which we dedicated to our fallen comrade. After a simple soldier's breakfast we marched to the cemetery. A simple coffin adorned with flowers enclosed the mortal remains of our good comrade. Now he rests peacefully in the beautiful earth of Flanders.
>
> UNIDENTIFIED GERMAN SOLDIER, WESTROOSEBEKE, 30 OCTOBER 1914

6

Blighty/*Die Heimat*

I can see by the papers that peace is mentioned now in lots of ways but they will have to come to our terms and I think they will come to that as they are starving in Germany.

PTE ROBERT W. PRICE, 10TH WELSH REGIMENT, 1916

I am fine so far, but I hope there will be peace soon. When our enemies finally realise that they can't defeat Germany in the field they will have to conclude an honourable peace.

CHRISTIAN KAUFMANN, GERMAN SOLDIER, 19 NOVEMBER 1917

The war officially ended with the Armistice of 11 November 1918, after a succession of hammer blows that had fallen on the German army since the opening of the Battle of Amiens on 8 August 1918 – the beginning of 100 days of continuous advance. During this advance, the Allied armies pushed the Germans back to a line that was broadly similar to the one where it had first met the British 'Old Contemptibles', four years before. With the Armistice agreed, the war on the Western Front was to end abruptly, and the British Fourth and Second Armies commenced their advance into Germany as an occupying power on 17 November. The news of the end of the war was received in many ways – for the British soldiers at least, its occurrence was almost a matter of fact: 'Armistice signed with Germany' was the only entry on this fateful day in the diary of Pte Fred Walker, King's Own Yorkshire Light Infantry. It was a feeling of relief, an exhalation of a long breath.

Nevertheless, the British prepared for offensive action against the Germans on 11 November, just in case:

The men were in their usual good spirits. Many discussed the situation, some arguing that the Boches were bluffing. But optimism and pessimism centred more on the question whether or no a sequence of four rumless days would be broken. We could not realise that the War was coming to an end. Every now and then officers and signallers would furtively glimpse at their watches. At last the hands pointed to the hour, and I called out to the Company the words: 'Eleven o'clock!' Thus the most dramatic moment passed, as we marched on in silence.

CAPT. F.C. HITCHCOCK, LEINSTER REGIMENT, 1918

Yesterday, we were to have pushed on and captured another town – Ath – which would have been a bloodless victory, since the enemy was retreating so fast that it was difficult to keep pace with him. A screen of cavalry was to have advanced in front of us, and this in itself would have been a novel experience, being the first time, I imagine, since 1914 … However, a stop was put to the proceedings by the signing of the Armistice, which took place in the morning. As we marched away the band played a tune well known to the men, who are accustomed to accompany it with the following words:

> When this ruddy war is over,
> Oh! How happy I shall be!

LT-COL ROWLAND FEILDING, 6TH CONNAUGHT RANGERS,
12 NOVEMBER 1918

On this fateful day, Pte George Lister of the Royal Army Medical Corps saw fit to break his routine of sending postcards simply depicting the 'Flowers of France' for the collection of his wife and son. On 11 November, he sent two cards that revealed his relief that it was all over, that he could once more rejoin 'Mum and Kiddie':

> All the very best wishes and hopes that today brings us closer together soon. From Dad to Kiddie, Belgium 11/11/18

> Here's hoping that your path will be strewn with the flowers on t'other side. From Dad to Mum, Belgium 11/11/18

PTE GEORGE LISTER, RAMC, 11 NOVEMBER 1918

For the German army that had fought long and hard on the Western Front, and had come so close to ending the war in 1918 with the hope of an honourable negotiated peace, the end came with mixed feelings:

What will the people do when they return to their homes in peacetime? They will throw themselves on the ground and they will cry. They will find that nothing, nothing at all, remains. To rebuild on the same spot will be impossible, everything is blocked by rubble and debris which will be impossible to remove. These villages, once prosperous and thriving are now dead and will remain so forever. How foolish are we people to wage such wars that destroy everything and absolutely everything

HAUPTMANN GOTTFRIED ESSER, INFANTERIE-REGIMENT NR. 53, 1918

The World War is over! No one seems to be able to rejoice about it. Even the thought that now one might be able to see the *Heimat* again has no calming effect. The Armistice is in effect, but at what cost ...

The terms of the Armistice! Shocking, humiliating, terribly sad! For this I have spent four years of my life fighting in this most horrible of wars! All those irreplaceable losses, all the sacrifices we made! The enemy occupying the Rhine, Cologne, Coblenz, Mainz ... it makes me want to put a bullet through my head.

OBERLTN. MAILLARD, INFANTERIE-REGIMENT NR. 51,
11 NOVEMBER 1918

After the Armistice, the men of the German army straggled home from the front to face tremendous uncertainty. Its terms left no doubt that there was a price to be paid. With the abdication of the Kaiser and the collapse of the Hohenzollern monarchy, the German Empire had ceased to exist. The nation was now a republic, one that eventually would have a constitution that made it one of the most liberal democracies in history. Equality for all Germans; the political power would be only in the hands of the nation, a cabinet and chancellor elected by a democratic majority vote and a president elected by the people. But in Germany, the soldiers of the Great War trudged home to a nation that had fallen into political and social chaos, a nation where left-wing Marxist groups battled with right-wing nationalist *Freikorps* units. Many of them would have thought their world to have been turned upside down. It had turned into a world they could not understand anymore. There was an all-encompassing atmosphere of rancour and frequently smouldering hate. Amid this political turmoil, in June 1919, the Treaty of Versailles was signed by the victorious Allies and then dutifully ratified by the new German government. For one man at least, Leutnant Heinrich Schmidtborn, this was hard to take:

In the early morning hours we arrived at Hillegem to set up a defensive position. There are only a few of us left. The major part of the troops is now granted a well-earned and bitterly needed rest, as the enemy will not appear before nightfall. The battalion's staff was preparing to take its quarters when the small, friendly vicar cheerfully tells us that the war is over! There had already been rumours of a ceasefire, but hearing about it in such a straightforward and honest manner takes us by surprise.

At 10 in the morning, Leutnant Habich enters my room and tells me that there is a telephone call for me. There will be a ceasefire starting at 12. So this is the day, the day we have often talked about in the difficult years that lay behind us, the day we had longed for, always beset with the doubt if we would survive to see it. And now it is finally there and the news leaves us shaken and speechless. The old vicar asks if he would be allowed to ring the church bells. I grant him his wish. I see countless Belgian flags, hear the church bells ringing and feel the triumphant stares of the local population. One thing I know: this armistice will not be on honourable terms.

Inside the regimental HQ a gloomy atmosphere prevails and there is plenty of chaotic news. The Kaiser has abdicated, revolution in the *Heimat*, in Frankfurt a *Vizefeldwebel* is supposed to have taken command of the regiment, we are to hand over all our aeroplanes. It can't be true. And yet it was all true. We prepare to march home. My small and brave flock of men is assembled in front of me. I read Hindenburg's declaration to the Army and then address the men personally: 'Men of the 87th. I need to thank you all, thank you for your gallantry and loyalty, for your stubbornness and your will to fight especially in those final and difficult days which now lie behind us. You have done your duty and held your ground. Take the reminiscences of the honourable deeds of the regiment with you into peacetime. You are undefeated, did your duty to the last man and for that I thank you. We are facing an unpredictable future, but I have not the slightest doubt that you will act and conduct yourself like what you have been and always will be – true German soldiers!'

On 12 November the companies are ready to march out. We know that we are being watched with sharp-eyes, so everyone is willing to do his best. I do not need to remind anyone that we have been allowed to march out in honour and thus the men move with a wonderful precision just like they did in better days. Our mood was subdued. We were marching into a dark and insecure future. We learned more and more details of the enemy's terms, of the frantic situation at home and the possibility that we were marching into a civil war. Our thoughts drifted back to memories of the four years that lay behind us, to the comrades that had marched on our side when we had advanced through Belgium in August 1914. We knew that we had done our duty and that we were about to enter the *Heimat* as upright and honourable men. We will not return home like a beaten army, because we do not feel as such.

On 23 November we crossed the Meuse. On the following day, we continued our march in glorious autumn weather and then came the day on which we were to enter German territory again. The mood of the troops began to improve slightly when we entered Aachen. Here the people welcomed us as good as they possibly could. Hordes of stray soldiers had already crossed through before us and the citizens seemed to be happy that with us, order and discipline had returned as well. At Neuss we had to camp in the open probably to avoid clashes with revolutionary units. As we were moving directly into the industrial heart of Germany we were expecting the clashes with them any day, so when we crossed the Rhine near Düsseldorf on 29 November we received orders to make our machine guns ready to secure the crossings, but luckily the Düsseldorfers welcomed us with cheers and gifts.

The ranks had thinned noticeably as all soldiers living in the Rhineland had been discharged. Now the remains of the company disbanded. It was time to say farewell. Time to separate from a circle of people with which we had shared joy and pain and in which we had experienced the most horrible, but also the greatest and most wonderful years of our lives. Many a tear was shed but promises to reunite one day were given as we all knew that nothing would ever be able to break the bonds of comradeship that were forged in those years of fire, blood and sweat.

LTN. HEINRICH SCHMIDTBORN, INFANTERIE-REGIMENT NR. 87, 1918

The war was over; there were many struggles to come. For the old soldiers of the Great War, there would be memories. Post-war, pilgrims started to return to the now healing but once mortally wounded battlefields of France and Flanders:

The plainest relics are the two thousand cemeteries that lie thick just behind the line that we held … yet I do not want to seem to walk through a graveyard. It is something very much more vital. Some of those very cemeteries are named for a section of trench that meant more for Britain and something Britain stands for than any of the defences on our own island. Things were done where now there is nothing but an enclosure of stones with a few names inscribed (or merely 'An Unknown Soldier ... Known unto God') which have entered our history. They are a permanent part of our English-speaking world. How much more permanent are the memories of those who took part in that extraordinary adventure, and the story of it that will have to be told to all who ask ...

R.H. MOTTRAM, *JOURNEY TO THE WESTERN FRONT*, 1936

They came to remember, to thread their way along the ribbon of the old front, to examine the relics of war, and to remember comrades, lost in battle:

No memorial speaks for us.

Our deeds and our suffering, our successes and our dead left no trace in the country in which millions of German soldiers threw away their lives. No stone heralds their deeds, only a few huge fields, which they call cemeteries, bear witness to their fate. A fate which is tragedy. The tragedy of the ones that failed, the drama of the unlucky ones.

But we shall remember:

We will never forget, that on the battlefields of the Western Front, in France and all over the world, at the wayside cross and behind the slope and in the woods we find the monuments of our deeds. Invisible monuments for you, who we salute.

Dead soldiers, brothers and comrades, that stood on our side to the trenches, shielding the fatherland; we salute you! All for one and one for all we stared into dark nights and across sunlit land. No-man's-land in front and the *Heimat* behind us.

Whereas we returned home, death threw you on the field of battle.

You the comrade on my right and you the comrade on my left, now resting in the land of the dead, to you we bow our heads in reverence.

Oh brother of mine, dead comrade, Germany remembers and will never forget.

MAXIM ZIESE, *DAS UNSICHTBARE DENKMAL*
(*THE INVISIBLE MONUMENT*), 1928

Das letzte Aufgebot (The final levy) – Young Fritz, *c.* 1918.

'Men of 18 in 1918' – Young Tommy. A significant percentage of the British army was made up of fresh recruits in 1918, as the need for manpower became critical.

Postscript: The Men

The men whose voices feature in this book are listed here. Some were casualties; others lived to meet the challenges of the post-war world. It is extremely difficult to distinguish German casualties from existing records, so as a mark of respect for all these men, we make no distinction here. We remember them all.

Alpheus, Werner
Andrae, Berthold
Appel, Fritz
Assmann, Karl
Astbury, W.
Balzer, Arthur
Barth, Ludwig
Beaver, David
Becker, Friedrich
Behrendt, Gustav
Bell, D.H.
Benn, John H.
Bielert
Blencowe, Oswald S.
Blum, Wilhelm
Blumenfeld, Franz
Blumschein, Walter
Bolwell, Frederick
Borgräfe, Otto
Bornemann, Heribert
Brenner, Karl
Bridgewater, Conyers
Brieger, Oskar

Brown, G.M.
Brücken, Peter
Brüls, Willi
Bucky, Hans
Compton, Frederick J.
Cook, A.H.
Cotter, William
Daly, Jeremiah
Delaney, John J.
Dennis, Gerald
Dernore, Bertrand J.
Dibben, R.
Diekmann
Dintelmann, Gustav
Döhner, Otto
Douie, Charles
Dünker, Heinrich
Dunne, Laurence
Eberhard, Heinrich
Edmonds, J.
Edwards, Percy
Einsiedel, Hanns von
Emmerich, Rudolf

Esser, Gottfried

Feil, Hans Christian

Feilding, Rowland

Forst, Wilhelm

Friede, Werner

Funck, Eduard

Gehner, Gustav Willy

Geller, Paul

Gibbs, Philip

Gillespie, Thomas C.

Golden, Hellmuth

Görtemaker, Johann

Gremler, Emil

Guckert, Joseph

Hacken

Hartland, Percy

Hautumm, Ignaz

Hay, Malcolm Vivian

Healy, James

Hegemann, Werner

Heigl, Wilhelm

Heinzmann, Gustav Adolf

Herrman, Johann

Herwig, Wilhelm

Heubner, Heinrich

Hilger, Paul

Hill, R.G.

Himmes, Wilhelm

Hitchcock, F.C.

Höbener, Eduard

Höcker, Paul Oskar

Holtz, Georg von

Hoppe, Wilhelm

Horrocks, William

Howard, Albert

Hunting, Victor

Jahn, Peter

Jünger, Ernst

Keay, Kenneth D.

Kiefer, Otto

Kieser, Herman

Klein, Erich

Kleine, Friedrich

Koeppe, Franz

Körding

Kortzfleisch, Bernhard von

Kratz, Anton

Kronenberg, Egon

Krüger, Richard

Lamb, Arthur H.

Lambert, Arthur E.

Leipner, Otto

Lindner, Karl

Lister, George

Lloyd, R.O.

Lügke, Norbert

Maillard, Herbert

Mason, Humphrey N.T.

Meyer, Kurt

Mitchell, F.

Moorat, S.A.

Mößner, Gustav

Mottram, W.H.

Muir, Ward

Müller, Martin

Munday, Ernest W.

Munz, W.

Murphy, Jack

Näter, Peter

Nett, Fritz

Nichols, G.H.F.

Orschler, Wilhelm

Pauer, Walther

Price, Robert W.

Quigley, Hugh

Rausch, Peter

Rehnisch, Gustav

Robbins, Albert

Roe, Edward
Rommel, Erwin
Schäfer, Hanns
Schlechter, Otto
Schlieper, Wilhelm
Schmelzer, Paul
Schmidt, Gustav
Schmidtborn, Heinrich
Scholder, Rudolf
Schombardt, Richard
Schreiber, Werner
Schrever, Karl
Schuster, Karl
Seegers, Franz
Seitz, Nikolaus
Sinawitz, Richard
Sorley, Charles Hamilton
Stanley-Clarke, Arthur R.
Stevens, Vivian V.
Stichert, Gustav

Stosch, Albrecht von
Street, C.J.C.
Sturhahn
Taffs, William C.
Talbot, Henry W.
Thomas, E.
Thorp, Arthur
Thuir, Wilhelm
Trehbe, Adolf
Trounce, H.D.
Vanselow, Max Berthold
Vietmeyer, Paul
Vossdellen, Werner
Walde, Hans
Wallace, E.
Wegener, Georg
Weidenhaupt, Gustav
Whitehead, Philip
Wientzek, Richard
Williams, M.

Acknowledgements

We are grateful to all those who contributed to our work – directly or indirectly. Petra Schuir, Werner Kodorra and Wilhelm Himmes allowed us to make use of their extensive collections of German wartime letters and diaries. Individuals gave us access to precious family diaries in their care: Kate and Gill Hutchinson for the moving letters and diaries of William Taffs, killed on the first day of the Battle of the Somme; Andy Nurse, custodian of the diaries of Pte J.H. Benn; Kenneth Bone for the 1914 diary of Pte H.W. Talbot; Paul Rodger for access to his grandfather Sgt J. Compton's diary; Martin Howard for his grandfather Cpl Albert Howard's diary; and Pete Whitehead for his grandfather Pte Philip Whitehead's diary.

We thank Giles MacDonogh for allowing us to use his translations of German wartime poetry, and Vanessa Domizlaff, great-granddaughter of *Feld-Oberpostmeister* Georg Domizlaff, commander-in-chief of the German Field Post Service during the First World War, for help with the transcription of German handwriting of the period. Paul Reed is thanked for his help, advice and enthusiasm for the project; Nick Britten, Stuart Disbrey, Mike Edwards, Chris Foster, Taff Gillingham, Wytzia Raspe, Horst Schäfer, Maximilian Seidler and Julian Walker also assisted us with wise words, advice and support. Jo de Vries at The History Press gave unflinching support and unequalled enthusiasm for the book at all its stages.

Bibliography

Archive Resources

Archiv MSTP – Post & Telekommunikation
AVD-Nachrichten, für die im Felde stehenden Angestellten der Aachener
Verlags – und Druckerei-Geschellschaft während des Kriegsjahres 1914–1915
British Newspaper Archive
Hauptarchiv Bodelschwinghsche Stiftungen Bethel, Bielefeld
Imperial War Museum, London
Landesgeschichtliches Informationssystem Hessen
National Archives, Kew
Rheinisches Volksblatt, November 1914
Stadtarchiv Paderborn

Europeana Soldiers' Papers

www.europeana1914–1918.eu. Contributors, where known, are given in
brackets; quoted under CC-A-SA 3.0:

David Beaver (Stuart Leaver)
Oswald S. Blencowe (Doug R.)
Beathe Burckhardt
William Cotter (William Power)
Jeremiah Daly (Frederick Noel Daly)
Laurence Dunne (Anon)
J. Görtemaker (Etta Wittmeier née Görtemaker)
Percy Hartland (Anon)
James Healy (James Healy)

W. Horrocks (Doris Harrison)
Kenneth Douglas Keay (Sheila M.E. Andrews)
Arthur Haughton Lamb (Martin Lamb)
Jack Murphy (John Bruton)
Robert William Price (Michael Payne)
Albert Robins (Steve Brown)
Hanns Schäfer (Wolfgang Schäfer)
Arthur Ramsay Stanley-Clarke (Jonathan Irwin)
W. Williams (Anon)

Private Collections

Kenneth Bone
Peter Doyle
Werner Kodorra
Wilhelm Himmes
Martin Howard
Paul Rodger
Robin Schäfer
Petra Schuir
Pete Whitehead

Published Memoirs

Aachener Verlags – und Druckerei-Geschellschaft (1914–1915) *AVD-Nachrichten, für die im Felde stehenden Angestellten der Aachener Verlags – und Druckerei-Geschellschaft während des Kriegsjahres 1914–1915.* AVD, Aachen

Adams, Bernard (1917) *Nothing of Importance. A Record of Eight Months at the front with a Welsh Battalion, October 1915 to June 1916.* Methuen, London

Anon [D.H. Bell] (1929) *A Soldier's Diary of the Great War.* Faber & Gwyer, London

Bairnsfather, Bruce (1916) *Bullets and Billets.* Grant Richards, London

Bairnsfather, Bruce (1927) *Carry on Sergeant!* Bobbs-Merrill Company, Indianapolis

Bolwell, F.A. (nd) *With a Reservist in France,* Routledge, London

C.-H.-Knorr-Aktiengesellschaft (1914–1918) *Knorr-Feldpost Archiv.* Knorr, Heilbronn

Chapman, Guy (1933) *A Passionate Prodigality*. Ivor Nicholson & Watson, London

Clapham, H.S. (1930) *Mud and Khaki*. Hutchinson & Co., London

Dennis, Gerald V. (1994) *A Kitchener Man's Bit. An Account of the Great War 1914–18*. MERH Books, York

Douie, Charles (1929) *The Weary Road. The Recollections of a Subaltern of Infantry*. John Murray, London

Downham, P. (2004) *Diary of an Old Contemptible*. Pen & Sword, Barnsley

Dunn, J.C. (1994) *The War the Infantry Knew 1914–1919*. Abacus, London

Edmonds, Charles [C.E. Carrington] (1929) *A Subaltern's War*. Peter Davis, London

Empey, Arthur Guy (1917) *Over the Top*. A.L. Burt Co., New York

'Ex Private X' [A.M. Burrage] (1930) *War is War*. Victor Gollancz, London

'An Exchanged Officer' [M.V. Hay] (1916) *Wounded and a Prisoner of War*. William Blackwood, Edinburgh

Eyre, Giles E.M. (1991) *Somme Harvest. Memories of a PBI in the Summer of 1916*. London Stamp Exchange, London

Feilding, Rowland (1929) *War Letters to a Wife France and Flanders, 1915–1919*. The Medici Society, London

French, Field Marshal Viscount of Ypres (1919) *1914*. Constable & Co., London

Gibbs, Philip (1920) *Realities of War*. William Heinemann, London

Gillespie, A.D. (1916) *Letters From Flanders*. Smith Elder & Co., London

Hall, James Norman (1916) *Kitchener's Mob. The Adventures of an American in the British Army*. Constable & Co., London

Hewett, Stephen H. (1918) *A Scholar's Letters from the Front*. Longmans, Green & Co., London

Hitchcock, F.C. (1937) *'Stand To' A Diary of the Trenches 1915–1918*. Hurst & Blackett Ltd, London

Höcker, P.O. (1914) *An der Spitze meiner Kompanie. Drei Monate Kriegserlebnisse*. Ullstein, Berlin

Hodges, Frederick James (1988) *Men of 18 in 1918*. Arthur H. Stockwell Ltd, Ilfracombe

Jünger, Ernst; Kiesel, Helmuth (2010) *Kriegstagebuch 1914–1918*. Klett-Cotta Verlag, Stuttgart

Lambert, Arthur (nd) *Over the Top. A 'PBI' in the 'HAC'*. John Long, London

MacGill, Patrick (1916) *The Great Push*. Herbert Jenkins, London

Mainwaring, G.B. [G. Mainwaring Brown] (1918) *If We Return. Letters of a Soldier of Kitchener's Army*. John Lane, London.

Mottram, R.H. (1936) *Journey to the Western Front*. Bell & Sons, London

Muir, Ward (1917) *Observations of an Orderly*. Simpkin, Marshall, Hamilton, Kent & Co., London

'Quex' [G.H.F. Nichols] (1930) *Pushed*. Constable & Co., London

Quigley, Hugh (1928) *Passchendaele and the Somme. A Diary of 1917*. Methuen, London

Rogerson, Sidney (2006) *Twelve Days on The Somme. A Memoir of the Trenches, 1916*. Greenhill Books, London

Rommel, Erwin (1937) *Infanterie greift an: Erlebnis und Erfahrung*. Voggenreiter Verlag, Potsdam

Williamson, Henry (1929) *The Wet Flanders Plain*. Faber & Faber, London

Official, Regimental and Unit Histories

Baldenstein, Werner Rinck von (1927) *Das Infanterie-Regiment Freiherr von Sparr (3. Westfälisches) Nr. 16 im Weltkriege 1914/1918: ‚Hacke tau!* Verlag Gerh. Stalling, Oldenburg

Edmonds, Brigadier-General Sir James E. *et al.* (1925–1948) *History of the Great War based on Official Documents: Military Operations, France and Belgium 1914–1918* (14 volumes). Macmillan & Co., London

Foulkes, C.H. (1934) *'Gas!' The Story of the Special Brigade*. William Blackwood & Sons, Edinburgh

Grieve, W. Grant & Newman, Bernard (1936) *Tunnellers. The Story of the Tunnelling Companies, Royal Engineers, during the World War*. Herbert Jenkins, London

Maillard, Herbert (1935) *5. Westfälisches Infanterie-Regiment Nr. 53 im Weltkrieg 1914–1918*. Sporn, Zeulenroda

Mangels, Max (1939) *Königlich Preußisches Reserve-Infanterie-Regiment Nr. 215, II. Teil: Vom Einsatz vor Wytschaete bis zum Rückmarsch über den Rhein. Aus Deutschland großer Zeit*. Sporn, Zeulenroda

Meyer, Artur (1937) *Das Reserve Infanterie Regiment Nr. 236 im Weltkriege. Nach amtlichen Kriegstagebüchern und nach Kameradenberichten*. Sporn, Zeulenroda

Mitchell, F. (1933) *Tank Warfare. The Story of the Tanks in the Great War*. Thomas Nelson & Sons, London

Reichsarchiv / Reichskriegsministerium / Oberkommando des Heeres / Kriegsgeschichtliche Forschungsanstalt des Heeres (Hrsg.) (1925–1939), *Der Weltkrieg 1914–1918. Die militärischen Operationen zu Lande*. Mittler und Sohn, Berlin

Vischer, Obert z.D. (1921) *Das Württ. Infanterie-Regiment Nr. 180 im Weltkrieg 1914–1918*. Belsersche Verlagsbuchhandlung, Stuttgart

Wyrall, Everard (1926–30) *The Diehards in the Great War*. Harrison & Sons, London

Collected and General Works

Anon (1908) *Felddienstordnung vom 22. März 1908; D.V.E. Nr. 267*. Ernst Siegfried Mittler u. Sohn Hofbuchhandlung, Berlin

Anon (1909) *Exerzier-Reglement für die Infanterie (Ex.R.f.d.I.). Vom 29. Mai 1906. Neuabdruck mit Einfügung der bis August 1909 ergangenen Änderungen (Deckblatt 1-78). D.V.E. Nr. 130 u. Anhang 130a*. Mittler, Berlin

Anon (1915) *Lehnert's Handbuch für den Truppenführer*, Berlin

Anon (1918) *Wegweiser durch die deutsche Kriegswirtschaft*. Schweighofer & Herle, Berlin

Barton, P., Doyle, P. & Vandervalle, J. (2004) *Beneath Flanders Fields. The Tunnellers' War 1914–1918*. Spellmount, Staplehurst

Borchert, M. (1931) *Der Kampf gegen Tanks. Dargestellt an den Ereignissen der Doppelschlacht bei Cambrai*. Mittler & Sohn, Berlin

Chapman, Guy (1937) *Vain Glory*. Cassell & Co., London

Churchill, Winston S. (1931) *The World Crisis 1911–1918*. Thornton Butterworth, London

Cron, Hermann (1923) *Die Organisation des deutsches Heeres im Weltkriege*. Mittler & Sohn, Berlin

Cron, Hermann (1937) *Geschichte des deutschen Heeres im Weltkriege 1914–1918*. Militärverlag Karl Siegesmund, Berlin

Dietz, Otto (1919) *Der Todesgang der deutschen Armee. Militärische Ursachen*. Curtius, Berlin

Doyle, P. (2013) *Great War Tommy*. Haynes Publishing, Yeovil

Doyle, P. & Foster, C. (2013) *Remembering Tommy. The British Soldier in the First World War*. Spellmount, Stroud

Eisenhart Rothe, Ernst von & Tschischwitz, Erich von (1933) *Deutsche Infanterie: Das Ehrenmal d. vordersten Front*. Sporn, Zeulenroda

General Staff (1914) *Field Service Regulations Part 1. Operations, 1909* (Reprinted with Amendments, 1914). HMSO, London

General Staff, 1914. *Field Service Regulations Part 1. Organisation & Administration, 1909* (Reprinted with Amendments, 1914). HMSO, London

General Staff (1918) *Handbook of the German Army*. HMSO, London

Gudmundsson, Bruce (1995) *Stormtroop Tactics: Innovation in the German Army, 1914–1918.* Praeger, Westport

Hammerton, J. (ed.) (nd) *The Great War I Was There.* Amalgamated Press, London

Holmes, Richard (2004) *Tommy. The British Soldier on the Western Front 1914–1918.* Harper Collins, London

Kraus, Jürgen & Rest, Stefan (2004) *Die deutsche Armee im Ersten Weltkrieg: Uniformierung und Ausrüstung 1914 bis 1918.* Militariaverlag, Vienna

Leonhard, Jörn (2014) *Die Büchse der Pandora: Geschichte des Ersten Weltkriegs.* C.H. Beck, Munich

Messenger, Charles (2005) *Call to Arms, The British Army 1914–18.* Weidenfield & Nicholson, London

Purdom, J. (ed.) (1930) *Everyman at War.* J.M. Dent, London

Simkins, Peter (1988) *Kitchener's Army. The Raising of the New Armies, 1914–16.* Manchester University Press, Manchester

Stosch, Albrecht von (1927) *Schlachten des Weltkrieges. Band 21: Somme – Nord. I & II. Teil.* G. Stalling Verlag, Oldenburg

Transfeldt, Walter (1984) *Wort und Brauch in Heer und Flotte.* Von Spemann, Stuttgart

Index